Misfit
An Autobiography

Captain J.R. White

LIVEWIRE PUBLICATIONS
Dublin

First published 1930 by Jonathon Cape, 30 Bedford Square, London and 91 Wellington Street West, Toronto, Jonathon Cape & Harrison Smith, 139 East 46th Street, New York.

This Volume published by, Livewire Publications Limited, PO. Box N° 9902, Dublin 6. Published. Livewire Publications. 2005.

The moral right of Captain J.R. White to be identified as the author of this work has been asserted.

Designed in London, Great Britain, by Adlibbed Limited.
Produced by Publish and be damned. www.pabd.com
Printed and bound in the UK or Canada.

ISBN Number: 1-905225-20-2

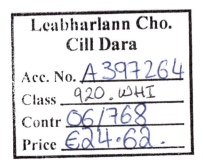

Livewire Publications will publish short stories, small novels or documentary accounts of an unusual nature in an Irish context. Our objective is merely to publish what is excellent in writing today in a social context. We feel there is a lacuna in Irish publishing and feel we can produce material that is not available to the general public. We are willing to take a chance.

We intend producing a volume relating to child abuse in Ireland, a volume of short stories and a novel plus other material of a historical nature. We have independent funding for our projects and so are not dependent on the Arts Council although it is our intention to seek a grant from this body.

Our first volume Misfit by Captain Jack White, the co-founder of the Irish Citizen Army, has not been republished since it first appeared in 1930, neither in print nor on the internet. It is an account which we believe has an appeal to anyone who is interested in the early history of Irish social movements. More than that it is a book which has a very modern feel to it and one which addressed the inner as well as the outer revolution. We feel that this very personal account should be out there alongside all the other accounts of this period since it describes events and a background that is not readily available elsewhere.

CONTENTS

FOREWORD

I have hinted on the last page of this book that it isn't finished. I want to say so definitely on the first. It isn't finished, because I'm not finished - not by a long chalk.

People like things finished. Why haven't the psychoanalysts discovered the most fatal arid final of the complexes, the termination complex? The Oedipus complex is a pimple by comparison. Finish your father by all means, but keep moving yourself.

All the same, it isn't easy to explain that one may be in movement, directed movement, between unsolved contradictions, not just oscillation.

I end this book on a hunting simile. Suppose I begin it on the same. What sort of a hound is it that keeps on giving tongue when he's doubtful of the line? I have followed two lines in my life, roughly speaking, the lines of Christ and Lenin. They do not yet visibly converge. Visibly and vociferously they appear to diverge. Right! Let the pack split if it must. I am going to keep my nose down and my tail up. The whips may whip me after one pack or the other. Maybe some of the keenest hounds will have to come back to me.

Did it ever occur to you, fellow-hunters, that a true scent might lie deep in the heart of cover, and be picked up again in the open, but overlaid in all the cover between?

Lenin obviously knew what he was talking about, and he said it all. Because he *knew,* his word has become flesh.

I venture to suspect that Christ also *knew;* but He didn't say it all. He told us He didn't. He gave us the scent in the heart of cover. We've got to pick it up and follow it in the open.

The really interesting thing about me is that I have followed a scent 'found in the heart of cover' into the open, *against the whole pressure psychic and material of an obstructing social system.*

You couldn't expect anyone but a lunatic to do that; and even I am not lunatic enough to tell all about it just yet. But I want to tell it, and I haven't told it in this book. Sufficient for the day is the evil thereof I make trouble enough for myself as it is.

This morning, for instance, I received this letter from a lady:

'My dear Jack,' she writes, 'I believe your book is likely to be in the shops here in about a week's time; at least, a bookseller told me so. I should like to know from you direct, although I hate your book being published, especially coming out in Dublin, broadcasting a character of yourself (in your own imagination) all over Dublin and Ireland.

You are just blackmailing yourself in public, that is all. I have stood up for you here in Dublin as well as I could when I was fit and able to fight, and you have made it all nothing by letting your flaring imagination loose like a great fire raging over the land.

I want you, now I have given you my mind on the subject, to send me one of the first copies of the book, and please write your name inside it from yourself. I will send you 10s. 6d., price of copy, when I hear from you.

You have dug yourself a grave here in Ireland, put a red flag on it, but you will never lie in it.

Good-bye, dear Jack.'

Now, that's a good letter, the kind of letter I like. There is an unsolved contradiction in it also; therefore there is the principal ingredient of Life. Perhaps that is why the writer refuses to let me lie in the grave with the red flag. I have no predilection for graves anyway.

On one of the rare occasions when I heard my father express his religious views, he made a remark which has always stuck in my memory.

'Crucified, crucified!' said he. 'Why, lots of plucky fellows would be crucified to save a pal, let alone to save a world.' That was a soldierly view, but it missed the point.

One is not crucified to save the world, or one or more pals. One is crucified to save oneself from the world. God may be the other side of the cross. Only one's Mother, the isolated earth, and her unripe fruit, the physical body, are underneath and upon it.

Whereas obviously one belongs to a larger system. If in some form or other one chances the cross, God and Mother are blotted out at the crisis. 'My God, my God, why hast Thou forsaken me?'

The world-saving process, and the assumption of the blessed Mother) doesn't begin till after the resurrection.

Even then it is slow.

It is inconvenient, but to know anything about the resurrection one must be crucified first, and for one's own sake, which is so egotistic.

The bourgeois, since they dislike working for themselves, want the resurrection without the crucifixion.

Lenin won't let them. 1 am prepared to help him. Like him, I believe in the resurrection of the dead and the life of the world to come.

Amen.

J. R. W.

Empire Day, 1930.

CHAPTER I.
THE SOUTH AFRICAN WAR

In January 1899, I was gazetted to the 1st Gordon Highlanders (the old 75th) then quartered in Edinburgh Castle. From the time of joining the regiment to the outbreak of the South African War I was profoundly unhappy. I did not like my brother officers and my brother officers did not like me, or if they did, they concealed it.

South Africa changed all that. The regiment was into the battle of Magersfontein, 11th December 1899, less than a fortnight after landing.

We started out as escort to a convoy that was to be taken through to beleaguered Kimberley, when the Boers entrenched at Magersfontein were swept away. But it is not so easy to sweep underground.

We stood around our convoy overlooking a great plain which crackled with musketry like a fire of dry sticks. Beyond was a large edition of the South African kopje.

A staff officer rode up to the colonel. 'Have you got a whole regiment here, sir?' 'Seven companies' I heard the colonel reply.

'Send four at once to support the Highland Brigade.' We did not form part of the Highland Brigade; that had started out overnight, and, as we knew later, been decimated before dawn. It was about 8 a.m. when our four companies started to join the remnant of them. My company was among the four.

We extended to about five paces between men, and set off in three lines with about three hundred yards between them.

It struck me as odd at the time, that the only instructions I got were to follow the line in front commanded by my skipper, for obviously people were not going out of their way to wave signals down in that crackle.

By the end of that day, and thereafter, nothing struck me as odd. The first surprise I got was to pass groups of Highlanders belonging to different regiments, mixed up, and lying about playing cards. This was about the point where the crackle began to be accompanied by an occasional hum. Somebody asked them what they were doing. I caught the words, 'Bloody well fed up.' Odd again, but none of my business.

We passed on. The hums were frequent enough now, getting sharper and higher pitched. Dear me! They were bullets. They began to strike close by and throw up dust, sometimes into one's very eyes. Rather exciting, though; nobody seemed to mind much. We walked calmly on.

The line in front lay down. We followed suit. It advanced in a short running rush. We did the same; plenty of other Highlanders in our path now; some of them very still, their limbs at queer angles.

The line in front got lost. I could have told it that it would, though I had never been under fire before. Singular mechanical military mind! All the better; this was rather fun, and my section, nearly all old Dargai men, seemed to enjoy it too. We got within a few hundred yards of the Boer trenches. In front of us was a more or less coherent group of the Highland Light Infantry. We were up to the organized remnant of the Highland Brigade caught in the morning's disaster. We found the fattest ant heap each we could, and lay down. A great giant of a sergeant got restive.

'Come on, sir, he called to me, lead us into the trenches.' I wonder what would have happened if I had. Quite possibly victory and a V.C., for I honestly believe at that time most of the Boers were clearing off. Their fire was not really hot; but my whole personality was not engaged in this war enough to take over command from Lord Methuen, and at least five commanding officers of regiments. So I calmed the sergeant down. Later he nearly got me killed, standing up to bring me a share of a tin of rabbit he had opened with his bayonet.

Aha! Lord Methuen was interested after all. A red tab appeared on a horse some distance to the rear. He was not well received. 'Get off your horse, you bloody fool' reached me from some enthusiast for life, who was getting the bullets meant for the red-tab. He got off and the horse was immediately shot. I heard him shout, 'Where is Colonel Downman?' (Our C.O.) Naturally nobody could tell him. I presume he went to look. That is the first and last I saw of Methuen's control of the battle of Magersfontein. Oh! very singular military mind! Most amazing of all I could not find my dumbfounded wonder at it all reflected in the minds of those with whom I subsequently discussed it.

There was better to come. A hot enfilading fire opened from the right.

That meant the choicest ant heap was out of focus. We got out our bayonets and scratched up little mounds to protect our flanks.

The Highland Light Infantry men in front preferred other methods. They got up in a bunch and began to run through us. It was very sensible of them if they hadn't bunched so, but it outraged my strong sense of military discipline, which the reader has no doubt noticed.

If I were not prepared to lead an unauthorized attack, neither would I permit an apparently unauthorized retirement.

I told my men to cover them with their rifles, which they did. Most of them subsided inconveniently close to us. One intrepid fellow came on and I pointed my own carbine at him (the officers carried carbines to prevent their being singled out and picked off).

'Where the Hell are you going?' I shouted.

'I want to go to the rear, sir, I'm bustin'.'.

He was past me before I had time to recover. As my eye followed him I observed that every one was doing it. The plain was alive with khaki dots and their direction was not forward. Not far away to the right rear I observed my colour-sergeant. He, too, was 'homing.' I spoke to him with unnecessary violence; that a bulwark of discipline could so far forget it! With some exculpatory heat the colour-sergeant yelled to me that the order had come to retire. Whether it had or not became a matter for interminable dispute until every one agreed to put the indirect responsibility on poor Downman, our C.O., who was killed as he got up to wave a line of men round to face the new enfilade fire. It is a likely explanation that his signal was misinterpreted, as he appears to have been killed in the act of giving it.

Methuen disclaimed giving any such order, as well he might. He had no means of giving any order at all. It was before the days of loud speakers. Having made quite a creditable bid to stem what I believed, and between ourselves, still believe, to have been an unauthorized retirement, I did not hesitate to join it when I saw it had the support of common consent if not of authority. Even then we were not heavily fired at. Probably the sergeant and I could have taken the trenches.

Having retired a suitable distance the regiment closed in quarter column and piled arms. What was more to the point, the officers' mess-mules arrived, and we began a scratch meal at about one thousand eight hundred yards' range from the Boers. When a really funny thing happened; the Boers mounted a gun, or remounted one, they had taken away. It is my belief most of them were halfway to Kimberley and came back from sheer curiosity to see what astonishing thing we would do next.

The first shrapnel shell did a lot of damage to a mule-team belonging to the Black Watch. The second burst about ten feet over my head, but as I was at the rear of the regiment, then hurriedly unpiling arms, it did no harm to anyone. We then extended and continued to retire. A staff officer rode up to the colonel, a new colonel now. I heard him say, 'Don't you think this ill have a bad effect, colonel?' I did not hear the colonel's reply.

If I remember right we halted for a little, but soon retired again, this time with a sense of re-established discipline and order under superior control.

This is a true account of a battle, probably the first ever written. Certainly the first ever written of a battle in South Africa. The regiment lost three officers, one killed and two wounded, and about fifty men killed and wounded. But to my humble observation it lost more than that.

At Magersfontein any of our men that I saw showed a nonchalant gallantry that was beyond praise. They were as good as the stories in the papers. They would have charged anything or gone anywhere they were told. But nobody told them to go anywhere. Nobody made any preparations to render it possible to tell them to anywhere, should the need arise. I was in action with the same men at intervals of every few weeks for the next eighteen months. I never saw them the same again. They were plucky enough, but they were different; and so was I.

This is not a history of the South African War; it is a history of myself in relation to various environments. Its egotism is only softened by some note of various environments in relation to me.

So I make no apology for skipping from the Modder River across the Vaal to the Rand and Johannesburg.

A very pleasant skip, take it all round, interrupted only by two nasty breaks, from the time Bobs left the railway in Cape Colony on the general advance.

Paaredeberg was one nasty break and the epidemic of enteric at Bloemfontein the other.

At Paaredeberg I got a little glimpse of what the Great War must have been like, for we had about a week in mud-filled, corpse-surrounded trenches, sapping up to Cronje.

The last day of Paardeberg I heard to my joy that Ladysmith was relieved and my father safe.

At Bloemfontein I was left behind for a bit after the regiment had started for Pretoria, as my hands and legs were covered with veldt sores. Those who suffered from them were supposed to run a better chance of immunity from enteric. I retain a ghastly impression of visiting one of our fellows down with enteric in a hospital bell tent. It contained sixteen men. I started back when I entered for I thought there was some mistake; this tent was evidently the mortuary for dead niggers. Assured it was not so, I re-entered. Every man's face was so covered with flies that not a speck of white skin was visible. I found my man and spoke with him through a fog of flies.

Approaching Johannesburg we had the first of the only two real hot fights I claim to have experienced till I came to Ireland. Magersfontein was not a fight; it was half massacre, half farce. This fight at Doornkop I am going to describe had its farcical element, but ' it did deserve to be called a fight. Doornkop is, I believe, the exact scene of Dr. Jameson's defeat in his famous raid. The Boers held the ridge of the Rand. Ian Hamilton's cavalry we were with his wing of the advance - had a sniff at them and decided it was a job for the infantry. It was not, but no matter. The regiment was ordered to advance up a long glacis, sloping upwards towards the Boer position. The slope was very gradual and a veldt fire burned in our direction about halfway up it. The Boers held the advance ridge of a plateau about 250 yards wide at the top of the glacis, with ability to retire to the rear ridge and drop away to their horses under cover of a steep slope.

We started in fourteen extended lines. I was in the tenth. There was a hundred yards or so between the lines. The charge was sounded, and the Boers were cleared off the front ridge by the lines in front of me. Up to the time of reaching the front ridge and coming on to the plateau I don't remember my line losing a man. From then on it was red hot.

All the front lines were mixed up and the ground strewn with dead and wounded. I thought it very unhealthy. With a few stalwarts (I found on these occasions the drunkards and the religious fanatics had a way of standing out) I pushed on, looking for cover.

Suddenly we came to a line, an exact line, of motionless figures I took to be corpses. 'What execrable taste,' I thought. 'The Boers have got the range so exactly, they're dropping men in a line for sport.'

I plumped down on my belly next the corpse on my right. 'Are you dead?' said I.

No, sir-r.'

'Is the man next you dead?'

'I don't think so, sir-r, I'll ask him.'

There wasn't one of them dead. There was a little line of stones I had failed to notice, not much bigger than ostrich eggs, and the supposed corpses were behaving just like ostriches. As I lingered, two of them were hit through the rump. I decided to go on. I have a particularly good 'spring' for the kilt, as it is called. Two stalwarts came with me, Holland and Doran. If they are still alive and read these lines I greet them. Holland was hit through the foot and collapsed with a yowl. Doran and I got through to some real good cover. There were five men there already, all hit and all belonging to the Volunteer Company attached to the regiment.

Military discipline had not had time to deprive them of all common sense. Doran and I, both blackguards, confronted the Boers, a good fifty yards ahead of the regiment.

I began to think hard. The Boers were jumping up and disappearing over the back ridge in ones and twos.

'There'll soon be none left, thought I, as I took pot shots at them from an admirable cleft between two big rocks.

'What shall I do, then? If I start the charge and there are none left I might get the V.C. But if there is one left I might get shot. That, having come so far, would be a pity.'

The Boer fire slackened and slackened. I had almost decided it was safe to emerge and capture Johannesburg, for this was the last strong position guarding it, when my mind was made up for me by a blood-curdling yell from behind.

The regiment, whose thought processes had evidently been exactly similar to mine, had decided to charge. It was making this dreadful noise to strike terror into its foes, if any.

There was one. I saw his Mauser carbine sticking out from behind a rock before I saw him. I was extremely frightened, but reason did not desert her throne.

'The owner of that gun,' thought I, 'is either dead or too frightened to run away.' With that I did a belly-slide in fine rugby style and seized the offending firearm. It came away in my hand. Peering over the rock, I saw an extremely frightened youth of about seventeen years of age.

I asked him was he wounded, and he said he was.

'No, you're not,' said I, looking at him closer. 'Get up. ' He got up, sound as a bell. At this moment the van of the charging regiment arrived, led by a Glasgow Irishman. 'Bayonet the b -,' he yelled. I checked his amiable intention with authority.

Then arrived an officer, my superior in rank, and by this time there were ten or a dozen men around. 'Shoot him, shoot him,' yelled the officer.

A wave of disgust swamped my sense of discipline.

'If you shoot him,' said I, pointing my carbine at him, 'I'll shoot you,' and he passed on.

He is now a General, that officer, and I am a Bolshevik, or reported as such.

My mother naturally feels pleased when Generals speak kindly of me.

'I met General So-and-so the other day,' she wrote me not long ago. 'He spoke so nicely about you, though he said you hadn't always seen eye to eye.'

Looking back on the battle of Doornkop, I find it strangely educative. I recognized my own cowardice indeed cowardice begot the courage of self-preservation. I was naturally sympathetic, therefore, to the cowardice and self-preservation of others. But those who are unwilling to recognize their own cowardice hide it from themselves by cruelty to others. They will go to amazing lengths of self-deception -and mendacity. A letter appeared soon afterwards in the *Bloemfontein Post,* written by one of our jocks to a friend in Bloemfontein. It contained an account of Doornkop.

'I will now mention an incident that has made a good deal of bad feeling in the regiment. During the final charge, one of the Boers was seen to pick off five of our lads with his last five cartridges. Then he held up his hands and surrendered. Our boys were going to avenge their comrades when a young officer came up and insisted that his life should be spared.'

Not bad that. Small wonder I was prepared for the truths of psychoanalysis, when some twenty years later that science came to formulate the whole content of my experiences of life.

The regiment lost ninety-seven officers and men killed and wounded at Doornkop. St. John Meyrick was the only officer killed. He was hit by a long-range bullet at the very beginning of the attack. Sixteen men were laid out the next morning on the field, blankets over their faces, but their feet exposed.

There was strong competition for their shoes.

'Can ye no hae the decency to wait yir tur-r-n and the puir lads har-r-dly cold,' said the sergeant major. An elegant figure drew up beside me.

It was the Duke of Marlborough, known to me by sight, for my crammer was at Woodstock and we had sat immediately behind the ducal pew in church. He gazed at the ranks of death. 'C'est magnifique mais ce n'est pas la guerre,' he said.

No, your Grace, it was not even magnificent. Its magnificence was of the same order as your own.

We took Johannesburg and Pretoria, and after that marched east to Komatipoort.

One little spell, when left with my company within twenty miles of Komatipoort to guard a stretch of railway line, remains with me.

It was bush-veldt country, full of strange birds and beasts; the honey-bird that flies ahead of you whistling till he takes you to a wild bees' nest, then if you don't leave some honey for him he leads you next to a poisonous snake. So runs the story anyway.

The G'way bird, a ludicrous creature that invites you to 'G'way' with a note of weary sarcasm that first convulses with laughter and finally irritates, it is so super-humanly human.

The blue wildebeests (gnu). I wounded one badly once but failed to come up with it. Hyenas galore making night hideous, and an odd lion or two.

Through the queer monotonous bush, where even a native not bred in the country gets lost, runs the Crocodile River. I owe to that river the most complete sense of physical well being I have ever known. The stream ran a few feet deep over a bottom of warm sand. I used to lie down with my head just above water and let the current roll me over and over. The river is not called 'Crocodile' for nothing. But these beasts lurked in the deep parts, and avoiding them, one was safe enough.

After Komatipoort Bobs went home and said the war was over.

Kitchener started to organize mounted infantry on a large scale,

War according to textbook may have been over; hard and continuous fighting was just beginning.

I joined the 6th M.I. composed of a company of ours ' a company of the Welsh Regiment, a company of the Wilts and a company of the Bedfords, the whole, with an Australian contingent and some odd details, forming De Lisle's column.

The M.I. was at first and for a long time pure bliss. An Irishman, Findlay of the Bedfords, commanded us; Cameron, another Irishman in spite of his name, was my fellow-subaltern in our company. Our skipper was a bit fussy but innocuous. We led the life of filibusters and stole everything we saw. De Lisle was a dashing soldier. His most frequent order was a laconic 'Gallop that kopje,' and gallop it we would, Cameron - generally a hundred yards ahead - then myself, then the skipper and the company. Cameron was the one man I ever met completely without fear. But his number was up. In June 1901 we were trekking about the Orange River Colony in search of what we might devour, somewhere near the Basuto border. There wasn't much left to devour by then. The 'pastoral' columns had been at work, taking the women into concentration camps, burning the farms, destroying every living thing, except the men, whom we couldn't catch.

A big Boer convoy was reported in the offing, and two hundred rifles, about the whole strength of the 6th M.I. under Sladen, who had taken over command from Findlay, were sent out some hours before dawn to cruise around and capture the convoy if we could.

Sladen was a cheerful soul who took his responsibilities lightly. He had a habit of asking advice from the man nearest him and accepting it without question.

As dawn broke we sighted a huge convoy trailing over the veldt as far as eye could reach.

'What shall we do?' said Sladen to his bugler.

'Gallop them, sir,' says the bugler.

'All right,' said Sladen. 'Sound the charge.'

It was a gallant affair, or would have been, but that only the more aged and uxorious Boers were sleeping in the wagons with the women. They burst out in various stages of dishabille as we approached, and on to their ponies to escape.

We captured some forty of them without a life taken or lost. We were much too good-tempered to be bloodthirsty.

Featherstonhaugh, a subaltern, in hot pursuit of a bearded Boer, found his chase cut short by the Boer's pony tripping in an ant-bear hole. The Boer scrambled to his knees. 'Oh please, sir, not make dead.'

'That's all right, old cock,' said Featherstonhaugh, "got any biltong?" (S*trips of dried beef.*)

There were some ninety ox-wagons and fifty Cape carts in the convoy and several thousand cattle accompanying it. We 'laagered up' the lot in a Kaffir kraal and waited for our main body to come up.

About mid-day mounted men in scout formation were seen on the skyline, in fact on two skylines, at least one of them in the wrong direction for our people, and their formation was a bit too loose even for us. Still it was about time for our people to be coming along. The chances were it was they.

Sladen sent for one of the Boer prisoners and lent him his glasses.

'Are these your people or ours?' he asked.

The Boer pointed to something he said was a gun team and invited us to look.

I had a look myself. Sure enough it looked like a gun-team; I couldn't see the gun but it was a long distance and a gun has poor visibility. If it was a gun, it was conclusive evidence that the newcomers were British, for the Boers had lost all their guns long ago. Then I must needs butt in.

'Look here, sir, I said to Sladen. 'If those are our people and that's a gun its going to shell us. How do they know we've captured this convoy? It's the first time we ever have; they'll see the wagons and start to shell. Better send someone out to tell them we're their own people and the convoy's captured.'

'All right, White,' said Sladen. 'Jump on your pony and out you go.'

So out I went. To give my own pony a rest, I jumped on a Boer pony I'd annexed that morning. The brute had a mouth like a mangle. If I had known what I know now, I wouldn't have gone on. I had a strong intuitive inhibition. But instead of making me wary it preoccupied me with inner conflict. 'Don't be a fool, I kept saying to myself, 'that was a gun-team right enough.'

Fifteen hundred yards or so from the laager the country broke into a series of short switchback undulations. As I cantered to the top of one of the undulations, two very odd-looking persons cantered up from the other side. They were within ten yards of me before I saw them and reined up. They had straw hats with little flags stuck in the ribbons, too unconventional a headgear even for De Lisle's M.I. The mangle mouthed pony seemed glad to see his friends. 'Hands up, ' commanded the strangers. I kept one hand on the reins, debating with myself in a most painful way whether I could pull Mangle-mouth round before those very alert-looking carbines were against my chest. I decided I could not. One hand didn't satisfy my captors, so up went the other.

'Dismount, off-take your gaiters. I did so. Then they demanded my breeches. I was feeling very ashamed. My hypersensitive conscience was accusing *me* of rather disgraceful cowardice. I should have let myself be shot in order that the shot or shots to stop me might warn our people of their mistake. Well, I would atone now to my own pride anyway. I would not divest myself of my own breeches; so I sat sulkily and made no move to obey.

Those Boers were good fellows. They never threatened me. They just cut my bootlaces, pulled off my boots, and my breeches after them, and gave me back my boots.

It was a lovely pair of breeches made by Thomas.

Then a posse of some forty or fifty Boers came up. They dismounted and surrounded me. Their attitude was distinctly unfriendly. They mentioned the word 'Skeet', which means 'Shoot', and I gathered some of them were in favour of shooting me as a protest against our habit of making war on women. Somebody inquired was I 'Kapitan.' I made it very clear I was the most insignificant kind of lootenant.

The unpleasant discussion was cut short by the sweetest sound I ever heard - British bullets whistling overhead aimed at my captors or some of their friends, visible nearby.

Thank God! My cowardice had done no harm. Somehow or other our people had learnt the truth.

I learnt afterwards how it had happened. My capture had taken place out of sight of the laager, but my skipper had been sent out to another lot of Boers, supposed to be British, approaching from another direction. He had been captured in full view and had been seen to bend down and take off his bandolier. Then our people opened fire all round.

When firing began, my captors took my breeches and gaiters and left me. They were mounted in a second and in a canter in another. 'Smart work, I thought. It took the 6th M.I. a distinct interval to get out of the trot.

I remained alone in a very inadequate costume.

What a bitter enemy of reason is pride! I was sore with myself, anxious to atone by some stunt of courage for my drop in my own estimation.

I actually ran forward after the attacking Boers with a mad idea of getting in amongst them unnoticed, and slipping through to our own people. Some of them spotted me following. They pointed their rifles at me and made it clear I was to desist. Then pride and the herd-instinct baffled, I began to think. The path of reason was obvious; it converged with that of modesty. I should make with all possible speed for De Lisle's main body and hurry them to Sladen's relief. Incidentally I should procure, if possible, another pair of trousers.

The Boers, or somebody, had set light to the veldt. There was a wall of smoke a bit off the direction from which De Lisle was expected. Luckily I knew that direction, for I had looked at a map in the laager, found our position, and noted the line from the previous night's camp.

I would not set off purposefully. I would meander about aimlessly till I got behind the smoke and then leg it.

There was an odd Boer or two about with ammunition Cape carts. One of them drew me to him with a pointed rifle. He went through my coat pockets, took nothing, not even my pipe, and signified his indifference to my further movements. I meandered very aimlessly away from him. Once behind the smoke I corrected my course by the sun and broke into a steady trot. I was dressed for running.

I passed under a ridge on which was an inhabited Kaffir kraal. The natives saw me coming and flocked from their huts to the crest of the ridge overlooking the spruit that I followed. I had good reasons to avoid ostentation.

They stared at me, those natives, men and women alike, and little pot-bellied children with umbilical cords like miniature pig's tails. Stare they never so intently they could not comprehend, they could not place in its category this strange figure now striding with assumed nonchalance beneath them.

Then, led by the intuition of a woman, came revelation. This apparition that was no white man, for white men wore trousers, and was no black man, for black men had not white legs, had a category none the less. It was a god. A woman ' s first to prostrate was herself, but the revelation was practically instantaneous to them all.

Had I been above them I might have assumed that worship was phallic. As it was I am satisfied that I stumbled on a root-religion older than that, and eternally new, the deification by the human mind of its own ignorance. And in the recesses of my being an idea was born. The herd deify what they cannot understand, but the true sons of God will not own their Father till He proves His paternity to their intelligence.

I acknowledged the act of worship with a divine salutation and passed on chuckling.

Soon afterwards my divinity was reminded of the precarious circumstances of its earthly tenement. I saw a fairly large body of mounted men riding parallel to my course about a mile to the right. I was not anxious to meet them. I thought they might be Boers beaten off by Sladen, and I remembered my prisoner at Doornkop. Beaten men, or men who have undergone severe punishment, are ill tempered. There was a field of tall mealies just ahead, I dived into it and lay doggo. From my hiding place in the mealies I looked up and saw a helio winking from a rise in front. That must be De Lisle. I had come dead straight. I broke cover and ran towards the helio. Soon I ran into De Lisle's advance guard.

I was now full of my mission, so full that I forgot my costume. I forgot also the military mind and a certain levity that alleviates its pressure on its humbler victims.

The wing of the advance guard I had run into was commanded by a subaltern. I told him of the urgency of the situation and begged him not to wait for orders, but to give me a horse and gallop on with me at once. I could hardly make myself heard for the uproarious laughter that greeted my appearance.

There was a doctor with the advance guard, from Cork. He was the weakest link in the chain of levity and mechanical discipline that obstructed me. I pulled him off his horse and got on it.

If you'll give me my horse,' said he, 'I'll give you my orderly's.' One point gained, but the subaltern wouldn't come on without orders. He sent, however, for the commander of the whole advance guard. On that officer's arrival the subaltern was told to take his orders from me and gallop like hell. We galloped. In a quarter of an hour we were within sight and sound of the laager. I had come about six miles. What I saw both shocked and puzzled me. The whole convoy was gone; not a wagon, a Cape cart nor a cow remained. How could the Boers have recaptured the convoy without capturing Sladen and his men? Sladen must be captured or annihilated and the Boers in possession. The heavy firing audible must be by the Boers at us, and the absence of bullets whistling past because they hadn't yet got the range.

Perhaps I can tell the rest of the story more vividly in a portion of a letter to my father written immediately after, which my mother has preserved. it may give a better impression of the kind of boy I was than my present sophisticated retrospect.

Thank God! It was not so, although the Boers got access to the wagons, as I will explain later. First I will continue about my own experience. On nearing the kraal firing became very heavy, and for a second, it bore out my previous fear that the Boers were in possession and firing at us, but no bullets came over, and I soon saw that it was our fellows firing at the retreating Boers, and then a cheer dispelled my last doubts. Poor Sladen's people had had a terribly hot time. Cameron (Gordon Highlanders) was killed, as was Mair, an Australian attached to the 6th M.l., Strong, of the Bedford company, was dying with an expansive bullet wound through the stomach, and Findlay, the adjutant of the 6th, had two ounces of brain knocked out by a Martini, but still lived, and I am thankful to say now seems to be going on well though he is paralysed down one side. Sladen himself was the only officer of ours unhurt. The kraals were strewn with dead and wounded of both sides, some ten dead Boers being left by their comrades in our hands as well as some wounded. The prisoners, with two exceptions, we retained, they having been driven into a straw palisade surrounding one of the kraals and promised a bayonet for the first man that moved. This excellent piece of work was done by a corporal in our company in charge of the guard. The exceptions were a parson named Kestell and his son, the former having been the predikant at Harrismith. He had given a lot of trouble at his capture in the morning and had been insolent to Crawford and the men. I had pointed a revolver at his head and eventually given him a pretty sharp rap thereon with the muzzle, but had remembered on hearing his name later on that he had done a most gallant thing in putting McGregor of the 92nd under cover when he was wounded on the 6th of January at Ladysmith. So I apologized to him for my rough treatment, and said I would do what I could to make him comfortable. This reverend gentleman, however, after waving to the Boers to come on, managed to escape, and making a dash for a rifle, shot one of the Australians before he got away. Though his action was hardly consistent with his calling, I can't help feeling him a better man than I am for his sturdy bearing and subsequent escape. I know now what a different thing it is to face death at the head of your own men in the flush of a fight to courting it in cold blood rather than be taken. Though everybody tells me I did the only sensible thing in putting up my hands, and Sladen has been kind enough to recommend my action in getting away to De Lisle and bringing him up, I must confess I have sunk in my own eyes.

I will give you a rough account of the fight before I go on, and illustrate it by the plan below:

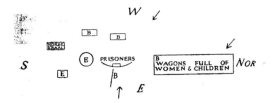

The circles and squares are the usual little sod wall or mud enclosures about a Kaffir kraal. Those marked B were rushed by the Boers; those E were held by us. The line B, low right, was a low wall facing the wagons, which the Boers got behind. The horse kraal was full of our horses, mostly off-saddled, but a good many horses were standing about in the open. The arrows are the three directions from which the Boer attack developed. In strict confidence, our outposts were sketchy in the extreme and were immediately driven in. Sladen counted on being able to hold the line of the parked wagons, as he thought the Boers would not fire into their own women. His first move appears to have been to run to the end of the wagons to organize a defence there, but he found the men on the ridge to the north-west of the wagons had already been driven in, most of them being killed in retiring, and that the Boers were rushing the wagons. He ran back shouting to every one to hold the kraals, Findlay with him and also, apparently, Mair. Findlay was hit, and Mair stayed with him, being almost immediately surrounded by Boers. Mair and two men with him put their hands up, but he was shot dead - his last words: 'Have mercy, you cowards.' As for the men, the same bullet passed through the nose of one and killed the other. It seems to have been cold-blooded murder.

For the rest, my plan will show you more or less what happened, the Boers rushing the kraals marked B and firing being mostly at about ten yards' range. One incident is interesting. A man of ours was captured in the first forward rush of the Boers, and sent in with a white flag to Sladen, demanding surrender. The Boers took advantage of the flag to push a lot of men closer up, and Sladen, of course, told them to go to Hell. The man went back with the message and was ordered by the Boers on pain of instant death to raise the white flag again on the end of a long ox whip. As such close range the men might have thought that the flag was being raised by Sladen's order, but a sergeant of ours, Rothnie, got a dozen men to cover the unfortunate holder of the flag, and shouted him to drop it or he'd be instantly shot. The poor fellow with fifteen Boer and twelve British rifles within ten yards of him, dropped the flag and fell flat on his face, eventually escaping unhurt. I believe it would have gone hard with all surviving officers had the Boers gained the day. One brute, after shooting an Australian through the chest, jumped on him and bashed his ribs in, the man dying as much from the latter as the former. De la Rey was in the firing line himself with a Mauser pistol, but on the man next him being shot dead, he left hurriedly. I find now C. de Wet was there, and a doctor at a Boer hospital we struck the other day in the wilds between Senekal and Bethlehem said he got three bullets through his clothes. If so, it is a pity a fourth couldn't find a more central position.

De Lisle was up not long after me in the kraals and shouted for every one with a fit horse to get on and retake the wagons that had got away. Somebody drew his attention to the casualties. His answer was characteristic: 'I don't care a damn for the casualties, every one with a fit horse come on.' I was dazed with the loss of so many good fellows, especially Cameron, and the prospect of doing something to avenge it pulled me together a bit, and finding my own pony one of the few not shot, (I told you I rode out to the Boers on a captured one) I got him saddled up and galloped on. We re-took the whole lot of wagons, and I don't think more than five Cape carts in all got away. I was dressed for this gallop in a pair of Boer trousers given me by a man in the kraals. Fortunately I had another pair of breeches and putties in my kit, so the next morning could appear perfectly equipped.

On the evening of the 7th we buried our dead in the cemetery at --,a town cleared of its inhabitants some time ago. It was a ghastly scene, twenty of our fellows and Australians and thirteen Boers being buried on opposite sides of the cemetery path; the men and the Boers in two shallow trenches; the officers in separate graves; our men in blankets, the Boers as they were, as the women weren't inclined to part with any of their bedding, and contented themselves with loud lamentations as the dead were lifted out of the wagons. The prisoners remarked, on its being suggested to them that they should dig the graves for their countrymen, 'Why should we dig graves for Transvaalers?' and they didn't take the trouble to fill the trench properly in, a duty which was left to them. Cameron we buried wrapped in his tartan rug, as was his wish. His loss is a deep one to me, as his pluck and decision in action had made me very fond of him. The men loved him.

Strong of the Bedfords was just about the best officer ever saw, always absolutely cool and absolutely sound. In Cameron dash predominated, as to my mind it now should, but he was sound as well.

De Lisle spoke to me in the strongest terms about the loss he was to the regiment. He - De Lisle – makes enemies by the sort of remark I have related about the casualties, and his manner is frequently hectoring. I should be sorry to lose him as commander, for his worst enemies believe in him, and he gives one a sense of doing some good. He would do more, if the other columns were under as good a soldier. For this day's work they gave me the D.S.O. To do myself justice I did my best to prevent them. I told Sladen and De Lisle and every one else that I had behaved like a coward. In fact, I think I was quite hysterical about it. But Kitchener seems to have been so tickled at the idea of my running away in my shirt that nothing would do him but to recommend me for the D. S. 0. It pleased my father, anyhow, for that gave us every possible military decoration between us. My father had all the others. As for me, I was already becoming accustomed to the non-acceptance of my standards of merit or demerit.

Enough for South Africa.

The war there taught me two things - the weakness of my spirit when alone, and the strength of my body. I was never sick nor sorry as long as we marched fifteen miles a day or more. I began to feel rotten as soon as we halted and a short march wasn't enough to tune me up. That lesson I have never forgotten.

As for the weakness of my spirit cut off from the herd. I have had to tackle that; I have sure had to tackle that. For details consult the sequel.

CHAPTER 2.
INNER REVOLUTION

My father had had the Governorship of Gibraltar held open for him until he returned from South Africa and recovered in health from the effects of the Ladysmith siege. He took up his duties in Gibraltar some time in 1900. I left South Africa with a draft of time-expired men in August 1902, and joined my father as personal aide-de-camp soon after taking the draft to the depot at Aberdeen.

I say I was A.D.C. to my father, but I was really A.D.C. to my mother; what is called invitation A.D.C.; managing the invitation list, making out the plan of the table, writing the menus and dancing with the plain women.

My three years at Gibraltar were the great playtime of my life. My job was by no means a sinecure, but it left plenty of time for amusement. I hunted, raced, and played polo. I shared digs part of the time with the chap who commanded the torpedo-boat flotilla; for shooting expeditions in Spain or Morocco, some naval exercise for a torpedo boat could usually be arranged. I had the run of my teeth at the gubernatorial table and free forage and stabling for two horses. I kept four.

In such a background began the real interest, joy, and tragedy of my life.

One of the accepted beauties of the place was Mercedes (Dollie) Mosley. She was Spanish and Catholic on her mother's side. I was Protestant on both sides, Ulster Protestant on my father's. There is a story told of an open-minded stranger listening to a conversation of local stalwarts in a public house in Portadown. The subject of discussion was the Roman Catholic religion. The stranger was so shocked by the lack of moderation in the views, he heard expressed that he felt obliged to chip in.

'Gentlemen, said he, I think you take an extreme view. You must not forget that the Church you condemn so unsparingly kept the lamp of Christian faith burning through many centuries and handed it on to our own Church; that the saints we reverence were many of them nourished in her bosom, and as for the Pope, he is a man of saintly personal character, beloved and respected by the whole of Christendom.'

He was heard in an impressive but unimpressed silence. When he had finished he was answered, and the answer was final as only an Ulsterman's can be.

'Aweel, that may 'a be, but he's a very bad name about Portadown.'

My views of the Roman Catholic Church were at bottom, with some deceptive tolerance on the surface, those of Portadown. In spite of which I became engaged to Dollie Mosley.

Both families were uncompromisingly opposed. Readers of the preceding pages will realize that that did not mend matters. I was perfectly aware, though, of the vast gulf in tradition, temperament, and outlook between us. I was equally aware of an emotional determination to bridge that gulf.

This set up a conflict between my reason and my emotion so intense that at one time it frightened me very badly indeed.

I remember the exact time and the exact place when this conflict came to a head.

I have undertaken to write this book without introducing my own theories and I will try to keep my undertaking, but I must give the outstanding psychological fact and its-strange accompaniment, which changed the very mechanism of my consciousness, and the whole course of my life. Apart from that change in the mechanism of my consciousness and the remarkable correlative in outer life, which, as I will tell in a moment, became connected with that change, not one of the main events and actions of my subsequent life could possibly have taken place

I had gone for a walk alone up the Rock absorbed in the inner conflict I have described. It was so intense as to exhaust me physically. I lay down half-way up the Rock and fell into an exhausted doze for some ten minutes.

When I woke, the conflict was resolved, not by the slightest ray of light coming to the mind as to how to overcome difficulties which were as obvious and rationally insurmountable as ever, but by a reinforcement of emotion. This took the form of a most pleasure able sensation in the middle of my chest, as if I had just drunk a strong liqueur. May I be permitted to say that the fluctuations of that sensation guided my, life, to the almost complete exclusion in important decisions of the normal mental process, for the next ten or fifteen years. It guides it still, but now the mind has caught up with it and co-operates with it in obedience to a totally different set of premises, which the liqueur-sensation, for many years not only unaided but obstructed by the mind, pushed and drove and beckoned me to discover.

If publishers and public stand for this book, I'll give them another some day which interests myself. I see no insuperable reason why it should not also interest them.

I descended the Rock and went to the Garrison Library to read the Reuter telegrams about the Russo-Japanese War, which was then in progress. As I did so the liqueur-sensation intensified to something like ecstasy.

Having said this much I must say a little more. In what follows I shall have to describe a journey taken across half the world at the bidding of the liqueur-sensation, in flat defiance, not only of reason, but of apparent possibility. I shall have to describe how my movements, initiated by such prompting, synchronized and converged with those of another person in a way that achieved my object as at no other moment it could have been achieved. The liqueur-sensation played the biggest part in driving me out of the army, to Canada, into various prisons and awkward predicaments beyond number. Of your charity let me devote a page to recording the existence of this sixth sense, this irresistible if at first unintelligible driving force. Extend your charity to granting me permission to explain in a very rough outline its latent intelligibility. As I read the telegrams about the Russo-Japanese War and felt the swelling ecstasy within me, this idea was born: 'you belong to a whole. Your Dollie Mosley belongs to a whole. What you see of her now is only a tiny little section. It will develop and change and you will develop and change. And here is the vital point you will both develop and change in organic connection with universal worldwide forces, which this Russo-Japanese War is beginning to set in motion. Therefore do not bother about your silly little sectional mind and the little foreshortened sections which is all it can see. I, the liqueur-sensation in your chest, am you, and the Russo-Japanese War, and wars and revolutions beyond that again within you and without you. I'll take you through. I'll take your purblind pig of a mind through. And what I'll do for you I'll do for Dollie Mosley. Leave it to me.'

So I left it -and will leave it, but I owed it that much.

While undergoing this profound change, I continued to write menus and race ponies.

I had a great character of a pony called 'the Baulker.' A charming American guest gave him his name when I was breaking him in, in the yard of the Convent (as Government House was then called). That pony could stand either on his head or his hind legs like an acrobat, and was so engaged when the American lady looked out of her bedroom window' 'Say,' she called encouragingly, 'doesn't he baulk?' He won me my first race. 'My boy,' commented my father, who was really delighted - the one thing we had thoroughly in common was horses, a bit too much so for him when I lamed his – "My boy, your success will be your ruin." But it wasn't. The Baulker indeed gave me some bad moments. I lent him to Admiral Farquhar for an afternoon's ride, he (the Baulker) got bored waiting to go through the barrier at the Spanish frontier - the Governor's A.D.C.'s had the privilege of riding round the beach - stood on his head, and entangled his heels in the roof of an adjacent karotske. The roof had to be removed. The admiral never borrowed a pony from me again.

There was comedy in that. I invited tragedy by driving the Baulker as wheeler of a tandem from a very low dogcart. A splendid old lady who was staying with us, a Mrs. Limond, volunteered to accompany me in this turnout to one of the garrison race meetings. We got there all right. I was mad, plumb mad; to let her come home with me after the Baulker had been standing for some hours. He smashed the cart and her kneecap. He'd have smashed mine, but I was sitting on a high hassock and his heels hit my shins slant-wise, but he cut me pretty badly. Some comedy again when I drove Claude Camberlege, the torpedo flotilla commander, to his wedding in this death-inviting rig.

I was best man and we were both in full uniform. Being a state occasion we had requisitioned John, one of the Convent footmen, as tiger on the back scat. John was observed to be sitting, not with his arms folded in the regulation manner, but with his finger tips joined in an attitude of prayer. But the Baulker, like so many obstreperous natures, was gentle as a dove in the presence of Love.

Then there was 'Licurgo.' I bought him for £10 from Mr. Williams, one of the group of British wine merchants at Jerez. Williams had rescued him from a cab in sheer regard for the dignity of a well-bred horse; he was a grandson of Hermit's. I knew of a blister that would cure anything - Harvey's embrocation. I took Licurgo to Gibraltar, blistered his shoulder and all four legs. Later I won two £40 races with him and the Calpe Hunt Point-to-Point, riding him myself at 13 st. 7 lbs. in a field of sixty-three starters. My father finished tenth in the same race. He might have beaten me, but 'Welcome, the thoroughbred charger which the people of Belfast had given him after Ladysmith, had broken his knees the day before, to my mother's unconcealed relief. It was bad enough to have a son on a ten-pound horse without a husband on a four-hundred-guinea one the devil himself couldn't hold.

I sold Licurgo for £40 to Admiral May commanding the Atlantic Fleet. With the horse I sent a letter of instructions how to glue him together. I am told the admiral framed it. The great old horse won the Point-to-Point the next year, ridden by the flag-lieutenant, and died on his way home. May we all die as nobly.

They were great days. Into their atmosphere of gaiety and sport came some pomp. King Edward was there more than once, and the Kaiser twice, going and returning from his spectacular trip to Morocco. The royalties were the business agents to get their countries a place in the Moroccan sun, and Gibraltar was the jumping-off ground to the subsequent Algeciras conference. In one of the Kaiser's visits, the last one, I think, he arrived in a great North German Lloyd liner, privately chartered, with forty-two gentlemen of his suite, including Von Tirpitz, Von Plessen, and other notabilities.

Comparing the atmospheres of German and British Royalty, I was struck with the greater *naiveté* and greater sincerity of the former. That the Kaiser was a bit of a mountebank I could see even then. I am convinced that his gentlemen could not. When he (the Kaiser) would summon one of his suite to be presented to my mother with an 'Ach, you have not met *my* Admiral von Tirpitz,' even that be whiskered old pirate evidently became 'the proudest man that ever scuttled a ship.' These immaculate military or naval chromographs, hung with decorations principally for lunching with people, literally glowed with pride at any sign of the Imperial notice. And they spoke of the Kaiser

-with a reverence, watched him with a henchman's tenderness, that was obviously genuine.

Edward's atmosphere was quite different. His inner circle, or the men I saw nearest to him, were either intimate or privileged jesters like Lambton or Charlie Beresford, or very well-bred superior flunkies like ahem! Some others. Certainly there was nothing naive about either themselves or their attitude to their master. The flunkies could and did demand from others the reverential attitude they assumed themselves, but one felt it was an assumption. The jesters in their intimate gossip constantly undermined it. King Edward himself liked good cooking and the company of pretty women. I remember a story retailed by one of the jesters about His Majesty and a lady on Tommy Lipton's yacht. A mast or spar suddenly fell, narrowly escaping the pair. 'This is no place,' said the Scotch skipper, 'for kings or their por-r-cupines.' I imagine the King would have laughed as heartily as anyone if the story had been told him in the right milieu. Anyhow, he made no secret of his predilection for pretty women. His equerry, Stanley Clarke, actually came round the night after a big official dinner with a list of ladies, obviously chosen for their looks, whom the King would like invited to a private dinner the following night. They included Dollie, and I, as invitation A.D.C., sent out the invitations by special orderly.

There was a greater *naiveté,* shall we say a more selective dignity about the Kaiser's admiration of the other sex. He took a fancy to a colonel's wife with grey -hair and a rather noble type of face. Noticing her absence at some reception he said to my mother loudly, 'But where is my Mrs. H.? I do not see my Mrs. H.' And when Mrs H. was summoned post haste he told her he would like to introduce her to his Empress. Admitted his Empress wasn't there; but I think he meant it. It takes sex to be the touchstone of quality.

I was invitation A.D.C., a cipher, but in regard to Edward's private dinner, half of me was proud of the notice of Dollie's beauty; the other half of me said, 'This Pimping for princes might have its limitations.'

My time at Gibraltar contained the seeds of change in my subsequent life. I had seen two people too close - God and the King. I was more conscious of the contrast than the connection. By God I mean the Being in Whom we live and move and have our being. Whose nature is reported to be Love. Stimulated by love I had glimpse of this great organic Unity, as I have tried to describe. By the King I mean no particular monarch. My experience included Edward VII of England and William II of Germany, and one or two minor lights. It would be presumptuous to say I had seen through them and what they stood for; but they no longer interested me. I was inoculated against that particular form of hypnosis. They were no different from other people. They were the summation of, shall we say, the most ordinary and least interesting side of other people. Their function, I had seen as invitation A.D.C., was to bring out in strong relief an aspect of other people which at other times lurked in decent concealment. Far be it from me to claim that I was exempt from this undesirable aspect myself. I was as big a snob as the rest; but with one eye open. And my snobbery always missed fire; I threw myself into it with too much abandon. The morning of a big dinner when King Edward made my father a field marshal, a pony had come over backwards with me in the Gibraltar main street, and dropped me on the asphalt on the base of my spine. That may be some excuse for what followed, but I do not wish to press it. It was a hot night in more senses than one. I was detailed to see the Royal party off to their yacht in the launch. The landing stage swayed abominably. I swayed with it, rhythmically I hoped. Returning to the Convent I went in search of the family who I expected to find on the roof watching the illuminations of the Fleet. There was a spiral staircase up to the roof. I ran up it and I ran down. Then I started to run up the back stairs into the house. The rest of the story was told me by my sisters. The invitation A.D.C. was missing. Cries were raised of 'Jack! Has anyone seen Jack?' Agnew the military secretary assured my mother I must have gone to bed in the A.D.C.'s quarters. He did it in good faith, I think. But Currie, my brother A.D.C. who afterwards married one of my sisters, knew better. He pulled the curtain at the head of the back stairs, and nudging my sisters, silently pointed to a sleeping figure halfway down. I had fallen like a soldier. When their Excellencies had gone to bed they carried me home.

CHAPTER 3.
BLACKGUARD'S LUCK

My father's governorship of Gibraltar expired about June 1905. A month or two later I joined the 2nd Battalion of the Regiment in Peshawar, the other battalion to that with which I had served in South Africa. In the hope of getting some military diplomatic job which would enable me to marry, I applied myself to the study of Hindustani. Eventually I passed lower and higher standards and higher proficiency in that language. For the last I got a government grant of Rs. 1000, but I never got the desired job. Other things intervened. I have told of the strange conception that governed the marriage union I contemplated, namely, that the union would consist in the progressive transformation of us both. I have already threatened to write a book on the subject. Perhaps many books would be necessary to justify so inhuman, so monstrous, an idea. For marriage is regarded as the sweetest of stabilities. A settled life or at least a settled income is with decent responsible people a *sine qua non* of the undertaking. A stable foundation is necessary for this most stable of emotional contracts. Dear me, the reiteration of this word makes me think of horses and mares - or possible mares and geldings. Probably my love letters to my fiancée contained a great deal that was not only subversive but also boring. Anyhow, she wrote breaking off the engagement. I found myself in quite intolerable distress.

I was on leave in Simla when the letter came. That was a shrewd perception of the Psalmist, 'I will look unto the hills from whence cometh my strength.' Many people follow it automatically in great trouble. I have always done so, if I could. I warned my bearer to make preparations and started off into the Himalayas towards Kashmir. I made a place called Narkunda, forty miles away from Simla, installed myself in the dak-bungalow there, and decided to make it a base for expeditions.

The first day I walked to a little mission station ten miles away, of which I forget the name, and called on the missionary's wife, not without hopes of being invited to lunch. I was invited all right. While I waited in the drawing room my eyes caught a text on the wall, 'Go forth now and I will go with thee and show thee what thou shalt speak and what thou shalt do.' I got the general sense of it, but one word seemed to be hammering into me all over -Now Now Now. Hammer isn't the right word. Melt, dissolve, would be better. That liqueur-sensation in my chest had a converse, a bottle contracted frozen feeling. The text, and especially the word 'now' began to thaw me. Yes, that's it exactly, I began to thaw. I remember a logger in Canada with whom I was arguing some point, which involved the personal factor - as most points do, by the way - remarking with a shrug, 'Well, you may feel the same when you're asleep as I do when I'm awake.'

This possibility of completely different sensations, covered by the same words, is a great difficulty in conveying one's sensations to others. Do proper and respectable people freeze, and thaw suddenly, violently, and dynamically? Pipes do, and they burst unless you leave the tap running. I am like a pipe. In a hard frost I have to leave the tap running somehow. When the thaw comes it must turn full on.

'Go forth now.' - The frost in my chest seemed inclined to melt at that. When I considered it seriously, streaks of the liqueur-sensation took its place. But what did going forth now imply? As to that I was in no doubt whatever. it meant first walking ten miles back to Narkunda; that would make twenty for the day. Then it meant getting a horse, if possible, and riding forty miles more into Simla that night. For the British mail left Simla at 11 o'clock the next day. I was in no doubt whatever it meant that week's mail or nothing. To reach Simla in time was difficult but not impossible. English leave was, humanly speaking, impossible. The full complement of officers in the regiment for borne leave had already received it. There remained the alternative of going without leave. To apply to the regiment was, I knew, hopeless. Stay! there was a mightier answer than the colonel. There was a commander-in-chief, whose name was Kitchener, and whose domicile at the moment was in Simla.

I thanked the kind missionaries for their hospitality and set out back to Narkunda. It was a steep climb most of the way, and bodily fatigue began to speak. This was sheer lunacy; to go thousands of miles on the bidding of a stray text after a girl who didn't want me. In very wavering mood I reached Narkunda. I called my bearer and told him to get a pony of sonic kind, if one was to be found. He returned shortly to say there was no such thing in the district. 'That settles it thought, and began to open some letters that had arrived, forwarded from Simla. The first one I opened had the telegraphic address, 'Flinching, London,' at the head of the paper. 'That's what I am doing, sure enough, flinching,' said I, out loud, and sent my bearer out on another horse-hunt. This time he came back escorting a native who in turn escorted, not a horse, nor yet an animal that with any accuracy could be called a pony. It was a little bigger than a St. Bernard dog. My legs would with ease have reached the ground on either side but for the remarkable shape of the saddle that threw my knees in the direction of my mouth. 'It is well,' said I to my bearer, 'we go to Simla. I upon this horse! Thou in whatever manner thou canst devise.' With that I pushed some things into a pillowcase and started. That indomitable quadruped never flagged. He went at just the jiggle best calculated to flay me alive against the antediluvian saddle; but he continued to go. I longed for him to stop, for any excuse to cut short the physical torture I suffered. But my will was engaged in the matter now, and the whole setting and circumstance made for mental exaltation. Night had fallen. The narrow path or pipeline we followed was cut out of the precipice with thousands of feet above and below it. The animal disdained all guidance. It would go on the outermost edge of the track and nowhere else; for forty miles my left foot hung over dizzy space. When I realized -the creature's will was as set as my own, I left him to choose his own perilous course. The desperate risks the creature seemed set on taking accorded with my mood. 'Good,' thought I, 'you non-descript equine. We're well matched. Each of us in his own way likes to hang over the abyss.' Years later when I had isolated this quality in myself I put it in verse: -

I have been suckled on pain
And weaned on the ultimate slope.
Suspended above the inane, I bit at the end of the rope.
When the strands of it creaked with the strain
They strung me to hope.

How nice to be a nondescript equine instead of a nondescript human; to jiggle through the night over the abyss, but write no verse.

I forget what I did with that *equus diminutives* destiny. I did not take him, her, or it, to General Birdwood, Kitchener's military secretary, to whose residence I limped painfully about 6 a.m. the following morning.

Birdwood was friendly and helpful. He would take me to the chief at breakfast, and he did. Kitchener seemed friendly too. My father had lived in the same house, Snowdon) when he was commander-in-chief in India, and some of my sisters had spent a slice of their childhood there.

'Well, White, what can I do for you? I told him my trouble at once and my reason for wanting to go home. 'Does your father approve of the match?' 'No, sir, but I don't see what it's got to do with him.'

I think it was that did it. Anyhow, he gave me leave there and then without demur; then he gave me a good breakfast. I caught the mail tonga down to Umballa and the mail train for Bombay. I had wired from Simla to the adjutant at Peshawar that I had leave from the chief. At Umballa I received the adjutant's reply. 'Chief's leave not valid without the colonel's sanction. Colonel arrives Bombay (he was returning from home) such and such a ship, due such and such a time.' The colonel's arrival might or might not precede my intended departure. I did not wait to investigate. I boarded my own ship safely. No doubt the colonel disembarked as safely from his.

The sea voyage was the hardest part. I knew very well that Dollie had broken the engagement under more than mere external pressure, though that may have played its part. She knew we were thoroughly unsuited. It is a little hard to convince a girl that she is only an undeveloped section of her ultimate self. She may not thank you if you succeed. Of course, I didn't put it as coldly as that to myself, though that idea was latent. I meant to get her, that was all about it, but I was frightened at the lengths of abnormality to which this determination had carried me, and I knew in some queer way I couldn't undo the experiment with supernormal powers I was trying. I was frightened of finding my text or my action upon it had been nothing but self-hypnotic delusion. I was also frightened of finding it had been something more. The most terrifying thing in the world is to commit oneself, to commit one's living action, to powers beyond the present scope of the collective mind. It means such fearful mental isolation, such a sense of belonging to a different species.

I consorted on board no longer with those of my own outward species, subalterns going on leave and the like. I made friends with a man who had been a doctor, undergone some sort of conversion) and was now a Salvation Army major. He had been working in some medical mission. I went ashore with him at Port Said. The usual crowd of importunate pimps pestered us to visit their haunts of vice. Strung up as I was now every moment and irritated beyond endurance by one chap who refused to leave us alone, I turned round and kicked him. I half expected commendation from the Salvation Army major. I did not get it. Instead I got a lecture on tolerance and allowance for the circumstances of others. The pimp had to make his living. I never

forgot that lecture. It was my introduction to Marx and his maxim 'The economic is the determining factor.'

I did not know where Dollie was. From Port Said I wired to a sister in London to find out, telling her to wire reply to the ship at Marseilles. At Marseilles I received the reply. It ran: 'Dollie and Agatha sail from Gibraltar on 6th. It was then the 4th- I forget of what month. My sister's wire meant that my fiancée and her sister were going to board my ship, one of the P. & 0. Line, by which they always travelled. The text seemed to have known what it was talking about.

I cannot describe my feeling the next two days between Marseilles and Gibraltar. I was relieved by the knowledge that I would have to attack a convoy rather than storm a fortress. I had dreaded the latter. In psychological matters my military instinct is unerring. My first victories had been achieved within the fortress by sorties from its very citadel, Government House. An attack from the sea was quite another matter.

On a cloudless Mediterranean morning the ship rounded Europa Point and anchored in the bay outside the harbour. I lay in my cabin under an open port. I heard Dollie's voice and peeping out saw herself, her sister, and, last but not least, her father. I remained where I was. Directly I felt the ship under way, I ran to the purser: 'Can you give me the number of Miss Mosley's cabin?' He could not, for no Gibraltar passengers had been allowed on board. A lascar of our crew was suspected of plague. Crazed with disappointment I ran up on deck. The ship was well out- -but still in the bay. I was a fair swimmer and measured the distance with my eye. A pretty desperate measure that, I realized, not to be undertaken unless compelled.

I ran down to the purser again. 'What about the Gibraltar passengers, what's going to happen about them?' 'They'll come on the *Orient;* she's in the bay now and will be in Plymouth within twenty-four hours of us.' No need to swim, then. This might work out better than the girls coming aboard. I had a sister at Plymouth now married to Currie, the brother A.D.C. who had been showman of the sleeping-beauty tableau on the back stairs the night of the royal dinner He was Adjutant of Gunners at Plymouth. I would have a base to act from. So I went to the Curries on landing at Plymouth and Currie agreed to come and meet the *Orient* with me the next morning. Together we went down to the tender. Horrible to relate, there was 'Uncle Arthur's rich uncle of Dollie's, and with him were two stalwart policemen. My reluctant father-in-law elect, whose various functions at Gibraltar included the agency of the P. & 0. Line, had seen my name in the passenger list and wired 'Uncle Arthur' to stand by at Plymouth and prevent molestation.

But 'Uncle Arthur' lacked the military instinct. Indeed, as the event proved, he lacked the whole gamut of military qualities. He betrayed this from the first by leaving the two policemen on the quay, while Currie and I went out with him on the tender. We did not converse. I sent Currie on board first to break the news. He was away too long, So I followed. Sister Agatha, mildly remonstrant, barred my path but was removed. The text had kept its word; it had shown me what to do. It had now to show me what to speak. Seemingly it completed its promise. By the time the tender had got back to the quay I had won the day. I gather the two policemen got £1 between them. 'Uncle Arthur's' genius was financial rather than military.

I wired to my mother to meet the party at Paddington. There was a moving scene in the waiting room in that sober station. 'Uncle Arthur' washed his hands of an affair in which he had tried to perform, not of his own volition, an unpleasant avuncular duty. My mother gallantly shouldered the responsibility he laid down. Dollie came that very night to the care of my family at the Royal Hospital, Chelsea, of which my father was then Governor.

My action upon a text seen upon the borders of Kashmir had met with triumphant and incredibly prompt success. To the outer world jack White had done another mad thing and brought it off with his blackguard's luck. But to me there was more in it than that. The liqueur-sensation was vindicated. It was *en rapport* with intelligence very much superior to Jack White's, able to combine and synchronize movements over wide distances of time and space.

To the world Jack White might be madder than ever, but to himself he was proved sane after a period of very agonizing doubt of his own sanity. Also, he would pursue this larger sanity till his little mind got the hang of it. Then he would prove to his own satisfaction what he had always -suspected, that it was the world that was mad, not he; mad as a flock of stampeded sheep and blind as an army of burrowing moles. He went back to India almost at once, but he has not gone back on the lesson of the trip. I find in the old MSS. I am now re-writing to 'cut out the theories' in fulfilment of my agreement with the publishers, the following pages. I think they should go in. The public have had a good Story. Let them stand a page or two of what it cost to write and live.

'Heretofore though in action I had obeyed, I think been compelled to obey, my chest, in thought I sided half my time with my normal mind, and was ready to find myself guilty of mental aberration. But here was wonderful evidence of the intelligent foresight far beyond mine, of the supernormal power to which I had yielded. Yet I would like to say here, that even when this evidence of intelligent guidance in my supernormal leaps rose to certainty, the strain of it always remained. All action taken in advance of my reason, though the main action of twenty years of my life has been so taken, retained this element of strain, often for long periods at a time almost beyond the endurance of flesh and blood. I never experienced the absolute faith in "my voices" that is reported of Joan of Arc, perhaps because to this day I have never experienced anything that could be called actual clairaudience or clairvoyance. The impulse to action was always this sensation in my chest accompanied by a mental sensation of co-operation with a scientific law beyond my formulation or comprehension.

During my agitator days in Glasgow, long after the period I am now describing, there was a revolutionary paper *The Worker*, with "Knowledge must always precede action" for its motto.

I wrote a series of articles for it on the contrary theme, "Action must always precede knowledge." I stand by that yet but knowledge is the goal and the crown of action, though for the *real* knowledge there is no path but action to win and keep it.

Nor did I ever have Joan of Arc's humility and simplicity. I was often abject in terror, feeling that the new combination of forces to which I had committed myself made me somehow of a different species to the normal human being.

But during my confident spells, I enjoyed my singularity inwardly, and spoke of it outwardly, if I thought I could find a grain of understanding. How many and how humiliating disappointments have I not suffered looking for that grain, till for a while I cried with Nietzsche, and cried sincerely, "Give me another mask."'

One more paragraph I find in the old manuscript, which it seems a pity to waste.

'In the fight of Love against Money, the more vital force has one great advantage. It is keyed up beyond fear of publicity or unseemliness; it moves with the speed of desire outdistancing thought, and, if it is thwarted, it is ready to suffer or, if need be, to inflict "grievous bodily hurt."

During my short stay at home there was one incident too important in its bearing on my subsequent life to omit.

It was an interview with the Mother Superior of a convent in Kensington Square, where Dollie had been for part of her education.

The good Mother urged the obligation on Dollie to comply with the demands of her Church.

Finding me adamant, she turned to the penalties that I would incur by responsibility for her disobedience. The matter in question was the faith of our possible children.

'Fool,' you will say, 'having gone to such trouble to get the girl, to be obstructive about these premature details.' I thought otherwise. Remember, I had got the girl following a lead of my own that no organised religion hinted at. It felt like something new. I was ready to give up all I had gained rather than compromise the right of my hypothetical hopefuls to extend this new consciousness free of Dogmatic shackles. Rome ' too, stood pre-eminently for the subordination of the inner light to external authority, individual vision to collective prudence. Rome was the enemy despite this charming and remonstrant lady.

'So be it,' said I, and if I was rhetorical I was none the less sincere, for I felt in my bones the vast complex of inner and outer forces I challenged and defied. 'So be it. I take the responsibility. On my soul be the punishment.'

Thus having challenged Rome I returned to India.

CHAPTER 4.
PEACEFUL PESHAWAR

There are two distinct countries included in the map of India, just as there are two distinct species included under the same external human form. There is India and Anglo-India. The former I sensed as a strange and somewhat unfriendly psychic presence. I saw it in vivid colours, heard it in strange sounds, smelt it in innumerable stinks. I touched it in nothing but my study of the language. The real India, I felt, could absorb the stinks. Anglo-India could not. When I think of Anglo-India I think of the proverbial hot-weather dinner-party 'where everything smelt except the flowers and nothing was hot except the champagne.' I think of a night-commode prepared for the visit of the Amir of Afghanistan on a visit to Peshawar shown me by its proud creator, the political officer; the thing was shaped like a throne and decked with velvet and silver-beading. Why I think of these things I must leave symbolists to discover.

The regiment was still at Peshawar. I had better say something about my regimental soldiering in peacetime; so far it has been only war and staff service. The subject is painful, for to the best of my belief I was a careless and rather slovenly officer; slovenly even in matters of costumes that all-important touchstone of military quality. The permutations and combination of a Highland officer's costume were too much for me, whether through want of concentration or pre-occupation with something else I cannot say.

Perhaps a sketch of my character given me by Sandy Miller, the only one of my brother officers I vividly remember, may explain my defect in part.

Sandy is dead and his mother has written a book about him in which she said, truly enough, that religion was one of the silences of David's (Sandy's) life. Blasphemy was not, especially about a certain superior officer, whom he loathed. He was running him down one day to me in most unmeasured language. 'Oh come, Sandy,' I chipped in, 'he's not as bad as all that.'

Sandy turned on me as might a minister interrupted in a sermon.

'I won't say you're a good man, Jack, for you obviously ar-r-e not

' (Sandy preserved the Scotch burr and his individuality with it) 'but there are depths of infamy in that b -a man of your comparatively simple nature can neither fathom nor understand.'

Was it my simple nature made it so hard for me to get the right combinations of sporran, spats, headdress, and gloves? To this day my favourite nightmare is of finding myself singular on parade in one of these particulars.

The explanation I favour myself is that of M. Coué, who tells us that the imagination is stronger than the will; the will working without the imagination is apt to defeat its own object.

My imagination was never seized by the beauties and duties of peace-time soldiering; not even by the kit-inspection regulation which directs that the bristles of the soldier's tooth-brush shall face the back of the cover of his Bible. Thus the earnest efforts of my will fell short of permanent success. For a while I would attain. At such times I was deeply pleased, for I wanted to be efficient. Then I would find myself humbled to the dust by appearing on parade in a Glengarry when the fashion was helmets, or in khaki spats when by some herd instinct that I lacked, all but I were bespatted in white.

They would talk to me about 'orders.' No real help lay in them. For one thing I seldom read them- I have already spoken of my need to guard against certain degrees of boredom as morally dangerous to me. For another their directions only removed the problem a step further back. Such a trite phrase 'Drill Order' offered no real guide to the sartorial complexities I had to face. My imagination was not engaged. It must have been through their engaged imagination that others achieved a uniformity that remained a mystery to me. My imagination did not become engaged in what I may till I may call 'barrack-square soldiering' till I took to raising rebel armies later on. I always severed connection with the rebel armies before they got down to niceties of costume.

In spite of my incurable defect I was sent out from Peshawar in command of three companies for military training.

A native transport driver was brought before me on arrival in camp on a complaint lodged by one of our Jocks. The driver had refused to pull up when some of the regimental baggage kept falling off an overloaded cart. I gave the man a scolding in Hindustani and turned to go away. The man did not go away but kept chattering. There was some kind of Transport N.C.O. with him. I told him to make his man shut up and take him away. He couldn't or didn't. Then I began to get angry; I have always hated redundant speech. I knew nothing about the Native Transport service, and cared less. I'd given the man no punishment, had no machinery to punish him if I had wanted; why should he make this disproportionate noise?

'If thou dost not keep silence,' said I, 'I will give an order that thou shalt be beaten.'

The babble intensified. I told one of our Jocks to turn him over the wheel of a cart and give him a few smacks with a swagger-cane on the rump.' *(This incident may serve to show to the keen-sighted the necessity of my getting out of the army. I wanted smacking myself, but not with a regulation' cane.)*

This was done. In a few days I got a communication from the colonel forwarding a complaint from the officer or official in charge of Native Transport and asking for my explanation. 'The man,' said his white superior, 'was brooding over his wrongs.' He was evidently a brooding nature that is what had annoyed me so in the first place. Ultimately the matter reached Kitchener and Kitchener was furious. As luck would have it, he had just raised the Native Transport service to military status; my action had challenged his dignity in infringing a dignity he had just conferred. The sort of thing my action would do anyhow! I am not a violent or brutal nature. No brutality was alleged. The man's chastisement had been of the mildest, a mere smack to a tiresome child. Ordered by anyone else it would have been left at that. Ordered by me, it must reach a commander-in-chief and affect an important military measure. It is my fate to have the spotlight on me. As the don had said at Summerfield, 'Whatever you do White, you're always found out."

Kitchener ordered that a Court of inquiry should be held on my conduct.

The Court met under the presidency of a colonel of Native Cavalry. Witnesses were called. Gus Fowke, my subaltern, a great cricketer and athlete, was the principal witness for the defence.

Asked what he would have done under similar circumstances, he replied:

'Well, sir, if I'd had a revolver I might have shot him (the chattering driver) or if only a stick I might have just clubbed him.'

No wonder after that the Court found me to have acted with reason and moderation,' and exonerated me from all blame. Kitchener remained quite unaffected by my dove-like innocence. He had over-ridden regulations in my favour when he had given me special leave home. Now he would reverse the process. He ignored the Court's finding. He decreed that I was to have no home leave till further orders; that I was not to go to the hills *(i.e.* I must remain in the plains for the hot weather) for two years; and that my ability to keep my temper was to be reported on every six months. Right on top of which came a letter from Dollie breaking off her engagement for the second time; saying she had left my people and returned to her own) and that the breach was final.

CHAPTER 5.
KITCHENER OBSTRUCTS

Last time Kitchener had provided the means to surmount obstacles otherwise insuperable. This time Kitchener was the obstacle himself. Napoleon said of the English they never know when they are beaten. The Irish fight even when they do know it. The fight I put up now was purely Irish in quality, though at this time I hardly knew myself an Irishman. I fought to escape the torturing pressure of my own thwarted will and imagination. I fought for the sake of fighting, without hope of success. There is a Gaelic proverb, 'Fighting is better than loneliness.' That's true. The deepest sense of it is that a man, doomed to loneliness, because he's different, must fight for companionship. For him there is no contact with his fellows in peace.

A merciful God sent distraction and transport to the front together. I had to go up for my Higher Proficiency examination in Hindustani. That meant going to Calcutta, and going on duty, so the ban on my leave did not apply. It meant also being within striking distance of the enemy, for Calcutta was Kitchener's winter headquarters, and it was now winter. Odd that the first breaking of the engagement should have caught me in Simla, the chief's summer quarters. Wait till you hear the end of the story; it's a queer one. It goes somewhere near fitting the mad theory I mustn't talk about that God is Love; therefore Love is God for anyone who chooses to identify them. Where can they be better identified than in the love between a man and a woman that carries on creation? Anyhow, that was the idea that really possessed my imagination. Not that I believed in it. What was my possessed or obsessed imagination against these serried impossibilities? Apparently it believed in me, and kicked me on till I believed in myself and it. For I won out, fighting blind and hopeless, not for victory but nervous relief. 'Be of good cheer, I have overcome the world; a very positive statement. Nobody believes it, because nobody is positive. The world has got them all down, down and out. They console themselves negatively, 'Cheerio, old man, it'll all be the same a hundred years hence.' The singularity of this particular lunatic is that I was never allowed to say or act that.

I went to Fort William and asked to see the chief. He refused to see me.

I hung around seeing aides-decamp, staff officers of all sorts. Some of them had been my father's men during his commander-in-chiefship and they did all they could; but it was no good; the chief refused to budge. In the intervals of my examination I kept at it. Just before I had to go back to the regiment, the examination finished, my importunity produced a concession. A General Bailey, adjutant-general, if I remember right, gave me a message from the chief that he would not stand in my way, if I would go back to the regiment and get the colonel's sanction. They must have thought that would get rid of me for a bit anyhow, and that the colonel, having been over-ridden before, could be trusted to keep me chained up. I promptly returned to the Punjab. I got the colonel's sanction. Moreover, I got him to recommend me for six months' leave. Kitchener sanctioned that six months' home leave a few months after he had himself ordered my leave to be stopped till further notice. Why? I do not know. Does someone suggest, 'both the chief and your colonel hoped to God you'd clear out and never come back.' That was my own view, but 'the sequel contradicts it.

I went home in a leisurely manner, getting off at Marseilles and visiting Monte Carlo. I had no sense this time of a particular moment to be seized.

If asked why I went to Monte Carlo, I think it was as the gambler's Mecca. I knew I was engaged on the most terrific of gambles, a gamble with my own soul and another's. An Irishman said to me recently could prescribe for his case; he could not stick steadily to anything. If he started on any job he immediately got up and went to another. The only place he could get any rest was in bookmaker's offices. Nothing was any good to him unless it contained an element of chance.

I replied, 'There is only one cure for you. Model your life on mine and make it one vast gamble for some imaginative goal. Then you will be able to rest.' I was perfectly serious and he thanked me deeply.

At Monte Carlo I fell in love, but, in view of the mission I was engaged on, refused to admit it even to myself. Finally the lady made the running and I played the Joseph. I think of this now, not with pride, but shame and regret.

'Bah!' said the lady, 'your soul is not the size of a peanut.' I have remembered the phrase. In attempting to concentrate all one's *untested* amorous forces on one woman in obedience to what a friend of mine calls the 'monopolistic monogamy myth,' that is just about the size to which the soul is reduced. But the myth had got me. It is necessary to catch hold of life somewhere and live it, even to explode myths or to glimpse the truth of which they are the symbols. I had my prey marked down. My peanut of a soul was aimed as if in a peashooter; aimed at the needle's eye of marriage through which, sure enough, the spiritually rich must go, before they can attain the Kingdom of Love.

I went home overland from Monte Carlo and stayed with my people at Chelsea Hospital. From there I corresponded with Gibraltar and things began to come right. The engagement was almost on again when the religious question, supposed settled at the Kensington Convent came up again. It came up fiercely and finally; that was natural, for it really underlay the whole attraction and repulsion. I was Protestantism incarnate, the individual protesting against the inertia of collective forms. Dollie's soul inhered in the old forms, and of the pull of collective authority Rome was the most logical exponent. Of course we didn't understand all this then, though life brought it out clear and concrete enough later. Then with me it was just intuition, shot with glimpses of disconnected reason. A cable from Gibraltar announced final determination not to surrender. On this point and this point alone, focused on the creed of the possible children, of course, I gave up pursuit, because there was no further to pursue. It was the root-difference, in the war over which our union lay. There was a certain peace in coming hard up against it for the second time, after all other barricades had been twice carried.

My father, and even my grandfather, the Anglican archdeacon, urged me to give way. My dear old grandfather because his God was as mellow as himself and able to tolerate the most foolish practices in people who hadn't the discipline of a study of Sanskrit roots.

My father, because he was first and foremost a courteous chivalrous gentleman, regarded my refusal to consider the feelings of the girl I had so relentlessly pursued as cruel and inconsiderate. He was anxious about me too, fearing the effect on me of the thwarting of this all-absorbing chase.

For my part I was desperate but quite calm and decided. It never occurred to me to give way. It did occur to me to shoot myself. Indeed the night the cable came, I went upstairs ostensibly to bed and packed everything, except a revolver I had brought with me from India.

I had looked at it often on the way home; not with a serious intention of shooting myself, if things went wrong, but with a feeling that if I continued to live, here was the guarantee I did so by my own choice.

Tonight I faced up to it more definitely. 'Out of the question here, anyway,' I decided, so I packed, intending to slip out of the house in the small hours and think over it at leisure.

Packing always did exhaust me. It has the same effect as regimental orders or the permutations of a Highland officer's costume. It withdraws the mind from its natural home in the infinite. Thus it induces fatigue. I went to sleep in my clothes.

I woke up in the best of spirits, and perfectly confident that everything was going to come right. So confident was I that I wired that very morning inviting myself to stay with a friend in Devonshire. I did this to be near Plymouth to meet the next P. & 0. from Gibraltar.

I believe I went to meet the next boat on no better grounds than my own inner confidence, which - a quite new experience - remained steady, with little oscillation. I attribute this to being on the bedrock principle of fundamental Protestantism, on which I knew I must indecision, moral uncertainty, which breaks stand. It is the spirit. Any fool should be able to face hanging, once he knows there is no chance of a reprieve.

I was just a week too soon. Before the boat after that, I received a wire from Dollie that she accepted my conditions and was sailing. I met her at Plymouth. A few days later we were married at the Chelsea Registry Office. The only representative of the Mosley interest was an uncle, not Uncle Arthur, invited by wire. He replied in kind, 'Coming, but absolutely hostile.'

We went for a short honeymoon to Ireland to the family place, Whitehall, Co. Antrim, which reminds me that the coming discovery of Ireland by my spirit has loomed over me so big in writing this, that I have made no mention of the roots of my physical being in that country. I must link up my twice born and once born selves, when I come to the Irish part of the story.

I wish to God I were free to tell everything; horrible tyrannies and cruelties I was guilty of without meaning to be; all actuated by the pressure on me of the new self of which I was pregnant, which was not yet born. If a woman has allowances made for her in pregnancy, why shouldn't a man? Especially if he is pregnant of himself; for then a miscarriage is death.

I remember one fierce argument. It was about the nature of Christ. Was He different in kind or in degree from ordinary humanity? Dollie asserted, what I take to be the Catholic view, that He was different in kind; without argument but with finality. It caused me such anguish that I slapped her. Brutal madman, was I not? What a fate for a bride! Just so; but must all truth perish, because no one has the courage to expose the bottom of the cesspool from which they have dragged it, leaving the fools to go on looking down an empty well.

I say it caused me anguish. Is that strange? I was made so that I can see all the consequences of a principle in a flash. What did I see here? I saw death, stagnation, and spiritual divorce. If Christ were different in kind from man, how can love manifest in man. We are rats, vermin crawling under a God of a different species to ourselves. No wonder on this theory we have crawled over Him, eaten Him, till the lice batten on us as we crawl over and eat each other.

Yes! I slapped my wife; but I've had a few slaps since at the guilty parties. Now let me go on. This is my life as I have lived it in fierce pain, given and received; through every conceivable unbalance and folly. Take it or leave it, WHOLE. I cannot mince it.

I thought it best to return to India quickly and go on with my soldiering. I wired to the colonel -'Married; ready to surrender remainder of leave if I may bring wife out to Khanspur.'

Khanspur was the regimental hill station for that year. Remember that part of Kitchener's sentence on me was that I was not to be allowed to go to the hills for two years. I could not possibly bring a rather delicate wife out to the plains.

Now comes the last of this strange series of Kitchener conjunctions. The two breaches of the engagement had been overcome (i) by Kitchener of Simla and me versus the colonel (ii) by half of Kitchener of Calcutta allowing the colonel and me to beat the other half. Now it comes to me against Kitchener and the colonel. By what the fools would call an amazing 'coincidence' the night my cable reached the colonel, Kitchener was dining with the regiment at Peshawar. A hefty enough triangle. Simla, Calcutta, Peshawar. Work out the area if it interests you.

The mess sergeant handed my cable to the colonel. The colonel handed it without a word - or so he told me, though I doubt him - to Kitchener.

They drank my health. I received a cable granting my request without comment. Of Kitchener's sentence against me there remained only the instruction to report on my temper every six months. As I was now married, I suppose that was allowed to lapse as superfluous. It was really the least superfluous part of the business.

CHAPTER 6.
ON TRAPS

Something has happened since I made that intimate confession in the last chapter. I was writing for the publishers, not for myself. I was writing in a trap.

Imagine me - me of all people - writing in a trap. 'You mustn't say this. You may show the springs of the trap till they can almost be heard to creak, but you must not show the springs of your life.'

Marriage is the first trap. My life is the story of getting out of traps and leaving them, sprung, not set, behind me. I cannot make these bald statements and leave them unexplained. Therefore I cannot tell the Story at all, if I cannot tell why I got out of the traps, how I got out of the traps, and how I sprung them behind me.

'Are you preaching free love,' says somebody, 'that you speak of marriage as the first trap?' Free fiddle~ sticks! Free love is a gin, not a decent merciful trap; one of those things that catches a paw and holds you lacerated and screaming. Marriage catches you whole and gives you a chance to get out whole; if you learn the trick.

A little military instinct applied to psychology should make this clear. Marriage decreases mobility and increases the exposed front. For any sort of guerrilla warfare in life it is a fatal handicap

Whether, despite the increased mobility and increased exposure, it is a strength in pitched battles, depends on the internal cohesion of the forces. Since all life is war, that internal cohesion is tested directly the marriage touches life. If the internal cohesion is bad the 'allies' are captured *en masse*. The trap catches you whole.

Now about getting out whole. If a man has any latent sense he learns his own fundamental character in marriage. Love makes him give up as much of himself as he can to please a woman. What he *can't* give up is *himself*. Every bit of himself he finds reveals to him the environment where that bit can breathe; and conversely where it chokes. He finds that marriage isolated à *deux*, without sharing a mental or social environment is well described as 'that state of connubial bliss where two become distinctly less than one.' For two to become distinctly more than two, they've got to fuse with each other's environmental arcs. If there isn't the nucleus for that fusion, the environments will clash as soon as a friend of either comes in at the door, and the happy pair have to stop love-making. Their real union or disunion throws itself on the screen of environment.

Now take a case like ours. I am what is called an introvert, I believe. I look inwards to the roots of things; that is, away from environment, for a start anyhow, to principles; away from effects to causes. So I'm apt to find that things, looking solid enough to the outer eye, are to the inner eye dying effects of a dead cause. Dollie is an extravert, a very pronounced extravert. Most wholesome efficient women are. A lot of women pretend to be introverts nowadays, but they keep their balance - especially at the bank. No genuine introvert can keep his balance, till he has upset it. He starts life upside down - all babies are born head down, I believe. He must get right side up with ideas on top, and life reflecting them as far as he can make it. Not so the genuine extravert. She - for it generally is she - has not got this alternative balance. Her balance is that of the world she belongs to, changing with it but not ahead of it. It may be no balance at all, or at best that of a house swaying on tottering foundations. It doesn't matter. Till the foundations finally give way, that is her balance.

Thus a pair like us, when tired of hand-to-hand fighting, can go on fighting through the warring worlds with which our respective types have become aligned. What is more, there *is* some hope of final decision, if not final peace. What's that game they play on board ship crossing the line; two combatants sitting on a spar over a sail-bath and hammering at each other with bolsters till one of them falls in - sometimes both. Suppose they sat on different spars, and nothing on earth would stop them hammering till the spar of one of them broke. Then if they loved each other, for all the hammering, the survivor would pick the sparless one out. There is a picture of my marriage given in advance. I am now to get off the spar on which we sat together and get on another. Then a long spell hammering at her spar rather than at her, hammering at the British Empire, and that state of life in general to which it pleased God to call her -and pleased her to stick to all the more because I was hammering at it. Then a spell - I'm still in it -sitting back and waiting for the rotten spar to break, gripping and splicing my own to be the better able to pick her out, when it does.

Through it all the motive of that vision at Gibraltar in 1904, the vision of love completed through warring worlds - am I to keep all this up my sleeve? I'd sure need some Oxford sleeve!

You get out of marriage whole if the passion that drove you into it drives you out of it after your own spirit. Your spirit and her spirit, mind you, not your souls. Souls touch, so do sardines in a tin. Spirits hang poised at their right planetary distance. They are always united, though they never meet. They are one in and through the whole, in which each has found its exact place in finding itself. I am not making this indecent exposure for gold. There is something I want to tell people: the message of a Misfit.

CHAPTER 7.
OUTER REVOLUTION

Military textbooks, if I remember right, define strategy as the broad general lines of a campaign tactics as the disposition and movement of troops in particular engagements. If a man feels he is losing ground in the war of life, he must revise his tactics or his strategy. For about a year as a married regimental officer, I tinkered with tactics. At the end of that time I decided on a fundamental change in strategy. Something was wrong. Regimental soldiering had been tolerable with a few polo ponies and a purpose ahead. Without the polo ponies, and with the purpose achieved at the cost of them, there was nothing in it.

I put in for the adjutancy of the Territorial Battalion of the regiment at Aberdeen and obtained the post. Dollie and I sailed from Calcutta where the regiment had been moved from Peshawar. We sailed on a Brocklebank liner, a cargo boat carrying a few passengers. I remember one incident of the voyage. I was always trying to develop her intelligence. I hadn't learnt then that no intelligence worthy of the name is ever developed by anything but hard-shell first-hand experience.

Men of my type in marriage, when callow, try to develop intellectual comradeship in their wives on the principle of 'hit 'em and hold 'em.'

The schoolmaster in us hits with the whip of our supposed intellectual superiority. The marriage itself holds from all really first-hand experience.

Suddenly the chessmen were swept off the board and flung into the Mediterranean. The trap was getting too small. I suppose these sorts of things happen to other people. Why not tell them? The common burden is lightened by sharing it. The captain, if he is still alive, may see the humour and pathos of the situation better now than he did at the time.

We got a charming furnished house in the Canonry in old Aberdeen and I took up my adjutant's duties. To my own surprise I enjoyed them and performed them efficiently, or the part of them that concerned military training.

I had scope. Virtually I commanded the battalion, for I was the only regular officer. In camp all schemes for manoeuvres and training were left to me. For the first time in my life, unhampered scope and responsibility made me realize I had it in me to be a good soldier.

The men had not grown stale by habit. I managed to keep them interested and often amused, for I treated the whole thing as a game we were playing together.

I got on well even with the officers, when I had suppressed the volunteer officer's habit of yapping at his men to hide his own embarrassment. 'You can say more offensive things, ' one of them said to me with less offence than any man I ever met.'

At a camp singsong the colonel's mention of the new adjutant was greeted by a spontaneous burst of cheering that gratified me highly.

The colonel (a local comb manufacturer) pleaded for reserved judgment. Perhaps he felt I had taken command a little too completely and enthusiastically. A voice interrupted him, 'He's shaping richt well, onyhow.' That's as far as I got. I 'shaped right well,' but the mould wouldn't hold me.

There was heavy pressure on the economic front. We paid a big rent; lived not extravagantly but without management. Spiritually too I was dissatisfied, unhappy, once the annual camp training was over and I had nothing but office duties.

The 1904 vision was always fermenting in me, a ferment at once mental and physical, pressing me to find some unknown dimension that linked and reconciled the two.

I read a good deal, especially Tolstoy. My own condition was a good example of his simile of the bird seeing the light through the closed window of a room. It dashes towards the light, encounters the glass and falls back dazed. To me freedom for spiritual adventure was the light, the army and my complete economic dependence upon it, my lack of training for anything else, was the glass.

I felt that in the army I was in a cul-de-sac. Even the realized part of myself was up against the end wall. Supervising a month's field training was the best it had to offer. Having found myself capable of that only emphasized my sense that I was capable of a great deal more; that the end wall stood between me and realizing any unknown, untested capabilities at all.

For military success, for staff service, accelerated promotion, the ordinary prizes of the ambitious soldier, not only had I no ambition, I had a positive nausea.

There was an unavoidable signalling course ahead of me now. How I loathed those courses, their stupid parrot-like repetition of words and movements. On the negative side that signalling course loomed in front of me a dull intolerable waste of life and energy; almost a menace to reason by its meaningless mechanical boredom. On the positive side was the spiritual ferment in myself, partially expressed and rationalized by Tolstoy.

One day as adjutant I had to swear in two recruits. On the instructions of the sergeant-major I made them hold up their right hands and repeat after me something about allegiance to their liege Lord Edward, his heirs and successors.' The two lads looked infinitely stupid and I felt it. I felt something more. I felt a distinct spasm of guilt. The *moral* began to come to the aid of the mental revolt. Need I tell you, I did not suppress that moral revolt; I welcomed it. It was too tender a growth though, as yet, to stand on boldly. I would try easier means of escape before I set myself up in moral revolt against the whole social system and the profession which my father adorned.

I wrote to my father: 'Dear Father, I feel I am odd, and I cannot be odd in the army as your son without making more or less of a scandal. Will you agree to my leaving and help me to do something else?' My father replied: 'My dear boy, I think you have been quite odd enough; I should be a little less odd, if I were you, and go on with your work.'

Always the same story: 'be a little less odd,' 'be more like other people.' Besides, I hadn't got any work. It wasn't work to drop into the office for half an hour every morning and sign a few papers. What was work anyway? I'd never done any. I'd rather like to try. The more suffocated I felt, the more I was drawn to the moral side of the question. The more I went into the moral side, the more it fitted with the 1904 vision, and was ratified by liqueur-sensation in my chest. The fit was perfect.

In the 1904 vision I had glimpsed that love was an organic whole, each and all of us in process of evolution towards the condition where we would contribute to that organic whole.

Then I was an impatient young dog wanting a particular girl. Now I began to see that this organic wholeness of love had its laws, and they were *moral* in nature.

The wholeness, the integration of love depended on fidelity to love in its widest aspect. It was simply childish nonsense to seek love and draw a captain's pay and allowances for teaching people to kill each other; Swearing them in to allegiance to their liege Lord Edward, irrespective of Edward's moral condition; possibly in flat contradiction to their liege Lord Jesus Christ, whose heirs and successors, it suddenly occurred to me, were not particularly numerous. The more need to start the line. Some spiritual adventure that! Swear me in!

Having seen that, the rest came automatically. I gave myself two months' leave and went to London to my people. From there I sent in my papers. My sister Gladys burst into tears when I told her my decision to do so, flung her arms round my neck and said I knew it would kill father. Though inwardly shaken, I replied, 'Then it must kill father.' It did not kill father. Uncle Johnnie, the Queen's College Fellow, my father's brother, told me when the whole thing was over that 'There are things in that my father had said to him, boy, Johnnie, that you and I just can't understand; we must leave it at that.' A good many things have to be left at that.

Not that I failed to make every effort to be understood. I wrote and had typed a paper, which seemed to myself to be written in a state of illumination and to be completely convincing.

I showed it to my father. He handed it back to me with his usual high courtesy after he had read it. 'I don't deny you a certain skill in argument, my boy, but - ' I showed it to Uncle Johnnie. In reply he quoted Horace: *'Tantum religio potuit malorum.'* I sent it through a mutual friend to H. G. Wells. He replied he would like to thrash my governesses and schoolmasters. I would have had no objection to this, but to blame them for this particular aberration of mine was, I believe, unjust. It was a clear cut away from the lot of them, a voyage of discovery undertaken entirely on my own.

Tolstoy went nearer than anyone to a share of the responsibility. I sent my paper to him and he replied in a charming letter I regret I have lost, that I was one of those nearest to his spirit. He was wrong too, as the event will prove, for though I followed him as far as he could take me, I developed into his positive antithesis later on.

My papers were in. I got a hint that my father had suggested to the

War Office to hold up acceptance of my resignation to see if I would come to my senses.

Convinced that I had at last done so, the only thing was to clear out. Impossible to be too holy for one's father's profession, but not for his hospitality. Impossible at the crisis of conversion anyway.

I got a job as English teacher at a sort of Berlitz School at a place called Tabor about one hundred kilometres cast of Prague; that is in Bohemia, the Ireland of the old Austrian Empire.

I had followed Tolstoy, down to the vegetarianism. Shortly before my departure, I had been observed by a bewildered family to refuse all flesh food at breakfast. Much embarrassed, I confessed my motive for abstention. I was pressed to let an egg be sent for. The dogmatist came to the aid of the embarrassed Gordon Highlander, and I declared that an egg contained potential life. At that there was an outburst of hilarity. The way of the spirit was set with thorns.

I left for Bohemia on a diet of dates and proteid biscuits. At Dresden, bloated but not nourished with this loathsome fare, I got the most appalling pain in my stomach I ever remember.

In response to very expressive signs - I could speak no German - a porter showed me to the refreshment room.

I gulped brandy till I could stand up straight. Thank God I had kept clear of teetotalism.

CHAPTER 8.
THE DE ROHANS

There isn't much to tell about myself as a language-master. The school was kept by a woman, Mlle. Alouette, a lark with a sour side to her tongue. She lived, I think, in more than amity with the elder of two brothers, who were the French masters.

I had all sorts of pupils, from schoolgirls to university professors. I didn't dislike the work, except when the shop girls giggled. My salary was 120 kronen-£5-a month, a tight fit for my board and lodging. I had my meals at the local hotel and held out manfully against the smell of meat for six weeks in all from my start as a vegetarian.

Then I fell for a steak berçy and have never attempted to be vegetarian since. It suited me in neither body nor mind. It seemed to increase my natural introspectiveness to torture. The mind was always trying to fill up the hollow feeling in the pit of the stomach. I judge it better for such as me to give the stomach its natural work and the mind an occasional rest. One day at the hotel I saw a thin parson. 'That chap must be some kind of a Protestant,' I thought, 'for he's well under forty-five round the waist.'

I was wrong. He was private Roman Catholic chaplain to a certain Prince Raoul de Rohan. Over a game of billiards the chaplain told me all about his patron. The Prince loved the English, it seemed, and was sure to ask me out when he heard I was there. He was married to an Irishwoman, and all the children had spoken English from the nursery.

Thereafter the Prince sent a carriage for me every weekend to drive me out the eleven kilometres that separated his place from the town.

On Monday mornings I used to start at 4 a.m. and walk back through pine forests over a carpet of glittering diamond-sown snow to Tabor.

I only once lost my way. That was when, on the Prince's invitation, I had taken my colleague, the French teacher, out with me and had his company on the way back. We got hopelessly bushed in a thicket of young saplings. 'Ah! si nous avions une bougie,' exclaimed the Frenchman. I muttered to myself, 'Ah! Si je n'avais pas un bourgeois.' There are some instincts which can only work in solitude. The presence of another human being, unless dearly loved and understood, deranges them, as adjacent metal deflects a compass. The beggar had disorganized the stars for me and he wanted a candle. A candle to find his way out of a pine forest; how damnably symbolic!

Ultimately I got the sack. Nominally it was because I insisted on using German as a medium to translate *Dorian Gray* to one of the university professors who had asked me to read it with him in English. I could pick up German; Czech had me beat. The Czechs were furiously anti-German, and, anyhow, all teaching was supposed to be by the direct method; but no one could interpret *Dorian Gray* to a pupil, with the merest smattering of English, by pointing to concrete objects. Anyway, I got the sack. It did not break my heart. I went straight to the De Rohans, who had told me I could come to them whenever I wanted and stay as long as I liked. What's more, I believe they meant it. But for my pride, my principles, and my quick temper I might be there yet.

It's a big mistake to let a tiger taste blood. Every really devout Catholic is a tiger for souls, and the Prince was a devout Catholic.

One night, Christmas, I suppose, out of friendliness, curiosity, and sentimentalism combined, I went to midnight Mass with the family.

The next night at dinner, the Prince opened on Tolstoy in violent language by way of smashing the chief obstruction between my soul and grace.

I asked him to stop, but he went on worse. I got violent in defence, and the Prince, thinking he was making headway, began to mock at me and my spiritual seducer with that peculiar self-satisfied assurance that the spoon-fed mind uses to the first-hand seeker. I got up and left the table. The Princess, sweet soul, came after me.

Having mollified me a bit, she brought the Prince. Half-hearted apologies were given and accepted, but the spell was broken. I left the next morning. To this day I find it almost impossible to accept material kindness from mental inferiors. One's mental equals never have anything to give except themselves. Besides, on this occasion I had just received a cheque for £53 wind-up army pay, so I could afford to be touchy about my principles.

Yet why should I sneer at myself. There I was at the De Rohans', resting on a bit of flotsam of the French Revolution on a far shore.

Destiny meant to drive me out across troubled seas. 'There, me lad,' said Destiny, 'this is the sort of mentality that made the French Revolution and learnt nothing from it. I've got some other revolutions up my sleeve that will interest you in Ireland and Russia. Kick that venerable old French plank from under you and strike out with me.'

Thus Destiny leads and drives us through a mixture of our highest qualities and our lowest, our principles and our pride, our courage and our impatient temper. In the same way she brings about great mass-changes by a mixture of the inspired thinker and the unchained *sans-culotte*. It's no good arguing with her or blaming oneself.

What separates me from the other, and more numerous species is that they seem to think they run their lives themselves. I know that the kind of questions my mind asks determines the path I take in looking for the answers. The shape of my mouth determines the food I hunt and where I hunt it; and I did not make the shape of my mouth. Perhaps the other species don't ask any questions. I never could understand them and they're not my business. For myself I have only free will in two particulars. I can fight or I can funk. I can face the questions honestly or I can shirk them. If I face them, I can face the action the search for the answer involves or I can shirk that. Even that margin of free will tends to decrease. For as one goes on, one gets so terrifically interested, one loses the habit of funking and shirking.

The Catholics have a doctrine about final perseverance being a matter of divine grace, not mortal merit. I would put it more brutally - that after a certain stage in a spiritual investment one cannot sell out. The capital has all been converted into plant. Also there is no market. The public isn't interested; but one's own absorbing interest makes up for it. To use a mining simile, the public does not believe in the seam. The prospector goes on boring for his personal satisfaction. The public is just bored.

CHAPTER 9.
A TRAMP AT HOME

I went home to Chelsea, but I didn't stay long.

One day at Holt's, the regimental agent, I met an old brother officer, Fraser-Tytler, commonly known as the Bulger.

I had grown a red beard. 'Hullo, White,' said the Bulger, 'where have you been?'

I told him I'd been in Bohemia. 'Yes, you look rather Bohemian,' said he, with a glance at the beard. So that was that.

Later on when old comrades asked me what I had been doing, I got into the habit of telling them, often with truth, I'd just been doing three months; but by that time my sense of humour had fully recovered.

About now it was still sick; and I was as sensitive about my spiritual quest as a flayed cat. I have omitted to mention that, when first I sent in my papers, only one explanation would fit the facts for my family; there must be something physically wrong with my brain. So they asked me would I have any objection to going to see Sir Victor Horsley, if they paid the fee. I agreed to go. I even went so far as to allow my head to be X-rayed, family still paying. But when Sir Victor discovered some peculiar conformation and wanted to cut it out, I thought my complaisance had gone far enough; final proof of my unreason, no doubt. By now, however, I was accepted or becoming accepted as mad but not dangerous. I had absented myself for some six months and come back with nothing worse than a beard.

I soon absented myself again. I forget whether I took the beard with me this time. I went to Falmouth to investigate a school, the good will of which I had seen advertised for sale. I had tried one aspect of school mastering; suppose I tried another.

The man I went to interview was the most terrible example of the pressure of life on a sensitive spirit I ever met. His name was C -. The son of a very poor country parson, with no presence or training for anything but the lower walks of intellectual slavery, with a genius for morbid self-torture, he was handicapped by birth, by nature, and by circumstance, and admirably adapted to taste the dregs of all three. His soul was a camera obscura of suffering, lit by one little window of ring of genius, where his imagination let in the suffering of others and intensified it by his own.

In the Great War he wanted to be a conscientious objector, not from cowardice but inherent conviction. He asked my advice not once but many times, for our Falmouth meeting was the beginning of a friendship. I advised him to let himself be shot ten times over rather than go out to the shambles; but his sensitivity to the opinion of others wouldn't let him rest. Finally, in sheer pity for his indecision, I advised him to join up. He was drafted to a Labour Battalion. There he descended into objective hell and observed it with his subjective hell.

He produced one book afterwards, written lying on his bed in a room without a table. It was called *Ermytage and the Curate.* Wells said of it that it was one of three war books which would be remembered one hundred years after the war.

Such was the man I went to bargain with about taking over his school. Here was a spirit too passive to master environment, too sensitive to do anything but squirm under it. Let me, for God's sake, take warning by him, Open my sensitivity to the four winds of heaven, fall into the hands of God, not into the hands of man.

If anything were needed to clinch my decision, it was the local curate. He called to inspect the new prospective schoolmaster. The price of his patronage was to supply him with Church lads. The thing was impossible.

I had four shillings left in the world; not much to take over a school with, had I decided to do so; but I always assume that means can be found, if I know my end. Now I had neither end nor means. I put a knapsack on my back, posed to C - for a farewell snapshot, took the boat across the bay to St. Mawes, and started as a tramp.

About the third farm I called at, the farmer was sitting on an upturned bucket milking his cows. He had a face like Christ. After his natural suspicion and surprise at a man of my address and bearing asking for a job had worn off, we began to talk about theosophy. He had studied the subject in *Bibby's Annual, and* obviously the whole trend of his mind was towards the unseen. I became suddenly peaceful and happy. In my own particular way I had set out looking for Christ. It was very encouraging to find someone so like Him sitting on a bucket. I got that glorious sense in which alone I feel fully alive of 'underneath are the everlasting arms.'

A personal God has gone out of fashion. It seems to me that is because life has become so complex. He is crowded out. But once jump out of the complexity, especially if you jump semi-deliberately on the chance of discovering a God outside, and there He is sure enough. Not a blind impersonal force. To speak of my own experience, I would compare His direction of my movements rather to that of a rider with delicate hands. Sometimes one is hard in the mouth. Often he leaves the reins slack on the neck; but I have grown accustomed to feel He is there. If we call life a game of polo - and it's not unlike it - the best pony is the one that learns to follow the ball. I think that is possible in the end. Destiny ceases to be blind. The idea behind it emerges. It emerges so clear that it points to persons and even to places. I hope to bring that out later on.

My theosophical farmer could not give me a job; but he thought neighbour Pomeroy could. Neighbour Pomeroy did; so I hadn't to sleep a single night out.

Not only did he give me a job, but he gave me the best room in the house, and served me first at table.

I hoed turnips, milked cows very inefficiently, and fed pigs. In honour of the last I composed some verses.

A highly instructive task of mine
As a farmer's help is to feed four swine:
Potbelly Pete and Manure-heap Mick,
Verminous Victor and Dunghill Dick.

As I'm preparing his dinner, the habit
Of Potbelly Pete is to run in and grab it.
How many people one happens to meet
Similar mannered to Potbelly Pete.

Manure-heap Mick in his eager greed
Plants his snout in his brother's feed.
Was it you that taught us that elegant trick,

Or are you a mimic, Manureheap Mick?

Verminous Victor's peculiar charm
Is his naive display of extreme alarm,
Lest the last few splashes of wash be licked or
Disposed of by other than Verminous Victor.

I have forgotten the last verse. Dunghill Dick must go unsung.

Perhaps neighbour Pomeroy preferred good pork to bad poems. It reached my ears after I had been with him about two months that he had said 'he couldn't turn Mr. White out because he was such a perfect gentleman.'

This was about as nasty a knock as I could receive. I was training as a farm labourer to become a peasant in the approved Tolstoyan fashion. To be tolerated for my perfect gentility made a farce of the whole thing, or rather made it impossible for me to kid myself any longer that it was not a farce. I could do nothing but leave. Pomeroy rowed me across to St. Mawes, gave me ten shillings, and we parted. I made for London.

CHAPTER 10.
A TRAMP ABROAD

My next venture was directly connected with my reason for leaving my last.

I soon forgot my inefficiency at Pomeroy's and persuaded myself I was inured to a farmer's life. To lead it, two things were necessary, a farm and oblivion of gentility. Money, of course, did not enter my calculations. That was too mundane a consideration. Indeed money would spoil the purity of the business. I must get my farm without money and without price.

Where could I do so? I heard that the Canadian Government presented intending settlers with free farms. Good; I would go to Canada.

That I had to ask my father for the passage money that I took along with me second-class on a Donaldson liner from Leith, my wife, who was even less suited for a rancher's life than I was, did not damp me in my purity and consistency of life. It so happened that we had as fellow-passenger in class an ex-private of my old regiment, a man called Black. He and his mother invited us to their ranch somewhere in Alberta, while we were looking round. We accepted the invitation.

After about a week, Dollie cabled to her father for funds and returned home. She was appalled by the roughness and bareness of the country. For my part, I was almost relieved at her going; anyway, I recognized it as inevitable. I was in no sense a man for her to lean on. If we count the date of my leaving the army my rebirth, I was about one year old. My hands hardly knew where to reach for the feeding bottle of experience I desired. I sought contrast and I had got it. Captain White, late Gordon Highlanders, under the aegis of Private Black, was not yet able to look after himself, let alone a gently nurtured woman. I mention Dollie's coming out as an instance of her pluck and my idealistic selfishness; a quality for aught I know that dogs me yet. I cannot help it. I must find out exactly what I am; what everything is. In the year I spent in Canada I found myself out in various capacities. It was one long process of recognizing my limitations. Only one little triumph marked its beginning shortly after Dollie went home.

After leaving the Blacks, I went to stay with a relative of an old brother officer, a man called Meiklejohn. He had a ranch in the Calgary district and a horse called Bevan. Bevan had a reputation as a bit of a brute. At a local race meeting at Cochrane within sight of the Foothills of the Rockies, I won two races on him the same day, a flat race and a hurdle. When I heard a cowpuncher come up to Meiklejohn afterwards and say, 'I always told you that Bevan was a great horse, but he could never win a race because he was never *ridden,* '*I* felt pretty good; all the more so that I only had a few dollars left, and I thought my horsemanship would get me a job as a bronco-buster forthwith.

It did nothing of the sort. I hawked myself round at the race meeting, but the only job I could get was to put up hay for an ex-quartermaster of English Yeomanry. I remember one very unpleasant trait in my character, which came out with the quartermaster's sons, who certainly shone at blasphemy and obscenity, though I could have beaten them at Sandhurst.

I was trying to be holy. In what was really class-fastidiousness, mistaken for religion, I rebuked these coarse fellows. It was really the officer's dislike of the private using language in conversation with *him. No* wonder I was paid off when the hay was up.

So it went on; a job for a fortnight, then into the town or the railway, a visit to an employment bureau and booking for another.

I worked west all the time. About my third job took me across the Rockies to a place called Kamloops, a horse ranch at last. It was kept by two young Englishmen not long out, but they did the riding and put me to ordinary farm work. I shared a hut with two Irishmen, a Northern Protestant and a Southern Catholic. Both said their prayers religiously every night. When I tried to talk to them about my religion or the hunt for it, they thought I was crazy.

Next a logging camp at Revelstoke well into British Columbia. Two loggers with a bottle of whisky accosted me in the town and offered me a drink and a job. I refused the drink but took the job.

We all boarded some kind of a launch in the evening. Every one was drunk except me. A big Swede fell into the river and was nearly drowned. I was deadly sober. *Tantum religio potuit malorum.* After fifteen miles or so down a wonderful river,' skirted by great forests, we arrived at the camp.

The gaffer, a great pock-marked giant of six feet four took me on all right, though he looked at me disparagingly.

I was put to swamping; that is, clearing the brush and cutting through old fallen tree trunks for the teams to get in and get the newly felled logs. It was infernally hard work. One could not slack too much or the teamsters complained of being held up. My second day I was given a mate called Jack, a deserter from the English Army. He had come west by his own account of himself, because he had 'put a -half-breed up the stick.' The expression was new to me but the sense was clear.

I experienced in that camp the mathematical relation between energy and food and sleep. If I missed any sleep or failed to charge my stomach as full as it would hold, I couldn't begin to last the ten hours.

The food was varied and excellent; bacon and eggs, two or three kinds of hot cakes, jam and maple syrup for breakfast. Other meals on the same scale. The pay, or my pay as a swamper, was three dollars a day with seventy-five cents docked for board.

The nights were the worst part. We slept in a big tent fitted with wooden bunks -about forty of us. Winter was coming on. With the thermometer outside somewhere about zero, the men laced up the flaps to shut out every breath of air and crammed the stove with hard wood till it got red-hot. The heat roused the vermin on the men's bodies. I have lain awake for hours listening to a loathsome raking of hairy limbs. The noise was like a concert of corncrakes. One night I could stand it no longer. I took my blankets and slept in the hay tent. Was the snag in Tolstoy's philosophy or in me?

My comrades regarded me neither with hostility nor friendship. Some of my habits occasioned pained surprise. The nearest approach to a pal I had, seeing me washing stripped to the waist one bitter morning, felt obliged to remonstrate, 'What, your bare skin again, partner? I can't think how you kin do it.'

When the gaffer had hands enough to dispense with my services, he sacked me. I had fifteen cents and a gun brought out with me from home, which I had managed to hold on to so far. I missed the one train in the day into Revelstoke. A very drunk railway ganger offered me another fifteen cents. When I refused he seemed impressed and put me up for the night.

At Revelstoke I cashed my paycheck from the camp, pawned my gun, and took a ticket for Vancouver. My mind and body were badly at loggerheads. The theory wasn't working a bit. Instead of the body obeying the mind, the mind was sucking its limited energy out of the body, asking, asking, 'what am I doing? Where is this leading?' But mind and body were agreed on just one point: to get out of the cold before mid-winter. Hence the ticket to Vancouver.

The most prominent public activity in Vancouver was in the hands of the B.C.E.R., the British Columbian Electric Railway. It was controlled by Englishmen who were so kind to the flotsam of their own race, that the company was known as the British Crippled Englishmen's Refuge.

It was a refuge to me anyway. It took me on as a timekeeper, later as a 'go-between' with the contractors, and paid me sixty dollars a month. It freed me from manual labour, for which as a means of livelihood I began to realize I was unfitted. It gave me access to a few cultivated people on whom I could hammer out my confused ideas, and true to its charitable repute, it never gave me the sack.

CHAPTER 11.
I CURSE TOLSTOY

I begin a new chapter in the middle of the Canadian story, because Dollie came out after I had been with the B.C.E.R. six months, about a year in all in Canada. Marriage to me has not been a millstone, as it -is to many, but a Mill's bomb. It always has cleared me out of dugouts. It has had on me exactly the opposite effect to that for which it would appear to be designed. Whitman writes somewhere 'Whom I take, I rush along to sweep through the ceaseless rings and never be quiet again.' That's what marriage has always done to me from the time I first began to contemplate it; roused in me divine or demoniac unrest first to achieve, then to surmount it. A week after Dollie's arrival I chucked my job. This was a monstrous thing to do. It appeared the more monstrous to me then because I did not understands to find what I understand now; namely, that my job is to find some escape from what Blake calls the 'marriage-hearse' and 'tell the world.' Marriage in the creative-minded arouses not only an emotion but a vision far too big for marriage to hold. What says Shelley?

'I never was attached to that great sect
Whose doctrine is that each one should select
Out of the crowd a mistress or a friend
And all the rest, though fair and wise, commend
To cold oblivion, though it is the code
Of modern morals and the beaten road
Which the poor slaves with weary footsteps tread
Who travel to their homes among the dead.'

Shelley was lucky. I *was* 'attached to that great sect.' I don't see how anyone could help being so. Not only is, the sect too powerful, but the alternative, if there is one, is too dim and too dangerous for glib espousal.

Yet *malré moi* I was in revolt against the sect. From original sin in my nature, made more conscious by the Gibraltar vision, I felt and glimpsed love to be capable of organizing life as a whole; more than organizing, revealing its latent organism, the perfect living interaction of the parts, whereas a cold and impartial survey of marriage shows life broken up into stuffy and secretive compartments like the 'snugs' in a Dublin pub. The wine of life is drawn for secret drinking and the individual and social consequences are unfortunate. A dual personality divided between irreconcilable or apparently irreconcilable ideas and practice gives rise to violent oscillation. I once wrote of myself. -

When my tremendous consciousness swells out
I catch the seraphim a cheery clout,
And chuck the cherubim beneath the chin.

When my tremendous consciousness falls in
I am oppressed by such a sense of sin,
To be a bloody nuisance I begin.

I repeated these lines to my wife. 'I see you know yourself,' said she. 'I ask you, how could any woman live with a man like that?'

That is just the question for which I seek an answer.

Twenty years ago in Vancouver I was beginning to seek it.

After chucking my job or just before doing so, I got in touch with a fairly wealthy and cultivated rancher called Hilltout.

I wasn't satisfied to accept as final the cul-de-sac into which the Tolstoyan path had led me. I could not get through as an isolated individual, working my body too hard for a living with too little congenial company for my mind; but there might be a balance attainable in conjunction with others of similar purpose. Hilltout for some reason seemed sympathetic and interested. He actually collected some people whom I addressed on the subject of the model community in a Vancouver hotel. Dollie and I went to stay at the Hilltouts'. By way of justifying my existence, I took a contract from Hilltout to clear some land of light timber at ninety dollars the acre. Imagine playing spillikins with tree trunks, and you will get an idea of the hand I made of it. The great thing is to drop the trees parallel to each other. An expert can do it. I could not. I trapped myself in a crisscross chaos. Then I tried to clear it by burning. The flame hardened the wood without consuming it, and I was worse off than before. Giving it up as a bad job in the heart of the copse, I thought I would try on a clear front beside the road. Then I dropped trees across the telegraph wires and disorganized the local service. Begrimed and bleeding, I made for the local town to report my damage. Then I chucked it. I was not a backwoodsman. I was not a peasant. I was not a farm labourer. In respect to that abortive incarnation, I cursed Tolstoy and died.

Dollie wanted to take me home; she had better do so. She tells me she had her work cut out stopping me breaking back several times on the journey east. That was not for love of the backwoods, but lack of relish for the prodigal son business. I had grave doubts about the fatted calf. There would be elder brothers in plenty. Perhaps I was more afraid of my conjugal escort than of 'rejoicing' father or remonstrant elder brothers.

There is something so pitiless about a woman's common sense. Fully cognizant of my failure as I was, I could lick my wounds, comfort myself with a sense of elimination of blind alleys, possibly start on a fresh scent, if left alone.

The presence of a woman who had married a promising young officer and was now escort to an exploded Canadian 'hobo' was not conducive to the restoration of self-respect.

We caught a White Star Liner, I forget where. Dollie sat at the captain's table, so I sat there too; but I felt like a slice off Lot's wife.

CHAPTER 12.
THE PERFECT DISCIPLE

I hope I have made it evident that I was an ineffective crank. I hope - though with less confidence - I have made something else evident too - namely, that an ineffective crank need not be fundamentally a fool.

An ineffective crank is a crank that is not attached to its right piston, or whatever it is that cranks drive or connect. That was my trouble. I wanted to be connected up somewhere. Then I felt I'd drive. Meanwhile if I was driving my friends crazy with annoyance, they had no practical alternative to suggest. They couldn't connect me up where I'd come unstuck. All they could say was, 'Could you do this - or that?' The job suggested was seldom in their own gift.

So Dollie and I went to what we called by courtesy a chicken farm at a lovely place called Slindon in Sussex. On the only occasion when I tried to keep accounts, I found it cost us eight-pence to produce each egg. Luckily we didn't produce many. Even so, the chicken farm made a heavy drain on the small allowance my father had now granted me.

Slindon was notable for one conjunction. I had tried out Tolstoy for myself; I had not watched anyone else closely at the same experiment. I needed what they call in military sketching 'the intersection' between the subjective and objective experience. Perhaps I had been a faulty disciple. My time at Slindon brought me into contact with a disciple *sans peur et sans reproche*. His name was Arthur Voysey, a son of old Charles Voysey, the religious pioneer who had the Theistic Church in Swallow Street, Piccadilly. He had bought a farm of five acres at a place called Fontwell, a mile or so from us, shortly before we arrived. He had gone off the deep end about the same time as myself, throwing up a £1,000 a year job as electrical engineer to the City of London with offices in the Guildhall. His rebirth differed from mine in that it was not rooted in anything physical and passional. There was no analogue in him of my liqueur-sensation which made my body for me more important and reliable than my mind and a criterion of other people's minds. His great object was to make the body the most obedient possible tool of the spirit with the fewest demands, let alone orders, of its own.

In pursuance of this object, he stuck at nothing. Shortly after his arrival at Fontwell, he embarked on a fast for fourteen days to purge his body of the poison of the old Adam. After that, he adopted a diet of fruit and raw vegetables, which he had slightly curtailed when I stayed with him near Nice over Christmas 1928. His wife was the last word of contrast to himself. A hard-bitten little Welshwoman, daughter of a horse-dealer, she had won as a girl most of the jumping prizes at West of England shows. She knew a horse and a dog. A terrier pup of hers killed a rat on the day of their coming into residence at Fontwell. Mrs. Voysey rejoiced that the dog was game. 'Wings,' as his wife and I called her seraphic lord, deplored that the soil should be stained with blood. Wings was or is -for I hope he is still alive - descended from the Duke of Wellington. He perpetuates on his gentle visage the Iron Duke's nose and in his gentle nature the Iron Duke's will. Visiting his farm I wished I had no nose at all, for he declared that the Earth itself was naturally vegetarian and no animal manure should stain the purity of his fields. He substituted rotten cabbages. As a consequence the nostrils were assailed by a stench which left the foulest midden of the most fetid farmyard cold.

In the midst of this highly flavoured purity, Wings laboured unnourished but undaunted. The wife cursed and laughed but dished up the raw peas and carrots with unflagging efficiency. Dollie rather liked the establishment. It amused her. Wings was a 'gentleman,' anyway, which was more than could be said for most of my new soul mates, and he sang good things with taste and delicacy. There was one daughter, Joan, not the daughter of this wife. In the midst of conflicting simplicities, she had simplicity of her own. Dollie once showed her a crucifix. 'What is that, said Joan, 'a clock?'

I was there one day when Charles Voysey paid a visit to his son. The old man and I were sitting in the porch watching Wings wielding a pick with emaciated arms on the new drive. 'Captain White,' said the old man to me, 'if you have any affection for my son try to save him from the worst aberration into which the human intellect can fall.' I had 'had some' of that aberration myself. Perhaps I had undergone the only cure for it, namely, to go through with it. My Canadian experience had nearly got me sane, which perhaps the old man recognized.

Wings is certainly a hard case. He is fourteen years older than I, that is sixty-four, and he is at it still - 1930. This contact at Slindon was about 1911.

The antithesis between him and me is profoundly interesting. We started from what looked like the same point, convinced Tolstoyans. But I had a check on any external authority in the liqueur-sensation in my chest. Also for periods I had no money, which is not a bad aid to correct theology, and my wife had laughed so uproariously when I refused to destroy the potential life in an egg, that I never asked her to feed macaw peas. The really interesting thing is to see what happens; to judge these divergent paths by their destinations. Wings has tried to make the body a tool, not to say a slave. I took it into partnership from the start with a voice and a veto on the board of the directorate. It vetoed the raw peas early in the day. Later it vetoed some other, and less questionable, planks in the ascetic programme. When I last stayed with Wings we had to part, and we did not part friends. The conflict of direction starting from some fundamental similarity of quest was too terrific. My fleshiness seared him. His lack of it froze me.

Soon after I left him, Wings went to Tahiti. The little Welsh wife died some time ago. Joan's departure for Australia with a peasant husband late of the Chasseurs Alpins, freed Wings to go to the logical end of his Tolstoyan tether. I feel sure he is under a banana tree in a loincloth. It had got to bathing drawers in the summer even at St. Isidore, the place near Nice. Wings then, making a tool of his body looks to me very apt to let his body make a fool of him. The path of the East is not for the West. What terrible anti-climax if the Tahitians sing to Wings on arrival, 'Yes, we have no bananas' - They tell me the banana space is narrowing in favour of big American hotels.

I have told you of Wings' destination; I have not heard yet of his luck, but I wait to hear. I have told you with a purpose; because before I stop writing books, if not before I finish this one, I propose to tell of my destination and see whether Wings or White gets into the cul-de-sac. The study of comparative religion is worthless if the comparisons are not tried out in actual life. Wings and I are about the only two men I ever came across, who have gone Nap, Boney, on an idea. It's a pity to waste our educative value.

After some six months at Slindon, Dollie got ill and went back to her people at Gibraltar.

The wife of the perfect Tolstoyan should have perfect health. She has much to bear. Both Tolstoy and Wings passed the sin of property-possession onto the conjugal scapegoat. Whether I would ever have reached that stage of camouflage, if I'd had any property, I can't say. I think not, after Canada. Anyhow I was saved the risk two ways; lack of property and lack of the docile now, what Tolstoyan wife. Frankly, I thank God! Well, now what about it? Here I am free to take up a lost scent; Tolstoy subjectively and objectively at a discount; something very odd about me still. A general reputation for being odd which amounts to the same thing for practical purposes. Quite apart from the practical purposes, a burning unquenchable thirst to find out something. Find out what? Well, I was getting some notion of what I was not. I suppose I wanted to find out what I was.

CHAPTER 13.
MENTAL EVOLUTION

Talking of bananas, I heard a very instructive statement made by that big Abyssinian tipster in Hyde Park.

They say he is a prince in his own country. Over here he is a great humorist and philosopher. He ranges over a number of subjects of wide human interest before he comes to the tip. Dealing with the relation of white and coloured races he summarized the matter:

'My father was so stupid, he ate the missionary and left the bloody banana for the Scotchman to sell!'

My point is that his father was not in the least stupid. The first stage in evolution is to get the diet most stimulating to the evolution of the mind. The next stage, that of the Scotchman and others, is to get money to ensure that diet as a permanency to oneself and one's heirs and successors The third stage, on which we may some day embark, and which assumes that mind has been evolved, is to ensure the enjoyment of that diet by humanity as a whole. When that day comes, the diet may be modified. Until then missionary is obviously preferable to banana.

It occurred to me reflecting on my recent experience, that my mind was not evolved.

With an inquisitive mind and amiable nature I had been shocked by the mechanical horrors to which humanity was enslaved, stimulated to seek some remedy and align my life with a higher principle. I had made the mistake of seeking the remedy, not in the realm of principles, but of parsnips and pork chops.

True, the latter had an important and indispensable bearing on the life of man. But the secret of the better ordering of man's physical life did not lie in itself. So at least I surmised, for my effort to find the secret there had been an unmitigated failure. Even Wings' more thorough and uncompromising effort, by eliminating the pork chops and the boiling of the parsnips, did not seem to me to promise success. I must institute a search for the principles that governed the life of man at its root, his relations with his Maker, if one could be found. Who would not disown the responsibility? I had found out what I was not. I was looking for what I was.' I remembered the phrase of Tolstoy's that had seemed to me the most irrefutable of all his trenchant logic. 'We do not know what God is. We only know what He is not.' On that negative basis I had left the army, believing that God was not identifiable with 'our liege Lord Edward, his heirs and successors.[1] Now, if I could find out something with which God was identifiable, I might see where I came in. The obvious place to look was in religion, in philosophy, -and all the higher ranges of thought, in the secrets of nature, as revealed by science, and if possible in personal contact with the people who conducted all these lines of investigation. I wondered I hadn't thought of it before. Never mind. I would make a thorough reconnaissance for God now.

Remember I took to the search a touchstone in myself, the liqueur-sensation in my chest, that would still get hot or cold with the presence or absence of any clue to the great unity, which seemed to be its hidden habitat. I tried some of the big libraries like the London and Mudie's first, but I found the scope of my quest too big for them. I got no sense of being a workman supplied with all his tools till I secured my reader's ticket at the British Museum. Then I practically lived in the great stuffy reading-room for six months. There were, of course, excursions to the Bloomsbury pubs in search of or in company with some of the living exponents of higher knowledge.

This is a very difficult chapter to write. I have styled myself a misfit. For such, a certain humility is seemly, and the quest of high truth is apt to lend a reflected arrogance.

I was not long in discovering one thing. I was not mad, or, if I was, I had the company of a numerous and posthumously respectable crowd of fellow-lunatics. Some of them, who hadn't gone too far in trying to live up to their equivalent of the liqueur-sensation, were even respectable before decease. Emerson, Carpenter, Whitman[1] were full of the liqueur-sensation, knew all about the early overflowing stages of it. They reflected the thing very much as I had it, a new world in the uncondensed nebula stage; glowing iridescent, inspiring to look at out of the study window on a dark night, but hardly solid enough to live on. No! The study window doesn't apply to Whitman; 'uncondensed' emphatically does.

I wanted something more than that. I was sick of trying to live on uncondensed nebulae. I wanted the new world to solidify or to get back to the old one.

[1] Ralph Waldo Emerson, Edward Carpenter, Walt Whitman

A little-known book, Bucke's *Cosmic Consciousness,* gave a thing a name and instanced a dozen great names as possessing it. That left me unsatisfied. *Cosmic Consciousness,* world-consciousness, confined to a handful of notorieties! I'd sooner have a little thing the many could share, than a big thing confined to the few. Still, the many had not got it and the few could not transmit it. Where was the obstruction?

A long impatient inspection of German philosophy: Fichte, Schelling, Hegel[2]: Being and Not-Being were one. I should think they were. There could be no real Being till Being reflected loving Intelligence. Aha Bergson,[3] a little light here; not much but a little Instinct and intellect two separate lines of development; the normal reason incapable of dealing with the movement of life because it had to stabilize things, strap them down on a dissecting-table, before it could examine them. That fitted my case. My liqueur-sensation could deal with things, deal with persons, in movement; could send me from India at a moment's notice in the teeth of apparent impossibilities, and synchronize my movements with those of another person. Bergson had some sense, if he would deal more with men and less with bugs.

But what was his substitute for normal reason? Intuition; little isolated flashes given to isolated individuals of the real Being beyond the dissecting table reason. That was good, as far as it went, but not good enough. I knew those flashes, their awful compulsion and their awful pain. They separated you from the others whose reason grew from dead things like hair grows on a corpse; and they never joined you up again, curse them. They took you to a higher reason growing not from dying and dead things, but from living things yet unborn. What was the good of labelling this halfway hell with a word 'intuition?' A man was a reasonable being. When he got sick of hair growing on corpses, how could he be satisfied with a glimpse of an odd hair of an unborn baby's head?

[2] Johann Gottlieb Fichte (1762-1814) developed a comprehensive form of subjective idealism in The Critique of Religious Revelation and The Science of Knowledge. Friedrich Schilling (1775-1854) developed Fichte's ideas towards a philosophy of identity in which subject and object were seen as united. Friedrich Hegel (1770-1831) developed the dialectical contradiction, thesis and antithesis and synthesis in which subject and object were at odds. Karl Marx was to use this to show the inevitability of radical change.
[3] Henri Bergson (1859-1941) who believed that time, change and development were the essence of reality. He won the Nobel Prize for Literature in 1928.

Yet for all the irritation with the redundant speech of philosopher and mystic, I got some good from them.

I have a friend, a lady who once belonged to the oldest profession in the world. She was good enough to eschew that profession in deference to the superior promiscuity of my spirit. I introduced her to a wide circle of London intellectuals. She was for several months attentive, inclined to be impressed. Ultimately she delivered herself as follows: 'Jack, I thought at first there was something to it, but I know now there isn't.' That is the intellectual's supreme vindication. He or she convinces the really intelligent that in the intellect alone 'there is nothing to it. I began to see that if action was no good without intelligence, intelligence was even less good without action.

The threads of intelligence must be interwoven with the threads of being; that is to say, that on some needle, which is neither, abstract neither intellect nor non-intelligent being, the two stitches must be picked up and combined. That needle is faith, keen-pointed enough to pick up stitch by stitch in their right order, strong enough to bear the weight of woolly substance always tending to rip off and rip up. Since obviously the first business of needle is not to visualize a pattern, and equally obviously a needle cannot do without a knitter, the whole crux lies in the connection between the knitter and the needle. We have got to pick up stitches without seeing the full pattern. We see it as we *make* it. But we cannot begin to make it *quite* blind. The human needle gets a vanishing fore glimpse of the pattern; that is intuition. Then he has to weave on faith and memory; that is the weaving of the living reason, which is also the reasonable life.

The connection between the knitter and the needle! I turned to the mystics for light on that. There was a 'Cloud of Unknowing' between the lower and the higher reason. There certainly was, but what I was concerned with was the dissipation of that cloud. I could not see why the lower and the higher reason should not be continuous, unless something had gone badly wrong somewhere. In a house you went in at the door, through the ground floor, to the first floor, to the second floor, and so on. But in this 'lower reason' life you went down from the ground floor, through the basement to the cellar, and there you stuck. The upper storeys were shut off by formulae no one could explain. The mystics seem to and got on to the roof. A parable in one of the Persian mystics pleased and tickled me. It was about three fishes, a fool fish, a half-wise fish, and a wise fish all swimming in a lake, when some fishermen approached with a draw-net. The fool fish and the half-wise fish were both caught. The fool-fish scurried backwards and forwards in the net, a fine simile of the wriggling of man caught in the mesh of a destiny he has not foreseen, does not enjoy, yet cannot escape. Of course the fool fish was the first to call attention to himself and be flung out on the bank. The half-wise fish had enough sense to pretend to be dead. The fishermen thought it was dead, and flung it back into the lake in case it might be rotten. That was exactly what I'd done in coming home from Canada, pretended to be dead; and from what I could see of it, if I'd gone on pretending much longer, I'd have gone rotten with no pretence about it. The wise fish was the only one to see the fishermen coming. He swam to a little waterfall, swished his tall and 'lepped' up it out of reach of the net. Well, more power to him! But why this netting of men like reluctant fishes foolish or half wise or even wise? A poor climax of wisdom to save oneself and leave the fools and the 'half-smart' to be netted! Couldn't the wise fish give the tip to the others, or, better still, organize them to rip the net?

I met numbers of extant mystics. I could understand they would have no great difficulty in pretending to be dead, but I couldn't see them swishing their tails and 'lepping' up anything.

The philosophers had got into a sea of Thought without Being. The mystics had got into some ocean of underlying' Being beyond Thought. Bergson, at least, got his finger on a possible starting-point of fusion. He had some truck with human beings instead of 'Absolutes' or 'Clouds of Unknowing.' A man could get in touch with the movement of his own life stream by intuition. If he wanted to stay in it he'd better 'get inside and pull the blinds down' to shut out all the external objects that tended to pull him out. That was not altogether satisfactory. It was something to be able to connect up with oneself, but I wanted to get in touch with other people as well, also in movement, and to know and feel that their movement was coordinated with mine to a common purpose. Movement coordinated to a common and living purpose, aiming at living things yet unborn! Here we are well on the road to revolution; leaving the backwaters and the backwoods of Tolstoyan individual'; coming through Bergson to Marx, but with a vast difference, due to the route travelled.

At that time I had not read Marx. My mediator between Bergson and Marx was a Polish Philosopher, who wrote in French about 1850, called Hoené Wronski. I have never met anyone in England who has even heard of him, though he has a little cult in Paris.

Wronski showed me that the medium for the medium for working of pure ideas was the collective mass-life and not the personal life isolated from it. He was a prolific writer. He wrote a lot about the philosophy of 'Messianism'. The time was not ripe for his messiahship, which was a bit obscure, anyway. He ran off into tomes full of mathematical symbols which were too obscure for me; but I got from him a definite sense of the convulsions of society as distilling a consciousness, which was destined to be their remedy and also of the nature of that undiscovered consciousness. Wronski called it 'La spontanéité de la Raison créatrice.' Kaiserling calls it 'the Creative Understanding'. I call it the human fish swishing its own tail to 'lep' out of the stagnant water.

To forestall my reading of his works, which has ever been very thorough, it will be admitted that Marx analyses the collective processes of society *in movement,* and predicts their direction. The very thing that Bergson pointed out could not be done by the individual for his or her processes because he or she had to stop the processes in order to examine them. If, then, it were possible to follow and combine individual processes in movement, a new dynamic consciousness would be attained, making personal and collective life an organic whole.

Here was the explanation of the Gibraltar vision of 1904. That gave me a definite experience of the organic connection between my own life-impulse and the mass-life. I had been dowered with a liqueur-sensation which freed me from the necessity to stop my processes in order to examine them. It drove me forward apart from, or in defiance of, my mind, and in my personal life had given me one salient instance of its power to synchronize and co-ordinate movements of separate persons beyond the power of their joint and several minds.

If there was some power which could start me off from India and cause me to arrive at Plymouth in the nick of time to transfer Dollie from the care of her family to that of mine - and I had proved to my own satisfaction there was such a power - it could not stop at these long-distance amorous assignations.

Why Wronski omitted to mention that ''La spontanéité de la Raison créatrice' was felt in the middle of the chest and not in the head, I could not imagine. The more need for me to remedy his omission, and explain myself to men instead of mathematicians. I say there is a vast and vital difference between coming to Marx by the ordinary external economic road and coming to him through the gap in Bergson.

The gap in Bergson is that whereas he establishes that the individual does not catch himself in the movement of his life-impulse by his normal objective reason, but only in rare moments of intuition, he fails to link up intuitions of separate individuals into an *interior* collective movement of a coherent nature.

Now, if I could be led for the interests of my personal love to strike the exact time and place to cut Dollie out from under the nose of Uncle Arthur and the two policemen, my deepening and widening amorousness might hit on the exact time and place, say, to cut a country out from under the batons of twenty thousand policemen, or a church out from under a Pope, or a class out from under a carefully-nourished lie. I would be led to meet the men who would co-operate with me as surely as I had been led to meet Dollie. We would be led together to the point to leap out of the stagnant lake. We would swish our tails and leap in unison. The immediate point was to meet the other tail-swishers.

I am a simple chap. I felt very much alive, and suspected that my life-impulse was derived from a highly intelligent Person, who was also alive. I decided more and more to trust my half-formed wishes and be done with half-warmed fishes.

CHAPTER 14.
WHITEWAY COLONY

Wings has a phrase, 'the creative union of the inverse,' by which he means that the masculine and feminine aspects of life, Thought and Being, 'fight bitter and regular, like man and wife.' In their conflict consciousness is born.

The fact is unquestionable, but I can't see it is anything to write home about. The baby is generally smothered at birth. Old Mother Being, beyond comparison the stronger of the warring partners, generally overlays it. The infant, if it remains conscious at all, is conscious only of its mother's oppressive avoirdupois. It's about time that the child began to bring the parents together. That would be something to write letters about or even to sing hymns. I mean, of course, if Life consciously combined and harmonized Thought and Being instead of being overlaid by the latter, we would be getting somewhere.

As things are, when Thought gets well away into the blue it is brought back in the blues by the butcher's bill or the bailiffs. Papa Thought has a most catholic temperament and a roving eye. Mamma Being is concerned with particular things at particular places and times, dinner, sorting the laundry, getting married. She is far too particular. Papa is a little too general to be effective. Now the only way the child could bring the parents together that I can see is this. The child (some undiscovered consciousness) must find in its mother's particulars an *exact* expression, Step by step, of its father's general plan. Matter must cease to overlay spirit. Spirit must certainly cease to get under the bed or up on the roof to get away from matter. Material events must fit in one by one, like the pieces of a jigsaw puzzle, to complete a whole pattern. Above all, personal meetings must be overruled by the pattern. Men or women following the same idea and having something to interchange must be drawn together by some force in Being, though in Thought they may never have heard of each other's existence.

It was in this manner, I take it, that I met Arthur St. John, for I have no memory of what external circumstances brought us together. St. John had swished his tail and leapt out of the British Army, actuated by the same general motives as myself. That is, as far as motives can be conveyed in words and explained in terms of theories, which is very little. St. John had rather liked the army and had some sentimental regret for it. I frequently wished I had never been born at this period, but I never regretted leaving the army.

My misfit in the army had been too glaring to be covered by any retrospective glamour. 'Ye must be born again.' To me the emphasis was on the 'must.' I could not creep back to any sheltering memories of my first birth. I must get on and be reborn, or wander, half unburied corpse, half-wailing embryo, through Limbo.

St. John passes. It was through him I discovered Whiteway Colony and Francis Sedlak. Outwardly, Whiteway Colony is a collection of shacks with an odd brick bungalow or two, in the Cotswold Hills. Inwardly it is, I think, a good deal more than that. It started on a basis of pure Communism, with the usual admixture of pure crankdom. The 'purest' specimens debated such points as whether it was lawful to support the State by Putting a postage stamp on a letter, or whether the moral legitimacy of gathering firewood in the adjacent landlord's game-preserves was invalidated by the risk of angering the gamekeeper. Meanwhile, the more mundanely minded did the cooking and the washing. Ultimately the latter kicked. By the time of my descent on the colony it had relapsed to individualistic holdings, but the members were held together by a loose spiritual bond. The place had a reputation for looseness that was largely unfounded. In its early days it had aroused the open hostility of the natives. One pure-souled, and withal intrepid, fellow had been addicted to mowing barley in a state of pure nature. I cannot see why anyone else should object if he didn't; but the natives had risen in revolt and driven off the two community cows, christening them 'Fraternity' and 'Free Love.'

Francis Sedlak lived on a holding of about half an acre; in a very adequate shack he had built with his own hands. With him lived Nellie Shaw, the lady to whom he once described himself as 'married but not legally, my wife objecting to chattel slavery.' This was when they interned poor Francis during the War as an Austrian subject, and wouldn't let Nellie visit him unless he would claim some kind of relation with her recognized by regulations.

Francis Sedlak was the only man I have ever met who claimed to have mastered and digested Hegel's logic. He had written a book called *A Holiday with a Hegelian,* which no one on earth but himself could understand, I as little as any; but I could understand that Francis understood. He had entered a world of pure thought with the key of Hegel's logic that suited him. He retained his giant's body, but he lived in his mind. He was no longer a groundling, but on the road to become a god. He declared he had found a key to the movements of the heavenly bodies in the fifty-two movements of thought in Hegel's logic and could make thereby slight corrections in astronomical calendars.

By birth, Francis was a Czech peasant. He had served in the Foreign Legion and successfully deserted; a rare feat, but his special kinship with me came out later in his service as a conscript when he returned to Austria. His account of his experience then has much in common with mine; the same gradual recognition of physical inertia, of intolerable weariness and boredom, as due to the spiritual inertia of a soldier's life, is present in them both. Let Francis explain his escape from Austrian military service in his own inimitable language:

'Pardié my friend, I very good soldier; I clean my belt and my bayonet. I do everything the corporal tell me, but I feel very sick, even my dinner not interest me. So I think to myself, "Pardié, you are sick, it is a pill you want," and I take many pills, but I get no better. Then I begin to see slowly, not my body sick, but my soul. Pardié, my soul no like this soldier business. My soul sick because it get no work. The corporal he do my soul's work, and the sergeant he work for the corporal's soul, and the captain for the sergeant. So I see the Emperor got my soul on a long string. When I see this, I fall in despair, for I see no hope. I take no more pills, but I sleep very bad. Then one morning it come to me quite sudden, there is no need be so sad. The Emperor he not keep my soul on the string unless I help him. I jump up from my bed and I shout, "Pardié, I am I." 'The corporal think I am mad. "Sedlak," he say, "you go back to bed." So I go back to bed, but my soul not sick any longer. When the company parade that morning I walk out of the ranks and I lay my bayonet at the captain's feet. The captain say, "Sedlak, what's this?" and I say, "My bayonet, captain, I not be soldier any more." Then I feel damn-fool and want to pick bayonet up. But the Captain, very nice man. He begin to argue with me, and his arguments so bad I leave bayonet lie where it is.'

That was very much what I had gone through *mutatis mutandis*, the gradual emergence of a moral cause to account for a condition of mental and physical discomfort. They put Francis in a lunatic asylum for a bit, and then let him out on his consenting to work in the orderly room. They sent me to see Sir Victor Horsley. I don't know whether I'll get out or be certified for life for the 'orderly room work' I've done on this book.

Another great link with Francis was his contact with and reaction to Tolstoy. He (Francis) had walked all the way to Yasnaia Polyana to see Tolstoy, who had asked him to lunch. They had had a long talk and Tolstoy had advised Francis to return to England to a colony of his disciples at Purley in Essex.

'All right,' said Francis. 'How will you go?' said Tolstoy. 'I walk,' said Francis. 'Have you got any money?' said Tolstoy. 'No, have you?' said Francis. 'No,' said Tolstoy. ' Pardié, I laugh,' said Francis, in describing the interview to me, 'somebody have money to pay for my good lunch.' So Francis had struck the snag in Tolstoy too.

Eventually three roubles were borrowed from the master's cook and Francis set out to walk back to Purley.

When he arrived he found the Purley Colony in a state of disruption. Aylmer Maude, who was in charge of it, had apparently interpreted the master's negative attitude to sex too severely. The more vital spirits had kicked, and there had been an exodus of the more amorously inclined to Whiteway near Stroud, in the Cotswolds.

Francis, drawn by destiny waiting in the shape of Nellie Shaw had followed in the wake of the malcontents.

Let Nellie take up the parable. She too has her distinctive speech.

'Well, captain, it was this way. We girls were sitting at the side of the road 'avin' our lunch off turnips, which was all we jolly well 'ad. In those days we was pure Communists. We only 'ad the one 'ouse, that one you see over there, and the men slep' on one floor and the girls on the other. We all worked the same land and we lived on our crop; it was pretty dam' thin living at that. Well, as I was sayin', we was eating our lunch one day when I looked up, and there was the queerest sight comin' along the road ever I seen in all my life; a great 'airy giant of a man as naked as 'is mother made 'im to the waist, and nothing but a pair of running-drawers, and sandals below that. You couldn't really say 'e looked indecent, 'e was that brown with the sun, as if 'e'd been in the wilderness forty years, let alone forty days. Long 'air 'e 'ad, too, right down to 'is shoulders. "Good Lord, girls," says I, put away them 'blinkin' turnips, 'ere's Jesus Christ."

When the first access of religious awe had passed, the stranger was viewed in more human perspective. He was given some of the turnips and ultimately Nellie herself. They had been together twelve or thirteen years when I first went to their shack as a P.G. in 1912.

It was from this Tolstoyan anarchist colony of Whiteway that I wrote the letter to the *Ulster Guardian,* which took me into the thick of the fight in Ireland. The very name Whiteway suggests that this poor pilgrim has his feet set on his own path after his long search for himself at the British Museum. But I do not think I was a museum specimen. I think I was very distinctly alive. Here is a sample of me at Whiteway:

Drunk as a spinning top,
Still at my centre.
I can go out at will,
You cannot enter.
Whisper, ye lea twigs,
I am the fallen log.
Frisk around, little pigs,
I am the sleeping hog.
In the Eternal Now
So am I mother sow.
Timid birds cheep at me;
She-squirrels peep at me;
Philistines weep at me;
Loves alone leap at me.
Drunk as a spinning top
Still at my centre.
I can go out at will,
You cannot enter.

From which it will appear that I regarded myself-, at moments, as having entered that underlying ocean of Being I had read about in the

Mystics; also that I claimed the power to get out of it at will, which was a lie. I could get neither in nor out then. The pilgrim had made some definite progress none the less.

I had tried out Tolstoy. Doing so had convinced me that if Tolstoy had tried himself out as a younger man, instead of breaking away to his death at the tragic last, he'd have seen the snag he left people like Sedlak and me to find out for him. He sent his mind out on adventures and left his body with his wife and that convenient cook. It had struck me already that if you send your body after your mind away from your wife and the cook, it compels readjustments. .

Your life force, of which one aspect unfortunately is physical sex, is keyed up, intensified, by the spiritual exercise of the quest. You are more alive than other people, because you are keener to lay hold on eternal life. You are more alive and more alone. In the strengthening and regulating of the keyed-up life-force by association with a woman or women, have you got to remain alone because your 'once-born' self was 'married and *its* wife thinks the twice-born self is crazy? Tolstoy's attitude on this matter was a stuffy version of Paul's, 'It is better to marry than to burn.' The more alive and the more alone I got, the more inclined I was to amend it. My amendment began to read, 'It is better to be unfaithful than to freeze.' Are the reborn entitled to remarry? Or are they bound for a bourne where there is neither marrying nor giving in marriage

CHAPTER 15.
THE WHOLE CIRCLE

My own revolt against the negative attitude of Tolstoy to sex had been gathering strength for some time. Finding myself in a Tolstoyan Colony, which represented a similar revolt acted as a check rather than a stimulant to my own tendency. For the experiments in free love of anyone not by birth an aristocrat or a gipsy lack the right balance of confidence or nonchalance. Francis was the most faithful of free husbands and his splendid mental and physical manhood left the amorous experiments of some of the other colonists a bit 'messy' by comparison. There was one notorious amorist in the colony who went by the soubriquet of Tod. Whether Tod showed signs of expanding towards Nellie or for whatever reason, he drew Francis from his god-like detachment. The interview was short. 'Tod, you are a prostitute,' comparable to the short rumble of thunder that precedes a storm, began and ended it. Francis had a gift of finality. He left all social functions severely alone, but one day, to please Nellie, he consented to attend a tea party of her friends in his own shack. He listened to the hum of small talk apparently unmoved; but after a while his philosophic calm was ruffled or his philosophic speculation was aroused.

'Pardié' he roared, why do you not stop that bleating?' Receiving no satisfactory answer he retired from the party.

It is time I myself stopped this bleating.

From Francis and Nellie's shack I am to write a letter to the Irish Press, which puts me in touch with my medium. Ulster was in a ferment of resistance to Home Rule. Winston Churchill, then a Liberal Home Rule minister, was to support his Government's policy in a speech to be delivered in the Ulster Hall, Belfast.

The Orange stalwarts barricaded the hall against him, and Churchill had to speak in a big marquee in Celtic Park. I have been at some pains to follow the thread of continuity of my own mental evolution, because I believe that my having done so will make my angle of entry into the Irish fight profoundly more interesting. I have exposed in a manner, which only its interest can save from indecency, the underlying sexual nature of my whole inspiration and impulse. That sexual impulse had been roughly and painfully torn from its immediate personal object in leaving the system of ideas and the social environment to which that still dear object still adhered. But the sexual, that is to say, the vital and passionate nature of my wider impulse remained. It was hungrier, sharp, and fierce from lack of a woman's understanding. Something that had started as physical in my body *was being hardened and pointed into a mind while still maintaining its centre of gravity and its passion force in my body.* This is simple sense, so every one will think it is nonsense.

The mind as we know it normally is self-conscious, not universally conscious, an instrument of separation rather than union. The body is the scat of more universal passions, the recipient of the great universal forces. The function of the normal mind is to check, to separate, to choose. It is then perfectly reasonable that in the transition from self-consciousness, and as the vehicle of cosmic or universal consciousness, the body should for a time supersede the mind. If the full energy of the life force is to drive and lead to its full consummation, it must be accepted first in the body. The failure to realize this fact is the cause of the failure if humanity to realize its hopes.

"In regard, firstly, to the tearing of my sexual impulse from its immediate 'personal' object. To what object had that impulse been transferred?

I might answer: to none as yet, but in continuity with my Gibraltar vision, I had begun to foreknow the Russian Revolution in the realm of idea, and to look forward to it in actual fact with a sense of pressure and pain as though my very being were pregnant of it.

No man could have been worse fitted than I by nature for the frightful patience involved in these cosmic premonitions, for as Ronald McNeill, now Lord Cushendun, once said to me: 'Jack, you're a very decent fellow, but there are three ways in which you make things very difficult for yourself and your friends. You want to change the whole world; you want to do it at once, and you want to do it all by yourself.' I admitted the justice of the criticism, as I always do anything that strikes me as true, especially humorously true. I could see no remedy, for Ronald's criticism neatly defined the exact state of the case.

I wanted to change the whole world because I was somehow physically pregnant of a change in the whole world. I wanted to do it at once, because far from the mountain labouring to bring forth the mouse, this was the mouse labouring to bring forth the mountain. Naturally the poor mouse wanted to expedite delivery.

I did not *want* to do it all by myself, but I couldn't find anyone else who was pregnant of the thing *whole*. Nobody but I seemed to have had that Gibraltar vision. Lots of people wanted to change things, but nobody else seemed to know there was a ferment working in the world towards predestined change along *definite predestined lines.*

Remember what the Gibraltar vision was. The change was going to grow out of the Russo-Japanese War. It was useless therefore to try and jump the pitch on the change ahead of the great central all-embracing ferment.

But for this I might have been hanged with Casement, whom I am soon to meet and co-operate with, for implication in his effort to free Ireland by alliance with Britain's enemies. But no! I had come to know by then that Ireland was one pole, Japan another, of a great predestined change, organic, universal, working everywhere from within. It was waste of time and waste of one's own life and other people's to try and incubate the egg before the full hatching period. In a way, too, you could watch the egg with an egg-tester, take it out of the incubator and put it back. I had an automatic egg-tester in my vision as to the progress of world-rebirth. There would be no hatch till the discoloration, or whatever it is, reached the poles, the apexes of the egg, Ireland and Japan, together. I am anticipating a bit. My vision only told me about Japan and Russia. My own action, still impelled by the same vision, had to link up with Ireland and link Ireland up with the whole scheme.

Why, then, did Ireland come in at all? On what I must now try to write, my whole life and the whole of this book and any future books of mine hinge, yet I almost despair of expressing it.

In the Gibraltar vision I had been shown the vital points, as it were, where the internal conflicts of society were going to expand into the dynamic mechanism of a universal all-embracing social change. This change was organically one with a change that had just taken place in myself.

World events to me therefore were no longer merely external, political, or geographical, but out-shadowing of a purpose that moulded and transformed me at the same time as the outer world. That purpose was moral, intelligent, making for the completion of my being and its harmonizing with my intelligence, simultaneously with the completion and embodiment of reason in the internal and external relations of peoples. Only I was ahead, a long way ahead from the point of view of interpretation. Since my inner being and the outer process were organically one, and I had an internal key to their correspondence, I could foreknow outer events, before they happened, from things that happened in myself. I said further back that I had the power of seeing all the deploying consequences of a principle in a flash. I had been deeply bitten with Tolstoy. I felt I had bitten deeper than Tolstoy, because I had tried him out as he had never tried himself. But I knew just how deep he had bitten. He dealt in principles, that is to say in creation or destruction.

He applied the principles of Christ literally to life. He made sense of the gospels at last by taking them literally; all except the miracles. He shirked the miracles, because he shirked the great miracle of Sex, in which God becomes man every minute. So he tapped the destructive power of Christ without the creative. He underbit the whole social system formed on pseudo-Christianity, and then tapered off with transcendental Buddhism. He, the great pacifist, brought, not peace, but a sword. Christ came to the whole world and the whole man. Tolstoy preached Him to the whole world from the half man. It must be admitted that Christ gave no guide in the teaching that has reached us to the close connection of mind and body in sex.

He failed to complete the inner revolution in himself. He undermined the outer forms of life with his explosive thought and kept his own inner life in a bombproof shelter. Marriage to him was a millstone, but he kept it round his neck. As I said before, to me it was a Mills bomb.

I knew the dynamic of Tolstoy in myself. I knew it was dynamite. So I foreknew the Bolshevik revolution before I had ever heard of the Bolsheviks. Material events to me were no longer material events. They were materializations of spiritual principles. If there was a snag or a flaw in the spiritual principle, it would be reproduced in the materialization and by reaction stimulate search for a more perfect principle. Somewhere, sometime, principles true or false, progressive or reactionary, would fight as naked principles, no longer under the mask of political or economic differences.

It was this naked fight of naked principles, prior to their reconciliation on a higher plane of consciousness that I glimpsed in Ireland. The fight between Protestant and Catholic in Ireland meant at the root the fight between the principle of Individualism and that of Corporate Unity. There in Ireland was my destined field of action, which would be the pure embodiment of Thought. It was, in short, the fight between me and Dollie.

I have spoken of the two great aspects of life, Thought and Being, 'fighting bitter and regular, like man and wife.'

I have dealt with the introvert and extravert types, which my wife and I so faithfully represented. If I have not suggested it before let me suggest plainly now that the introvert type, looking to ideas as yet discarnate, unmanifest, is distinctively male, and the extravert type looking to the *status quo,* its power to provide bread and butter for the kids and its habit of cutting off the bread and butter, if too much outraged and annoyed, is distinctively female.

Religious types, too, fell into the same sexual categories.

The Protestant, looking, in the main, to the inner light and individual judgment, was male.

The Catholic, emphasizing traditional continuity and external corporate authority, was female.

There was sex in me sidetracked into world issues. There in Ireland were the sexes fighting in big print with the sex-differences thrown on a big screen.

The Irish problem was the sex problem writ large.

Like the personal sex-problem, it was insoluble without a fundamental change in the relations of the partners. Ascendancy, male dominance must disappear and with it the submissive, irresponsible, or the nagging, hysterical woman. Comradeship must take the place of male dominance or female emotional hysteria. What agency could work this miraculous change? The partners must meet on a new basis. What could transform and renew the basis?

Here, then, is the indication of my subsequent action in Ireland and the explanation of its governing motives.

The warring creeds and races in Ireland had to be fused, and fused by some catalytic agent that had not yet emerged. Obviously they could not meet, while one partner was attached to a foreign king and the other to a foreign pope. What could break the empires of king and pope and free the partners to realize their latent union?

They tell me I think like a primitive man. Perhaps I do. Certainly since the 1904 vision, I have begun to know the tutelary gods, ruling over all things of like nature. The god of my free spirit knew the revolutionary workers' movement in the womb of time and moved me to work for its delivery. The same god showed me the secret links between my enemies, though outwardly they might appear to be bitter enemies to each other. He taught me, too, that all, which is not inwardly one with itself, and with the free spirit of man, must ultimately crumble or destroy itself. Russia then would unify and integrate the world as the vehicle, however faulty, of the unifying free spirit of man. Some agency would disintegrate the empires, spiritual and material, and compel them to disintegrate and destroy each other, no matter how urgently their material interests urged them to amalgamate. The final unification must await the final disintegration. This has been my ruling intuition. Since Russia stood for the negation of their whole system and power, the empires spiritual and material would try to combine to destroy Russia. It may sound mad to talk like this, writing of a period five years before the first Russian Revolution. Call me a liar, then, but the fact remains I knew it all in a dim sort of way then. I knew it in the creative principles which are the womb of facts.

Japan to me was always the destined agent to prevent the false, the anti-human integration the amalgamation of the spiritual and political machine against man.

How exactly my vision is working out, let the following cutting demonstrate. It is taken from *Workers' Life* Of 30th of August 1929: -

GROUPING AGAINST SOVIET
AMERICAN PROPOSAL TO GREAT POWERS
    'On 6th and 7th August the American Communist *Daily Worker* and a number of the Russian newspapers made disclosures of a secret note addressed by Stimson, the American Secretary of State, to the Capitalist Powers, proposing intervention in China against the Soviet.

The proposal was to seize the Chinese Eastern Railway, nominate a "direct representative" to control it, and conduct an "investigation" as a basis for propaganda against the Soviet Government.

When American journalists tried to have official confirmation or denial of the existence of this secret note, Stimson refused to see them, being "absent" for a few days.

Since then no denial has been issued, but some of the Press have tried to laugh the idea out of court as being a figment of Russian imagination.

Last Saturday's *Times,* however, lets the cat out of the bag, in an editorial article

It refers to this note, saying "intervention by the Powers such as recently suggested by Mr. Stimson, Secretary of State to the United States," was too distasteful to Japan.

This, of course, explains why the Powers cannot agree. Japan does not want American and British troops in Manchuria because she regards this area as her own special reserve. But the fact that that note was sent shows the intention of the Powers once the opportunity presents itself and exposes their aims in regard to the Russian Workers' Republic.'

It is easy to prophesy after the event. Let me submit myself to the test of prophecy before it. There will be war between England and America, detonated by Japan. In that war Rome will be ranged openly on the side of the British group of Powers. Catholic Ireland will be torn asunder between her Roman and National allegiance, but Britain's effort to rule and dominate Ireland through the Pope will fail and lose her the allegiance of the Ulster people. Extremes will meet in Ireland, when the secret affinity of the spiritual and material empires is exposed. Protestant Orangeman will stand side by side with Nationalist Republican, freed by his loyal republicanism from the domination of Rome. In the Irish Rebellion Of 1798, this combination took place in sympathy with the French Revolution. The Rebellion was crushed and the Union with England followed, inaugurated, to quote Lecky, by 'the greatest orgy of bribery in history.' I say '98 will repeat itself on a vaster scale and with a happier fruition for Ireland. For France substitute Russia.

CHAPTER 16.
I PREACH TO THE POPE

Such a ferment of ideas demanded action. True to my nature I sought action first in the realm of pure ideas. My first public speech was devoted to the examination of the root principles of the Protestant and Catholic religions in the pious hope of leading an advance guard over the transcendental bridge I constructed. Within eighteen months I was leading the Citizen Army over O'Connell Bridge, but as I said before, it is better to be unfaithful than to freeze.

The speech in question was delivered at a Protestant Home Rule meeting at the Memorial Hall Faringdon Street. On the platform with me were Bernard Shaw, Conan Doyle, and Stephen Gwynne among others. Before the meeting Stephen Gwynne caught me by the arm and rushed me to a balcony to address an overflow meeting in the street. I told them funny stories in Ulster dialect, which were greeted with roars of laughter. Then I went inside and delivered myself of the following amazing declaration to an audience which I am sure was at least eighty per cent Catholic. You couldn't fill a hall with Protestant Home Rulers, much less the street outside, except in one district of Ulster that I tapped later.

SPEECH DELIVERED AT MEMORIAL
HALL, FARINGDON STREET

'I am here to speak to a motion protesting against the stirring up of religious rancour and intolerance in Northeast Ulster. Gentlemen, any fool can protest against it. What I want to do, if I can, is to remove some of the ignorance and misunderstanding, which makes such a state of things possible. I am no advocate for leaving religion out of politics. As well, I think, to tell a man to draw water from a well but leave the bottom out of the bucket, as to expect a State to guide itself to its true destiny without the foundations of a religious purpose. Religion should be the wedded wife of politics, always inspiring, never interfering. And if she be not the wedded wife, she always has been, and always will be the dishonoured mistress, as she is now.

'Nor can I give you for what it is worth, my understanding of what religion means and its vital connection with the political issue for which we are met here to-day, if I pretend to think that all religions are equal, in the sense that it is a matter of indifference to which one belongs. To me the ground, which makes religious tolerance the beginning of wisdom and religious intolerance the most detestable of follies, is something very different. It is that all religions are the reflection of the needs of different human spirits or, perhaps, in their main divisions the needs of the universal human spirit at different stages of that gradual evolution of the spirit of which the evolution of the body is only the disjointed reflection. Now, what is the difference between the Roman Catholic stage and the Protestant stage of the evolution of the spirit? Is it not that the latter has arrived at a recognition of having within itself its own supreme law, has glimpsed within itself, however dimly, the Logos or higher creative reason, whereas the former has not, and consequently objectives its supreme law in a Church and priesthood external to, and having authority over itself. Both stages have their dangers, and we have only to look at both in their actual present day manifestation to see how many representatives of both have succumbed to those dangers. But I say that of the two, among the laity at least, the Protestant laity is exposed to the greater danger, because they have claimed a greater freedom. The man who claims the direction of his own conscience claims to be his own priest, and unless he does all in his power to prepare the way for others to attain the same liberty, his liberty is but selfish licence and he is false to the trust of a priest. What, then, is the right attitude of the true Protestant to his brother, his younger brother, if you will, who needs the support of an authoritative Church outside himself? Is it to mock at the support on which he leans, ay, and on which the elder brother leaned too before he ever dared to stand alone, and at the same time to put every obstacle in the way of his aspirations for further freedom? Is it to say: "I dare not help you to freedom, lest you should enslave me?"

'Gentlemen, no man who is truly free fears the results *to himself* of freedom won by others. He may fear the results of it *for them*. The best argument I ever heard against Home Rule, though it was a strange one from the user of it, was that of the Protestant Bishop of Down and Connor in his address to the Synod, that Home Rule in Ireland by destroying the power of the priests would produce in Ireland the same state of irreligion and secularism which the advent of democratic government had produced in other Roman Catholic countries. But the Bishop forgot this flaw in the analogy: in Continental Catholic countries, the democratic movement has had to fight the Church, allied to the old order in the State, and has regarded the Church as its enemy from the first. In Ireland the Church and the national and democratic movement may almost be said to be one. Have you ever thought of the significance of this fact? Consider a moment the root dogma of Protestantism, if such it may be called. What is it but that the individual is the direct receiver of truth? And what is the political manifestation of it? Simply this: that by extended suffrage and more accurately representative institutions, more comprehensive and comprehensible truth shall be realized from a greater number of individuals being placed under contribution. Here is the Protestant principle and the Liberal practice, the practice which, in spite of the necessary half measures and some unnecessary hypocrisies of its political exponents, in virtue of its principle still keeps Liberalism unruffled by the figurative and sometimes tangible missiles of its enemies. Yet lo! When the Roman Catholic Church appears as the advocate of that Liberal practice the application to Ireland of which is the direct outcome of the Protestant principle, it is not Catholics but some Protestants who exclaim hat is the that the forces of hell are being let loose. What is explanation of this portentous phenomenon? There is no explanation. Because only that which is rational can be explained. But it is a wonderful tribute to the wisdom of the Roman Church in insisting on the danger of liberating the reason, at least in the case of those who have not yet acquired proficiency in its use.

'I cannot be a Protestant, and I cannot be a Home Ruler, unless I repudiate, with all the force at my command, the claim that any power, human or superhuman, can be permanently independent of the consent of those on whom its authority is imposed. But there is such a thing as a power imposed on and consented to by the heart and imagination, before the mind awakes or can awake to understand and control the emotional nature. We see it exercised and exercise it ourselves in the education of every child.

From this point of view I would compare the Roman Catholic Church to the shepherd watching the flock, while the free-ranging reason is the sheep-dog collecting into a flock the more adventurous sheep one by one from the scattered pastures. The shepherd and the sheep dog have to work separate. The dog is often out of sight and the shepherd may shout at him and whistle to him when he is after some outlying sheep, which the shepherd does not see. But in the end the two flocks will join, and the shepherd will open the gate at last to let them both into the one pasture. All the while a man on a hill could see both shepherd and sheep dog, could sympathize with the doubts and impatience of the shepherd, though he saw the distant sheep the dog was ranging to collect. I want you to climb that hill, which you must climb yourselves and to which you must beckon others, before you can see at once the full divergence and the full reconciliation of the Protestant and Roman Catholic standpoints.

I will tell you what I see from my hill. I see a Church the representative of divine right, one with a people in demanding the human right of self-government. I see another pier in the bridging of the gulf that has widened down the centuries between the two complementary and, if they but knew it, mutually necessary parties, the party of divine and the party of human right; and I hear the spirit of Catholic Ireland crying to the spirit of Liberalism: "Give us some of the freedom you have won, and we will give you some of the reverence and beauty you have lost."

I read this speech with rapt exaltation. The predominantly Catholic audience cheered it to the echo. At that time I was so fresh and ingenuous I would have got a blessing from the Pope for a eulogy on Luther.

CHAPTER 17.
WHITEHALL, CO. ANTRIM

My spirit begins to be Irish. I am so incorrigibly spiritually minded that in the foregoing pages I had almost forgotten that my body was Ulster already. It was a queer thing to forget, for the old place, Whitehall in Co. Antrim, was the very vestibule of heaven to my sisters and myself as children.

We did not live there, but we spent there the greater part of nearly all the summer holidays. The aunts lived there, Aunt Fanny and Aunt Jane. Aunt Fanny was short, plump, and nearly blind. She could walk ten miles till she was seventy. She had a chuckle like the cluck of a hen, and it drew children to her like chicks. It was a robust chuckle. When the two Miss S.'s, the disreputable characters of the village, were rolling home up the Broughshane road, the least far gone of the two spotted Aunt Fanny. 'Hush, hush,' said she to her more uproarious sister, 'here's Miss White.'

The reply was retailed to us by Aunt Fanny, *sotto voce* indeed, but with every inflection of voice and brogue to the life. 'I don't give a G - d - for all the Miss Whites between here and hell.'

Aunt Jane was the invalid among my father's four sisters and two brothers, but outlived them all, dying only a year or two ago at the age of ninety-four. She was the exact opposite of Aunt Fanny in every particular. When Fanny's chickens ate the flower of Jane's horticulture, the former hoped to goodness at last they would get fat.

Aunt Jane had her own humour, a little dry and acid like herself. She had been president from time immemorial of the local Girls' Friendly Society. After some regrettable increases in the population, she was heard to murmur that she feared her girls 'were sometimes a little too friendly.'

The house itself is like a glorified farmhouse with two eagles perched at either end of the roof to blend the pride of the Whites of Whitehall with the 'homeyness,' almost the homeliness, which has made the family really beloved, a semi-sacred institution in the Braid Valley. The place is like a mother's lap. The lawn slopes down from the clematis-covered front steps to the pond. The pond is reached by many mysterious ways along borders full of Aunt Jane's special herbaceousness, or by walks roofed with arched laurels and over rustic bridges with a step or two missing.

The same God made Whitehall who made children, and He made them for each other. A soft protective motherliness is, the first thing you feel when you come down before family prayers and stand on the front steps to see if the postman is coming up the avenue. The great limes are like mother's skirts, and two soft lines of timber enclosing the sloping lawn are like mother's arms that hold you on her lap. But all around there is mystery, unfathomable, impenetrable mystery. Alec's Scrogg, that pathless thicket of brambles and rowans and guelder rose bushes: there is mystery and a spice of danger even in reaching it, for the steps of the rustic bridges get shakier and fewer. Once there you may sink up to the knees in a boggy bit just as you are reaching for a cluster of guelder rose. berries like polished scarlet wax.

Then the lofts, oh! the lofts, guarded from the timid by perilous entries, straight ladders above the stable and byre and the cumbersome trap-door above the laundry. But the grand tour of the lofts has been made. I can answer for it; made in wonder and delight and awe over chasms of missing floor-boards, disturbing families of wild-eyed piebald cats.

In the lofts there is a flavour of evil, were not sweet ness and safety so near. Alec, the old coachman, yoking the older brougham to take Aunt Jane into Ballymena, would exorcise any evil spirit. Further out there is definite evil. The bad fairy wood with its tangle of brambles and wild raspberries that never ripen, shut into inner darkness by great silver firs; under them a murmur of treacherous hidden 'laids,' as streams are called in Ulster, tributaries of a central Styx. Even so, the good fairy wood is just opposite, the other side of the avenue, aisles of orderly Scotch firs like a church with a carpet of pine needles so soft no one would hear you if you came in late. Such is Whitehall; no wonder it called me back.

The Clements family shared the run of Whitehall with us White children. Uncle John Clements had married Aunt Victoria one of my father's sisters, and by her had numerous and thrilling issue.

The Clements to me had something of the charm of the wild cats in the lofts. Even George, the eldest son, who never showed up, had some mystery about him though he was reputed to be rich, which is no passport to an Irish child's love. But he had had his fingers frost-bitten, and married his deceased wife's sister.

James, the next, was full of fascinating mystery, for he was always dying. He blew in to Whitehall when he wasn't so engaged, would take me out shooting, and bring down a dozen snipe with a dozen cartridges. Eventually he died, casually, as the Clements did everything, and allowed me to see him as a corpse. That was another Clements characteristic, a most flattering habit of taking children into their confidence, not in an unseemly way, but in readiness to share with them the realities of life. I think they inherited it from Uncle John, who invited me once to accompany him round the pond walk. He offered me a cigar, and told me how one of his sons had suffered from worms in childhood. His manner implied, 'What a pity I did not know you then; you would have been able to advise me.' I was about fourteen then. I suppose the subject had cropped up with reference to my terrier.

Henry, the next Clements, had been a cowboy in Texas and Mexico, and looked it. He was a pleasure to look at, a greater pleasure to listen to. He added to the civilized detachment of the Clements in general the wild and whimsical detachment of the prairie. His attitude to the solemnities of life was one of simple manly reverence illuminated by simple blasphemy. He was the quarry *par excellence* to stalk in the middle of family prayers. Not a muscle of his face twitched, but by whimsical allusions to the incident he could keep you laughing for a week.

Death and religion lost their terrors at Whitehall. First and foremost there was not a special tone of voice reserved for funerals and Holy Communion. That was of intense significance to me as a child. I think it would be to every child.

That differentiation was marked by me very young between Ireland and England, the spiritual Irish Channel. At church you always stood a chance of comic relief, if not from the clergyman in person, from some 'professed lunatic' of the village straying in to assist. Ann McVicker, who was on the most intimate terms with us all, from Aunt Fanny downwards, came once and actually mounted the pulpit to deliver a short prayer. Shall I ever forget my frantic delirious delight? I managed to smother my laughter, but in my rockings I kicked the wooden partition between the seats with a bang like a gunshot. Funerals at Whitehall were certainly not unrelieved gloom. The costumes of the mourners provided too much scope for humorous comment. I've seen a Clements - I think it was Henry - with faultless topper and frock-coat, so redolent of Bond Street that. I poked fun at him about it in the *cortège*. He vindicated his character by exposing a pair of brown tennis shoes at the base. In a word, even in stodgy old 'King and Empire' Ulster, Ireland could not be cut to pattern if it tried. Now I might quote Oliver Gogarty and say, 'Our function as a race is to resist being mechanized.' Then as a child I thought of Henry Clements' funeral shoes. Truth comes by many paths.

Whitehall was accustomed to lunatics, and treated them kindly. An advanced religious lunatic had once taken up his abode in the garden. He used to walk about naked, with a Bible in one hand and a golf club -he had once been a golf caddy -in the other. But Whitehall was pained when the heir of the Whites descended on it with a Bible in one hand and something very like a shillelagh in the other.

The description is apt enough for my debut in Irish politics heralded by the following correspondence in the Ulster Liberal Press: -

Extract from *Ulster Guardian* dated Saturday, 4th May, 1912
Striking letter from Captain J. R. White, D.S.O 'bigotry and stagnation' of so-called unionism. A protest the Belfast News-Letter would not publish.

'The following correspondence has been sent to us for publication by the recipient of the letters, who, for reasons which will be obvious to every Ulster Liberal, cannot afford to have it known that he even so much as receives correspondence of such a heretical character. The writer is Captain James R. White, D.S.O., of the Gordon Highlanders, and the only son of Field-Marshal Sir George White, V.C.I the hero of Ladysmith, and Ulster's distinguished son ' As will be gathered from the correspondence, Captain White wrote a letter to the *News-Letter* protesting against the abuse of Protestantism which the proclamation of the Liberal demonstration in the Ulster Hall amounted to. Having given our contemporary two months in which to screw up sufficient courage to print his letter, Captain White sent a copy of it to a friend in Antrim, with a covering letter, and gave permission for both to be published, which we do, we need scarcely say with the greatest pleasure.'

c/o Francis Sedlak, Whiteway, nr.Stroud,
Gloucestershire, 15th *April.*

I enclose a copy of a letter I wrote some two months ago and sent to the *Belfast News-Letter* with reference to the refusal to let Winston Churchill speak in the Ulster Hall.

I have been waiting and watching to judge by their fruits the claims to truth and progress of the respective parties over this Home Rule question.

My mind is now made up thus far, that whatever real obstacles there may be to the amalgamation of the two sections of the Irish people into one self-governing nation the leaders of the so-called Unionist Party are appealing to nothing but the spirit of bigotry and stagnation. The feebleness of their irrational position is only equalled by the vulgarity of abuse with which they make pretence of answering the rational and moderate proposals of their opponents, and it seems to me the duty of every man who loves Ireland and who can hope to exercise the least influence, is to strive to free Ulstermen from their retrogressive sway.

I write to you recalling the long and close relations of friendship between the people of Coreen and my family, and I hope if stirring times are in store for Ireland I may not be idle on the side of progress and Protestantism, which I take to mean the liberty of the reason, and to be represented by self-government or Home Rule in a nation, just as a free reason gives self-control to an individual. I hope to return to Ireland shortly. In the meantime make any use of this communication you think fit, and be kind enough to write to me, if you have any suggestions to make as to useful activity for the cause of Irish Home Rule.

Yours sincerely, J. R. WHITE.

P.S. - I never inquired whether the *Belfast News-Letter* printed the enclosed letter or not. No doubt they did not or I should have heard.

Copy of letter To *Belfast News-Letter*

'Dear Sir,

As a son of Ulster, a resident in Ulster, and as a man to whom the North of Ireland has always been the best-loved corner in the world, I ask for space in your columns for a belated protest against the part which Ulster has been made to play under the banner of Protestantism, to her incalculable damage in the eyes of all to whom the true spirit and mission of Protestantism is most dear. What is that spirit? What but the insistence on the power and right of the individual to sift for himself what claims to be truth, to verify by its appeal to his own reason and conscience the character of what is advanced as a divine revelation or a mandate supported by divine authority.

Protestantism, if it has any meaning other than any tongue may choose to impose upon the word, stands for the refutation of the claim of an ecclesiastical hierarchy to dictate to men their beliefs and duties, independent of their free and intelligent concurrence. This ethically unjustifiable pretence, reducing those who accept it if indeed its complete acceptance is humanly possible to the level of mere unthinking machines, has to be supported, as do all attempts to infringe natural laws, by unnatural interference and concealment. The double duty, composed of two inseparable elements, to prove all things and hold fast that which is right, is too stern a task for those who abandon their birthright for the ease or safety of spiritual apron strings, and their sheltered security is safeguarded by an "index" of things by no means to be proved. I will not venture to assert that this safeguarding is never beneficial for childish or overemotional souls, but if there is any body of men who have outgrown the need of it, the Protestant Ulstermen, if I know them aright, are such a body. To put a politician on the index for them is to give them an unmerited insult, a fact they will speedily discover to the discomfort of such as have encouraged their pugnacity to obscure their remarkably sound judgment. To thus insult them in the name of Protestantism is to fly in the face of history and significant language.

"The letter killeth but the spirit giveth life." That uneasy certainty in advance, which refuses a hearing to an opponent, is the naked spirit of

Popery. Let those who believe such a spirit to be life-giving shape their actions in accordance with it, but let them leave the name of Protestant to the heirs in spirit of those who called the word into being.

Yours, etc.,

J. R. WHITE

(Late Captain, Gordon Highlanders).'

The 'recipient' of the letters is now dead. He was a good man, kindly, broad, and charitable. He may therefore be assumed to be beyond the reach of the Ulster Unionist clique. He was a schoolmaster in a village above Whitehall called Coreen, a place whose inhabitants were deeply attached to the Whites, not without reason, for my Uncle Johnny, who was their landlord, on one occasion at least sent them back half their rent as a Christmas present.

It is worth noting, however, that a friend in Belfast to whom I wrote in the year of grace 1929, seventeen years after the date of the correspondence, asking him to look up the back files of the *Ulster Guardian* and send it to me, marks his accompanying letter 'strictly confidential,' and forbids me to mention his name in connection with his kindness.

There is a saying in Ulster, and a true one -'Rome is a lamb in adversity, a snake in equality, a lion in prosperity'; Belfast, with its pseudo-Protestant political popery, has become a mule in perversity, a jackass in pomposity. But the sacredness of a tradition is often in inverse ratio to its rationality. Whitehall was in the Ulster ascendancy tradition, and it failed to appreciate my breakaway.

CHAPTER 18.
BALLYMONEY AND CASEMENT

Some eighteen miles from Whitehall is the market town of Ballymoney, the centre of a district known as the Route. Over its fertile plains, broken by great stretches of bog, my cousin, now I am sorry to say my late cousin, Ion Montgomery of Benvarden, chased the elusive hare, as Master of the Route Harriers. A goodly company of the scions of the Ulster Ascendancy assisted him in the chase. Almost am I tempted in these barren days, when the light in Kathleen Ni Houlihan's eyes is dim, to wish I had confined myself to the hunting of hares as plentiful and by comparison as easy of capture, as the quarry of my cousin's hounds.

Sport of any kind I always loved. My tendency was always to go too far afield for too big game. What a much pleasanter life I could have lived, if I had never endangered the automatic invitation to shoot the Benvarden bogs, which quite commonly provided nine different sorts of game for an afternoon's shoot. Such regret is vain; especially out of place in the *Memoirs of a Misfit*. Let it be their function to chart the shallows and perilous rapids of an imagination that disdains to flow in its natural bed. Let the baying of the Route Harriers drown my useless moans and a libation of Bushmills whisky cleanse the spot, if discoverable, 'where I made one.'

With my Bible and my shillelagh I went to the Route to chase the most elusive of all hares, the spirit of '98. This spirit, though a potent intoxicant, is not the product of the local distilleries at Bushinills and Coleraine. To define it fully would take a history of Ireland and more than that. It would take one of those flashes of Kathleen Ni Houlihan's eyes, which have been known to bind even full-blooded Englishmen under a spell for life. To some these flashes come by way of the mind. To some they come lying out on a Donegal or Connemara mountain by way of - what? The aesthetic sense, a sexual susceptibility to something powerfully female in the Irish earth? Why bother to define it? Especially if, in these disillusioned days, one is almost tempted to suspect that Homer with his tales of Circe and the sirens knew at least as much about it as Yeats with his bean rows and his beehives. Enough to say that to the genuinely spell-struck, it disturbs the knowledge of how

114

many beans make five. It disturbs the balance. It lays a man open to the dry criticism of Ulster -'That man's had too much or too little whisky.'

The year 1798 was the year of the most formidable of the Irish Rebellions. It presented two new features, an alliance of Protestant and Catholic against the Government and the English connection, and a sympathetic *rapport* with the world-movement of ideas in the French Revolution. Its outstanding figure was Wolfe Tone, founder of the United Irishmen, an Ulsterman and a Protestant. The greater number of the leaders were Protestants, and the biggest fights against the Crown forces were waged by Ulster Protestants on Ulster soil.[1]

Returning to Ireland after the appearance of my letter in the *Ulster Guardian, I* brought to Irish politics the sense of taut expectancy that dominated myself. I knew little of the history of Ireland, nothing of her current parties and personalities. But I expected parties and personalities to respond to the predestined something I felt in myself. The division of Ireland was unnatural. The elements of union would be waiting for discovery. To be told that around Ballymoney some of the spirit of '98 still survived, that the Protestant farmers of the Route remembered with pride the combination of their forefathers with Catholic Irishmen to unite Ireland and throw off the English connection seemed to my sanguine youth as much information as was necessary for spectacular victory.

I visited Ballymoney and interviewed local Ulster Liberals, solicitors, Presbyterian ministers and such like. A fine old minister, J. D. Armour, gave me his wholehearted support, and Taggart, a local solicitor, seconded him. We formed a committee and decided on a meeting (confined to Protestants) of protest against Carsonism and Carson's claim to speak for a solid Ulster.

I cannot put my hand on the bills we got out for the meeting. I remember one crucial phrase, of my introduction, which the committee accepted but subsequently allowed to be altered under interesting circumstances.

I got them to avow the object of the meeting as a protest against the 'lovelessness of Carsonism.' That word lovelessness was important to me and sincere. Ireland to me was the point where the larger love was to triumph over the blind divisions and jealousies of men, in fact the

---

[1] I use the word Protestant to cover both Presbyterians and Church of Ireland Episcopalians. Locally it is often confined to Episcopalians as distinct from Presbyterian.

pivot of the millennium. Even now when I am forced by facts to admit the verisimilitude of a friend's suspicion that it is the place where all the damned souls are collected before being destroyed, the old faith is only scotched, not killed. My eyes have gone blind with seeing and my ears deaf with hearing, seeing disillusion and hearing the blasphemies of the ungodly, but some spark remains unquenched of faith in Ireland as the pivot of a great world change. It is certain that Ireland is a sympathetic centre. Her whole history shows it. Her little parochial rebellions achieve nothing but a morbid intensification of the martyr-mania of her people. Her real upheavals come in unison with worldwide movements and connect her effort towards internal unity with the unity of mankind.

There was another besides myself whose being was rooted in the National Being of Ireland, whose life was doomed to be cut short on the gallows because he failed to stretch his eager, already over-taut, soul to the hidden dimension of Ireland's destiny. I speak of Roger Casement. An Ulsterman by birth, a knight-errant by temperament, a diplomat, alas! by profession.

In the rift that opened between him and me over the arrangements for this meeting at Ballymoney lay the seeds of his death, and, for what it is worth, of my continuing life.

When Casement heard that the meeting was incubating, he descended on the town and the committee. He did not notify me of his intention or action. He made subtle changes in the spirit which I had intended the meeting to express. The most significant of these was the change of my phrase 'the lovelessness of Carsonism' to the 'lawlessness of Carsonism.' My appeal was to God. He changed it to an appeal to Caesar. When the British Caesar failed him, he appealed to the German Kaiser, who used him and left him to the mercy of his confrère. I knew by intuition, before I knew by reason, that the destiny of Ireland had nothing to do with Caesars or empires except to outlast the lot and rise on their ruins. My friends regard me as nervy, impatient. On one point Job was a restless neurotic by comparison. I have told you what it is. While the destiny of Ireland is unripe, I can wait. I can even overcome the Irish itch to die. Indeed on the only occasion I ever hunger-struck I knew I did not possess it.

The truth is, the diplomat in Casement spoiled the kingly gentleman, the self-devoted patriot. Do all diplomats think they can wangle anything? Casement did. Whereas in matters of high destiny you can wangle nothing, absolutely nothing; not even a prime minister nor a Kaiser, and God knows they are wanglable enough. You must go dead straight; get laughed at for a crazy impractical lunatic, and go all the straighter. Then God will send you a patronizing disciple or two, who will tell the crowd, 'This chap's not mad, he's only inspired.' Finally the disciples will take to literature, while the madman writes on tablets of flesh and blood. In his appeal against lawlessness, Casement was not even sincere. At Ballymoney he protested against the lawlessness of Carsonism. At Cork a little later he called for three cheers for Sir Edward Carson from a fervidly Nationalist audience, and explained - just in time to prevent the platform being stormed - that it was because Carson was the first in this generation to teach Irishmen to fight.

I was indignant when I heard of Casement's action, and made an appointment to meet him in Belfast. I believe it was the first time we met. The interview was pretty stormy. Casement was, of course, far ahead of me in experience and influence, a man of kingly presence, courtly address. One can imagine his horror at being informed by an ebullient boy, 'We'll get on all right if you're honest.' 'I think you're most insulting,' he replied. But we got over that. In our long subsequent association the note of that first interview was often repeated, but affection and a humorous tolerance on his part of my rival messiahship formed a pleasant accompaniment.

CHAPTER 19.
PROTESTANT HOME RULE

The meeting came off on the 24th of October 1913. Dollie and I drove over from Whitehall in a two-seater Ford in which I had recently invested. There were strong rumours that the Orangemen were going to put barbed wire entanglements across the road, but a later report that they had desisted out of respect to my father's memory proved true. A strong force of police guarded the meeting-hall. An Orange drum was being banged loudly in an Orange hall opposite as the meeting began.

Dealing with events now some sixteen years old, it seems necessary to reconstruct the general political setting, which the meeting was designed to influence.

The Liberal Government under Asquith was going to pass a Home Rule Bill for the whole of Ireland. Under the proposed Bill, the Ulster members would have sat in the Dublin Parliament and been, of course, outnumbered by the Catholic Nationalist majority. Sir Edward Carson took the lead of a movement that threatened armed resistance. Volunteers were organized all over Ulster. A general, I think on the active list, was procured to take command. A promising young English lawyer, who has since fulfilled his promise, if not his promises, became a dashing A.D.C. The motorcars of the Ulster aristocracy disembarked and distributed a ship-load of arms, while the Ulster Volunteers kept the police and coastguards in their barracks. In short, there was a very efficient and well-organized revolutionary movement, set afoot by highly-respectable people, and commanding the natural sympathy and respect of all other respectable people, including the ministers of the Government against whom it was directed. Had I not realized this, of course, I would have been in it.

Let the *London Times* of 25th October 1913 now take up the parable in its leader. Its further survey of the political conditions of the moment is all the more apposite, that the said leader deigns to mention our poor meeting at Ballymoney the previous night.

THE GOVERNMENT AND ULSTER
'We can conceive at this juncture no more momentous pronouncement

than that which the Prime Minister has to make at Ladybank today. He has to speak the word which will decide whether some fresh effort will be made to solve the Irish problem upon pacifist lines, or whether Ireland is to be plunged into a conflict, which will sow the seeds of further centuries of woe.

We do not doubt that Mr. Asquith will approach the issue with the deepest sense of responsibility and will handle it with the measured gravity it requires. He has never, like some of his lieutenants, poured scorn and insult upon the preparations of Ulster. He must be well aware that a situation full of perplexity will not be made easier by threats or' gibes. However much opinions may vary about the attitude of Ulster, at least it is an attitude which is entitled to be treated with respect. It springs from deep conviction, and is in no sense factitious. We have been told of late that the Government has always been well acquainted with the character of Ulster's opposition. The statement is one which we find it difficult to credit. Nothing is more certain now than that Mr. Asquith and his colleagues failed to realize the intensity of Ulster's determination, when they made their unhappy bargain with Mr. Redmond. Their mistake was not committed yesterday. They fell into it long ago, when they had to choose between defeat and the purchase of the support of the Irish Nationalist members. Evidently they have awakened now to a sense of their danger, but we have still to learn whether they have awakened in time. We are further told every day that Mr. Asquith is not to be bullied; that he will not yield to threats; that no ministry could be expected to abdicate its authority under pressure. The case of the Ulster Protestants, and of the whole Unionist party is that the ministry has never received due authority from the country for its Home Rule measure. Nor is it true to say that the ministry is being either bullied or threatened. The most remarkable feature of the movement in Ulster is its extraordinary restraint. No man's hand is being raised against his neighbour. We are witnessing in Ulster, not an outbreak of violence, but a calm grim series of steps, which are not to be translated into action unless the ministry pursues to the end its ill-omened course. Whether the stage of action is ever reached must depend upon Mr. Asquith and his colleagues. They have brought into existence an organization *(The Ulster Volunteers)* upon which they never reckoned. Upon them lies the onus of finding a way out of their plight.

The marked quietude of Ulster was relieved last night by a meeting of Protestants at Ballymoney in Co. Antrim to "Protest against the lawlessness of Carsonism." We are quite willing to make the Government a present of Ballymoney, and of all the Protestant Home Rulers it can find in Ulster. Ballymoney, as the late Professor Thorold Rogers discovered long ago, is probably the only place in the whole province where such a gathering could be held with any prospect of success. It represents a small and isolated "pocket" of dissident Protestants, the last few survivors of the Ulster Liberals of the old types. Ulster Liberalism is very like the Cheshire cat in *Alice in Wonderland*. It has vanished till only its grin lingers furtively in a corner of Co. Antrim. The one small effort of Protestant Home Rulers in Ulster serves, however, a useful purpose, because it reveals the scantiness of their numbers.'

So for once in my life I served a useful purpose.

The special correspondent in the same issue is a little more flattering. Here is his account

ULSTER HOME RULERS
MEETING OF OPPONENTS OF CARSONISM
A PROTESTANT GATHERING
Ballymoney, 24th October.

'Ballymoney, at which the meeting of protest against the lawless policy of Carsonism was held to-night, is a town of about three thousand inhabitants, situated in the North Antrim Division of the County about forty six miles from Belfast. Its interests are entirely agricultural, and it has large and important flax and cattle markets. The inhabitants of Ballymoney and of the, surrounding country within a five-mile radius are largely Presbyterians with Roman Catholic and Episcopalian minorities of about equal size. Just about this part of North-East Ulster many Presbyterians, particularly among the farmers, have always retained, to some extent, the Gladstonian faith of Non-Conformist Ulster, and this little town was in the old days a great fortress of Sharman Crawford's Ulster Land Reform movement.

Ballymoney was a good place in which to try the experiment of an Ulster Liberal meeting. There is drilling here among the Covenanters, but you see little sign of political enthusiasm in either camp. Every one seems to agree that all parties cultivate tolerance and an excessive amiability. In spite of this reputation for orderliness, about seventy extra police were drafted into the town earlier in the day. But it should be plainly understood that no Unionists assembled tonight to protest against the lawless policy of Carsonism.

Whatever significance may be attached to the meeting, it certainly indicated no new trend of Unionist opinion in Ulster. The promoters of the meeting could say - what indeed elections had already made known that there are a good number of Radicals, substantial people too, about Ballymoney and district. Probably these men dislike the methods of the Covenanters more than they like Home Rule, but that is another matter. The great feature of the meeting was that it was only open to Protestants. Admission was by ticket and no Roman Catholic might apply. This was good tactics since the propaganda of Sir Roger Casement and his friends is not amongst the Roman Catholics but amongst the Protestants of Ulster. They would like to find evidence of the conversion of Protestant Ulster.

Mr. Glendinning and others sent letters of apology, many of which referred in rather violent terms to Sir Edward Carson's provisional Government. The chairman Mr. McElderry, emphasized the fact that no Roman Catholics were present in the hall. Another speaker objected strongly to the view that the meeting had been engineered by the Russellite clique in Belfast. Then an old upholder of tenant right, a Mr. Carson, a local farmer, delighted the audience with humorous remark s. The late Sir George White's son, Captain White, had an enthusiastic reception from the four hundred or five hundred people present in the hall. He said it was not so much the lawlessness as the lovelessness of Carsonism which he disliked. Rome, he added, had always supported England in Ireland, and now England in Ireland supported Rome.

Mrs. J. R. Green, the historian, said that they had met together for the honour of the Protestant religion. She reminded the Presbyterian audience that Presbyterians had suffered with the Irish from Anglican and aristocratic ascendancy. But she touched her listeners most deeply when she declared that the Protestant farmers of Ulster owed their present prosperity to legislation obtained by southern sacrifice.

A speaker of a fame not less distinguished followed Sir Roger

Casement, who combines citizenship of the world with an enthusiastic attachment to romantic nationalism. He said that it was the first time he had ever addressed a meeting on an immediate political issue. Sir Roger spoke with feeling, but he avoided making bitter reference to Sir Edward Carson's movement. One thing was made clear by Sir Roger and his friends, namely, that the little band of Protestant Home Rulers refused to consider the exclusion of Ulster as a solution of the crisis.

In spite of the names and eloquence of the three principal speakers, the meeting as compared with the assemblies of covenanters lacked impressiveness. There is no need to deny, however, that the audience was fairly representative of local interests. It was composed for the most part of plain country people, who listened keenly to the speeches. The mottoes hung on the wall proclaimed that Ulster must be for Ireland and Ireland for Ulster, and that no provincial or provisional Government should be established in the north. Many of the orators, as befitted the occasion, laid stress on the anticlerical element in Irish Nationalists. A few local representatives of the legal and other professions took a prominent part in the proceedings, but one felt that the pick of the Protestant Home Rulers present on the platform, with the exception of Mr. Wilson of Belfast, were somewhat out of touch with everyday life and feeling in Ulster, and might be called cranks and faddists by the Philistines and muscular Christians in Sir Edward Carson's following.'

You're wrong there, Mr. Special Correspondent. The muscular Christians of Sir Edward Carson's following don't limit themselves to terms of endearment like 'crank' and 'faddist.'

A friend of mine in London, a great friend, luckily, told me that some years after the stormy times she met at dinner an Ulster R.M. hailing from near Whitehall. Hearing where he hailed from she asked innocently did he know Jack White? 'Oh that dirrty blackguard,' was the reply she got. But by that time I'd had a whack at a few policemen.

I would like to give one more extract bearing on the general situation at the time. The extract in question is a letter from Lord Charnwood to the *Times of* 23rd October 1913, and it is a very good letter. It bears out my contention that the high respectability of Sir Edward Carson's movement awoke an almost automatic sympathy in other respectable people, even 'inveterate Home Rulers,' as Lord Charnwood proclaims himself to be. For the same reason, it awoke an automatic antipathy in me, because I am a disreputable person. I could never feel happy landing guns in a Rolls-Royce.

But there is an aspect of Lord Charnwood's letter with which I am in wholehearted agreement, which has governed every step of my action in my contact with Irish politics and even Irish rebel armies. That aspect is his stress on the deep sincerity of the Ulster people and the fact that in the hearts of the rank and file 'the Ulster sedition' had in it elements of a higher character than English people find it easy to suppose. I agree also that 'the influences which the Pope symbolizes to Ulster have unquestionably their ugly side.' But Ulster's exclusion and isolation, her lack of faith in the dynamic quality of her Protestantism, have allowed those influences to envisage the conversion of twenty-six counties of Ireland into a Papal State, and to make some headway to date towards its achievement.

If Ulster is content to be isolated, excluded, and exclusive, let me assure the men of Ulster that 'the influences which the Pope symbolizes' have no such notion at all about confining their sphere to the Irish Free State.

The Free State is to them a base of operations, an experimental field, and a base of expansion after experiment.

By skilful use of the Irish language, not to revive the ideas of Gaelic Ireland but to oust Protestant tradition and handicap broader culture, by unheard-of powers for the censorship and suppression of literature, Rome Rule is asserting itself in the mutilated parody of Home Rule, of which Carson sowed the seeds, and his promising galloper garnered the crop. If the men of Ulster

I use the term men in vivid contradistinction to the gentlemen- think their little leaven is safe because they've buried it in a napkin, they're making a big mistake, England is backing Rome. All Governments are backing Rome. They'd be fools if they didn't. Better an omnipotent, infallible policewoman to chloroform the mind, than a lot of troublesome, expensive, possibly insubordinate policemen to bludgeon the people's bodies. And if the present clique-rule in Ulster goes on much longer, the Ulster people will be all ready for Popery except the name.

Which dissertation may give more interest to the report of my own speech at the Ballymoney meeting, which I take from the *Ulster Guardian* of 1st November 1913. I let it be preceded by Lord Charnwood's letter to contrast the respectable and disreputable points of view.

Times of 23rd October
LETTER FROM LORD CHARNWOOD
'The fact that I am an inveterate Home Ruler fresh from a tour among my Unionist friends in Ulster does not, I know, give any peculiar authority to my convictions, but it may excuse my unwillingness to be silent.

Among the conflicting estimates which I have read of the situation in Ulster, I believe that those which rate its gravity highest are nearest the truth. Quite apart from Belfast, a large number of country people of a sturdy sort have been submitting themselves with effect to drill and discipline. They are better armed and certainly better organized and led than might be supposed. They are prepared, I believe, for defeat and death upon the chance of political success in the end. It is beside the point to say that their resistance could easily be put down, and ought in the last resort to be put down rigorously. The real point is that the struggle may so affect the relations between Ulster and the rest of Ireland and the relations between Catholics and Protestants throughout Ireland, as to destroy or delay for generations the very objects for which Liberal and Nationalist statesmen alike desire Home Rule. Moreover, these people are entitled to a certain limited sympathy. Englishmen are apt to repeat towards Ulstermen the mistake which their fathers committed towards Southern Irishmen; they expect them to be like the English and are angry to find that they are not. The claims based by Ulstermen upon the deeds of their ancestors do not inspire respect, but they are not at all more unnatural than the insistence by other Irishmen upon the wrongs of their ancestors. Ulster bigotry is peculiarly offensive to the strongest English Protestants, who deliberately disbelieve that Home Rule means Rome Rule; but the fear that Home Rule means Rome Rule is not at all unnatural in Ireland, and the influences which the Pope symbolizes to Ulster have unquestionably their ugly side. Thus the Ulster sedition has in it elements of a higher character than English people find it easy to suppose. This fact is what makes it formidable; it also makes it impossible for Liberals to think that firmness is the sole quality required in dealing with it.'

REPORT OF MY SPEECH
From *Ulster Guardian,* 1st November 1913

'Captain J. R. White, D.S.O., who was received with round after round of applause, supported the resolutions. He was, he said, no advocate of peace at any price. There were things to which he held resistance to be a sacred duty, resistance at all costs and by all means in their power. If it were true that the most cherished rights and liberties of the Protestant population were being sacrificed by a cowardly betrayal, and that for no higher reason than the insensate lust of a corrupt Government for political power, then he would thank his fate that he had the tradition of arms in his blood and some knowledge and experience of the profession of arms stored up in his mind, so that he might offer himself unreservedly to the armed resistance organized rather than tamely submit to such an outrage. If the allegations were not false he would be the first to say to the Protestants of Ulster, "Arm, and let the hills of Ulster be so many fortresses prepared against a siege."

He was there that night to protest, not so much against the lawlessness of Carsonism as its lovelessness, its barrenness of ideas and of arguments, and above all its wholesale falsification of the facts of history and the facts of human nature. It was true that Ireland at the present time was giving fair promise of prosperity and happiness, but this was owing to the fact that a series of ameliorative measures had been passed, and these measures had been greeted with the same chorus of no surrender nonsense by the same party which was now opposing Home Rule. The Land Acts were the outcome of ceaseless agitation by the farmers of all Ireland to be freemen and not expellable serfs on the land they cultivated by their own labour. In that fight north and south fought side by side (cheers). The victory won, the Protestant farmers of Ulster were bidden to forget their allies. Let them listen, if they liked, but when the liberties which the north had gained by the help of the south were filched away from them one by one, he for one would rejoice that their meanness and ingratitude had been punished as they deserved.

When would Ulstermen see that the question of Home Rule was not and never had been a religious question, but a question of human rights? It was the policy of England for centuries to rule Ireland by fomenting religious divisions within her borders. Irish life, as they knew it today, hinged upon these divisions to an extent which to a stranger coming to Ireland seemed incredible. How was it possible to bridge these divisions, to establish a non-sectarian state education, when there was as yet no state and no ideal of a common state towards which Irishmen of all creeds could aspire. They could not blame the people for the existing state of things, but he blamed the leaders, who knew that there must be some meeting-ground before peace could be accomplished and yet resisted the efforts to find such a meeting-ground.

As a Protestant he admitted with shame that it was the leaders of the Protestant section of the people who were appealing now to the bitterest memories of the past rather than admit the need and wisdom of a ground of union to heal them. They were now at a great crisis in the history of their country, but at an even greater crisis in the history of Protestantism. If Protestantism stood for anything it stood for this, that each man believed he was so directly a son of God, that the final arbiter of right or wrong, truth or falsehood, was his own conscience and not any priesthood or any infallible power outside his own conscience. But let Protestants remember this, that the test of their sonship of God was their brotherhood with man, and those Protestants who could think and act towards their Catholic fellow countrymen as though they were their hereditary enemies had better for their own sakes leave the name of God out of the question. (Cheers.)

Afterwards a large number of those present signed the following covenant, which was read by Captain White: "Being convinced in our conscience that Home Rule would not be disastrous to the national well-being of Ulster, and that, moreover, the responsibility of self-government would strengthen the popular forces in other provinces, would pave the way to a civil and religious freedom, which we do not now possess, and give scope for a spirit of citizenship, we whose names are underwritten, Irish citizens, Protestants, and loyal supporters of Irish Nationality, relying under God on the proved good feeling and democratic instincts of our fellow-countrymen of other creeds, hereby pledge ourselves to stand by one another and our country in the troubled days that are before us, and more especially to help one another when our liberties are threatened by any non-statutory body that may be set up in Ulster or elsewhere. We intend to abide by the just laws of the lawful parliament of Ireland until such time as it may prove itself hostile to democracy. In sure confidence that God will stand by those who stand by the people, irrespective of class or creed, we hereunto subscribe our names.

CHAPTER 20.
DEBUT IN DUBLIN

The scene changes. The sands of my gentility are running out. What is a 'gentleman'? 'A gentleman, runs one definition is one who never gives offence unless he means to.' Exactly. Therefore one who always gives offence whether he means to or not is no gentleman, and to this latter condition I begin from now rapidly to sink. While a man confines himself to 'politics,' that is, to making speeches and circulating ideas even on the side of unpopular causes, he can remain a gentleman. His fellow-gentlemen have something solider on which to base their gentility than ideas and speeches, and if one of their numbers chooses to run a tilt against the ideology of their order, he is a foolish eccentric fellow, but at the right kind of dinner-party he may positively be a conversational asset. But supposing the eccentric fellow doesn't stop at that. Supposing he makes common cause with a lot of lewd fellows of the baser sort to threaten the solid basis of gentility, the unquestioned sway of the policeman's baton, the pointed persuasion of the soldier's bayonet in reserve, the ordered accretion and allocation of rents and dividends, can such be deemed a gentleman? He cannot. He has ceased to 'play the game.' He has become most vulgarly in earnest. The very preservation of the power to 'play the game' depends on his suppression. Pending his suppression, let him be cast into outer darkness where there is jailing and smashing of scalps.

Ballymoney made something of a stir. Far away across the Boyne, Dublin heard and wondered. The South of Ireland looks towards the North as Andromeda might have looked in the direction of Perseus' arrival. Very few Irish Nationalists will admit this; the merely political' Nationalist will strenuously deny it. It is true none the less. Take all the prophecies of the dawning of Ireland's destiny. They speak with one voice. A great light is to rise in the North. The hound of Ulster will be loosed and chase the Sassenach into the sea. There exist in Ireland a number of far from negligible persons, who await the fulfilment of prophecy. They might not admit it either, but they do. The political fight goes on governed by ordinary considerations of political expediency. The physical force movement goes on governed by no considerations at all but the necessity to keep hate alive, because hate is the only antidote professions strong enough to counteract England's false professions of love. But neither the constitutional nor unconstitutional movements believe in their own efficacy unaided. They work over-shadowed by predestination. The moment the strange unforeseen conjunctions for the fulfilling of destiny, are not of man's choosing. 1 hadn't been in Dublin a week before I sensed this. You can imagine what balm it was to me, and how disastrous to the last relics of my worldly prudence. I found myself an instrument of destiny. Here were a number of most intelligent and alive persons, many of them of wide repute in politics or literature, who were ready to take me at my own valuation.

The cause of my going to Dublin was an invitation to speak at the National University arising out of the interest evoked by Ballymoney. Of course I accepted it. On the platform also speaking were John Dillon, Tom Kettle and a number of leading lights of the National struggle.

John Dillon spoke before me. His speech was interrupted several times by suffragettes, whose rather rough ejection was greeted with approving glee by the occupants of the platform behind me. This angered me so much that 1 turned round and shouted 'Shame!' at them. I give Dillon's speech as part of my plan to reconstruct the general political setting and to let the Nationalist cause be pleaded by one of its own outstanding spokesmen at the time. I have given a very fair show to the Carsonite point of view. The opposite outlook and tradition should also be stated by an orthodox exponent before my speech with its unorthodox selection from both traditions.

MR. JOHN DILLON'S SPEECH

'Mr. John Dillon, M.P., in proposing a vote of thanks to the auditor, said they had in the history of their own country one of the most remarkable examples of the healing influence of liberty.

In the whole history of the world there was nothing more interesting than the recovery of Ireland in the interval between 1782 and 1793, and it was a remarkable thing that the history of that period had never been properly, fully, or sympathetically written. When one recalled the history of Ireland for the previous two centuries and the condition of Ireland when Grattan lament and the Volunteers secured the Parliament;

and when one remembered the difficulties by which that Parliament was hedged round and the limitations to which it was subjected, in his opinion, in the whole history of mankind and of civilization there was nothing so remarkable as the rapidity of the recovery of Ireland under that Constitution, such as it was.

But the Constitution to which he had been referring was not really free. There was one defect to its existence, namely, that the Executive Government was not subject to the Parliament, but was subject to the English Ministers across the Channel, and the revenue levied by the Irish Parliament was used by British Ministers to corrupt that Parliament and to sacrifice the liberties of the nation.

Then he did not know in all history of anything more remarkable than the rapid spread of religious tolerance under the rule of Grattan's Parliament. When it was created, Ireland had passed through a long period of penal laws of a savage character without parallel, and the Catholics were down in the dust, trampled under the natural foot. One would suppose that according to laws of human nature there would have been such a Catholics of spirit of animosity and hatred bred in the it would take generations to bring about peace between them and the Protestants who had oppressed them. But such was the healing power of the gift of freedom that within five years the Catholics and Protestants were close friends, and it was one of the most remarkable things in the whole history of the country that when in 1793 the Catholic delegates were on their way to London to present a Catholic petition, they were asked to go by Belfast, and the Presbyterians and Episcopalians took their horses from their carriage and drew the Dublin Catholics through the streets of Belfast on their way to London to present the petition.

There was nothing more infamous than the means by which that rising tide of goodwill and fellowship was destroyed, and the Catholics and Protestant of Ireland once more set at each other's throats. How different would have been the history of Ireland if Wolfe Tone and the United Irishmen and the men of that day were allowed to unite Protestant and Catholic - how different would have been the history of Ireland, and of the unhappy capital which was held up now as one of the most terrible sinks of iniquity and poverty on the earth!

What was the cause of the poverty of Dublin? Dublin at the date of the

Union was a great city with a Population as great as today. Belfast had thirty thousand, and Dublin had three hundred thousand. Dublin was the second city of the Empire, and one of the most brilliant capitals of Europe. If the machinations of English Ministers had not been brought into play to carry the Union and break the power of Ireland, this capital would be the second city of the Empire, and one of the most brilliant and wealthy in Europe.

If they were today the mockery and scorn of England and held up to foreign nations in the way they were they have been brought to this because they were suffering the fate every decaying capital had suffered.

What were the slums of Dublin but the homes of their nobility and gentry which had been decaying, and which had gone down to the present miserable condition. The city itself and the condition it had been brought to, was a standing monument of the infamy of the Union, and the means used to bring it about.

The Home Rule Bill to be passed next year was incomparably better than the Constitution that Grattan won, and would give Ireland power over the government of her own country which never rested in Grattan's Parliament.

"We hear", he continued, "a great deal about guarantees and about oppression of minorities. I am ready to give, and have consented to give guarantees, but 1 do not believe that the Protestants of Ireland themselves care three straws for guarantees. They have said so, and the Protestants of the rest of Ireland and of Ulster are not such weaklings as to be afraid of their faith in an Irish Parliament. They know very well, that under an Irish Parliament, freely elected, their position would be one of influence and power. The trouble is that the old spirit of ascendancy the poisonous spirit of ascendancy, exists in certain parts of Ireland, and among certain classes. Those who will benefit most under Home Rule, or at least as much as what is now called the majority, are those men who are clinging to an ascendancy which cannot be defended or maintained in any country."

The real truth was that the men in Ulster who were opposing Home Rule were living in the seventeenth century. In those days all Churches persecuted. He was ashamed to say that his own Church persecuted, but so did the Protestants; it was the spirit of the time. It was an evil spirit, but it all belonged to the past, and was just as dead as the Battle of the Boyne and the old cries that were clung to in the north of Ireland. What these men had to do was to make up their minds that they were living in the twentieth century, and once they did that and trusted to their fellow-countrymen, they would find that these fellow-countrymen would know no distinction of race or religion, but would judge men wholly by the honesty and ability of their services to Ireland. (Applause.)'

I spoke next. I give the report.

SPEECH OF CAPTAIN J.R. WHITE

'Captain J. R. White, D.S.O. (son of the late Sir George White), seconded the resolution. At the outset he congratulated the meeting on the gentle and chivalrous treatment shown to the suffragettes. Continuing, he said that he agreed with Mr. Dillon that five years after the passing of Home Rule the Protestants of Ulster would regard the mere mention of safeguards as an insult. The note of the Ballymoney meeting was the reconciliation of North and South, but it was plain that "North is North, and South is South, and never the twain shall meet," if each worked for reconciliation within its own borders, and no emissaries passed between them.

He was no accredited emissary, but he claimed to know the feeling of the North of Ireland. The saddest legacy of British rule in Ireland was that it fomented to such a pitch the religious divisions between Irishmen that the subject of religion was too delicate to be touched. He believed that this open wound in Irish life, however sensitive must be touched before it could be healed. The question of religion was, first and last the Alpha and Omega, the beginning and the end, of the Ulster question with every honest man in Ulster, and there were a good many of them. (Hear, hear.)

Dealing with the question of freedom, as defined by the Auditor, Captain White said it was true that liberty to be liberty must contain order within itself on pain of degenerating into licence; but while Catholicism seemed to him to lay stress on cohesion and the limiting of the liberty of the individual, which was necessary to secure the order of the whole, be it a nation or other smaller community, Protestantism laid stress on the liberty of the individual, which he held to be equally necessary, that each might be free by progressive experiment, the essence of which was to make mistakes, to extend and enrich the common life.

The resistance of Ulster, he continued, was based on the fear that the ground would not be neutral. They feared the claim, which was said to be advanced by the Catholic Church to assert supremacy over the State. It would be impertinence on his part to discuss the doctrine of the Catholic Church on the matter, but whatever that doctrine was, his own advocacy of Home Rule was not affected by it, for this reason, that - 1 believe that if the claim of supremacy over the State were not only made but attempted to be enforced, the Catholic people of Ireland would be no whit behind the Protestant in refusing it. (Hear, hear!)

The statement to convince Ulster, however, must come from the Catholic politicians themselves, and come in the clearest and most unmistakable terms. There were many sane and thoughtful men in Ulster who believed that if the Catholic Church made claim to control the State, that would justify armed resistance to government by a Catholic majority. Therefore, asked Captain White, cannot a supreme effort be made to set their fears at rest? He asked the question, he added, with a strong personal interest in the answer - he wanted to make his own plans for the future.

In the event of a fight, which he did not consider so remote as some others, he wanted to know to whom to offer his services. It seemed to him that they had three courses open: first, to convince at all costs the Protestants of Ulster of their good faith, and they would have all the help he (Captain White) could give them. Their chances of success in this rested, he believed, on their approaching Ulster direct, and not through England. The second was to prepare to fight their own battle for a united Ireland if Ulster stood out against it. He saw no reason why course one or two should not be carried out simultaneously. As to the third course - to leave the subjugation of Ulster or the Carsonites to the soldiers and police of the British Empire - in the event of their taking that course, and in that event only, he would offer his services, as leader or private trooper of irregular horse or any body of horse or foot, to Sir Edward Carson.'

PROFESSOR T. M. KETTLE'S SPEECH
'Professor T. M. Kettle moved a resolution recommending the Literary and Historical Society to the support of the students of the College. Referring to some of Captain White's remarks, he said the problem of Ulster was not a problem of irregular horses, but a problem of regular asses. (Laughter.) He could assure Captain White that there were in other parts of Ireland, besides the four north-eastern counties, persons who knew at which end of a rifle to put in the cartridge. (Laughter.) He thought what Ireland had suffered from was a lack of civil wars (laughter), and he should ask nothing better than that the staunch and grim and determined men of Ulster should have an opportunity of discovering that there are staunch and determined men south of the Boyne.'

The short extract from Tom Kettle's remarks 1 have given make it evident that my speech did not command unqualified approval from him or the body of Catholic Nationalist opinion, of which he was a very virile representative.

The suggestion that Rome 'in prosperity' might persecute again was resented. Naturally, too, the more virile Irish Nationalists felt that the highly respectable revolution or threatened revolution in the North had been given rope enough. If the English Government was not prepared to deal with it to carry through its own Statutes, southern Irishmen were prepared to deal with it themselves. Yet in a few months from that National University meeting, Tom Kettle was fighting England's battles in Flanders, while I was drilling Irish volunteers in an Ulster county. That is odd, is it not? Yet the explanation is simple. For the real fight, as I was soon to discover, was not between England and Ireland at all, nor yet between Ulster and the rest of Ireland. Kettle and his like never got down to the real fight.

So when England fought Germany in defence of Catholic Belgium, they fought for Belgium, not Ireland. For the roots of Ireland's wrongs and the point of leverage for Ireland's rights lay beyond their ken, even if under their noses.

Wherein lay the real fight? Let us see if the dear old dispassionate *London Times* can help us again.

Its leader of 22nd October 1913 headed 'The Condition of Dublin' reads as follows: -

THE CONDITION OF DUBLIN

'We are glad to record the movement for a public inquiry into the slum problem of Dublin, for there are few more tragic documents than Sir Charles Cameron's report upon the state of public health in the city during 1912. It moves compassion, not so much by what it says as by what it implies. Its stolid figures and bald statements of facts furnish unconsciously the true explanation of the innumerable sorrowful and hopeless faces which make Dublin just now the saddest city in the United Kingdom.

Long before the strikes large portions of Dublin had become haunts of misery and want and premature death. There is no need to rely upon general statements. The acknowledged facts published under the authority of the Dublin Corporation suffice. The average death rate in the city of Dublin during the past decade has been 24.6 per 1000; in London the annual rate is 13.6. Last year 43.3 per cent of the deaths took place in the various workhouses, hospitals, lunatic asylums and prisons of Dublin; the proportion of deaths in public institutions in large English towns only averages 18 per cent. About one-fourth of the inmates of Dublin workhouses die annually, making a death rate of 250 per 1000. When one reads Sir Charles Cameron's description of the condition of the sanitary arrangements of the North Dublin Workhouse, one begins to understand how it is that the mortality among paupers, rarely very good lives, is so terrible. But the gravest cause of the unhealthiness of Dublin is its tenement houses. The population of the city is estimated at 306,573 and of this total close upon 70,000 are dwelling in tenements of a single room. The number of occupants of each room varies considerably, but only 3604 one room tenements have single tenants. There are 6000 people living seven in a room, and 9000 people living six in a room. Such conditions are subversive both of health and morality. They suffice to account for the haggard and despairing men who gather daily outside Liberty Hall or on the banks of the Liffey. They would not be tolerated even in a modern Oriental city without desperate attempts to remedy so deplorable a state of things. The irony of the situation is that Dublin; still by far the richest city in Ireland maintains an elaborate staff to look after the public health and the sanitation of its precincts. There are 146 persons, most of whom are exclusively engaged under the direction of the Corporation in professedly caring for the health of Dublin. The city possesses twenty-two medical officers of health and thirty-six sanitary sub-officers armed with impressive certificates in sanitary science. The Corporation has ample funds, and is backed by laws, which give it all the powers it requires. The net result of all this simulation of endeavour is the state of Dublin as we see it today.

The effect of the conditions under which the poor of Dublin live is shown in the physical characteristics of the slum children. Most of them wilt at a very early age, and the infant mortality in the slum areas is very great. The problem is not insoluble. The trouble is that, despite the efforts of Lord Iveagh and others far too little has been done, and that the pace of improvement is impeded by the vested interests, which find their chief stronghold in the Dublin Corporation. What is needed in Dublin is an awakening of the conscience of the public regarding the iniquitous conditions existing in its midst. Home Rule will not right the wrongs of the Dublin poor. These are woes of Ireland on which the Nationalist party has always been studiously silent. Ardent Members of Parliament are always streaming from Westminster through Dublin, but they have never found time or inclination to expose grievances far worse than were ever found in Land League campaigns, grievances for which they know full well the remedy lies ready to hand. We do not, however, seek to make political capital out of a situation, the blame of which does not rest with the Nationalist party alone. The reproach for the condition of the city of Dublin must lie chiefly at the doors of the better classes of the city, whose apathy and lack of public spirit has so long permitted nearly a third of the population to live in an environment which should long

ago have been dealt with. The churches, the employers of labour, the public men, the wealthy private folk, none can escape their share of blame. . . . Dublin ought to be one of the healthiest cities in the world. It is swept by life-giving sea breezes. Its surroundings are more lovely than those of any city in the three kingdoms. It has ample room for expansion, yet people die like flies in the squalid slums, while even the broad expanse of Phoenix Park remains for the most part deserted and desolate.

'Home Rule will not right the wrongs of the Dublin poor.' 'The reproach for the condition of the city of Dublin must lie chiefly at the doors of the better classes of the city.'

Illuminating *London Times!* Only partially illuminating perhaps. No mention of the condition of the London poor, no stern reminder that the reproach for their condition must lie chiefly at the doors of the better classes of that great city; a definite suggestion none the less that the real fight may not be a political fight at all, may not even be a National fight but a class fight.

Certain Irishmen had seen this before the illuminated *Times* leader-writer. Wolfe Tone saw it when he wrote of that large and respectable class, persons of no property.

Certain Irishmen were seeing it now, James Larkin and James Connolly. They saw, too, or certainly Connolly saw that the National fight and the class fight were connected, but the class fight was the greater containing the other within itself.

'The cause of oppressed nations and oppressed classes, Connolly was about to write in *Labour in Irish History, is* one and the same. In the struggle for liberty of any subject nation, the owning and employing class are forced by economic pressure, to make terms with the oppressor, with whom and with whose system they become linked by a hundred golden threads of investments and the like. Thus the onus of the struggle is thrown more and more on the working class.'

The working classes of Ireland had been subject to a double pressure and had in them the potency of doubly powerful recoil.

They had suffered from the ordinary exploitation of their own possessing class, in addition and in common with the native possessing class they had suffered from industrial overshadowing coupled with agricultural vampirization by England. Moreover, their resistance to English domination was hampered by no sense of common patriotism but rather intensified by the racial hostility of centuries.

When I was invited to speak in Dublin, the first great movement of revolt on the part of the southern workers, the Larkin strike of 1913-14, was in progress, had been in progress for some months. Before I realized that here in Irish Labour was the medium destined at once to unite Ireland and link her cause with that of humanity at large, an incident occurred to plunge me into contact with the strikers from my own particular angle of approach.

In the North I had raised a protest against the perversion of Protestantism to deny political freedom to a subject nation.

In the South I broke away from politics down to the real fight in indignant horror at the perversion of Catholicism to deny even the freedom to control their own children to an economically subject class.

The strikers were hard pressed, terribly hard pressed. A movement was set on foot by Socialist sympathizers in England to relieve the pressure on them by taking some of the strikers' children to be cared for during the duration of the strike in English homes.

A Mrs. Montefiore, who afterwards became my friend, an elderly lady of gentle birth and unexceptionable character, and a Mrs. Rand were sent over to Dublin as representatives of the English movement to select children from the hardest pressed families and arrange their transport to England.

A day or two after the National University meeting, a loathsome agitation convulsed Dublin. The priests, with unspeakable indecency, became the open tools of the bosses, who were slowly starving out the parents and used their 'sacred' office to ensure that the children should starve with them.

The following, taken from the *London Times* of the 25th October, will show to what lengths of illegality and violence they went.

'All the steamers leaving the North Wall tonight were strongly picketed to prevent the deportation of children. A large number of men, including some clergymen, watched each steamer. A telegram, which is published in some of the evening newspapers, from the Rev. James Leech of Liverpool, is the subject of much comment tonight. In it Father Leech says, "Had the priests and people of Dublin known the atmosphere - anything but Catholic - to which the children have been taken, and in which I was forced to leave them, because the parents had tied the hands of the priests here, their opposition would have been even more strenuous. I blush, as a priest and an Irishman, to think of what I saw yesterday morning - that Irish parents could forget their sacred duty as the parents of these children have done."

This evening the deportation of fifteen boys was stopped at the Amiens Street railway station. A large number of Roman Catholics, including some clergymen, assembled on the platform, and when the boys arrived, accompanied by a lady and some men, they were immediately surrounded. The priests appealed to the men to allow the boys to return; and appeals were also made to the boys. The men declined, and the crowd, which appeared determined not to let the boys go, became very excited, The priests continued their appeals, and amid growing excitement the train went out, leaving the boys, their guardians, and the clerical party on the platform.'

That is a delicate touch in Father Leech's telegram. 'The atmosphere-anything but Catholic - to which the children have been taken, and in which I was forced to leave them!'

And the atmosphere from which their precious little souls had been taken, the atmosphere no doubt eminently and unquestionably Catholic. We have heard about that. 'The effect of the conditions under which the poor of Dublin live is shown in the physical characteristics of the slum children. Most of them wilt at a very early age, and the infant mortality in the slum areas is very great.' (See *Times* leader, p. 212.)

A few more explanatory extracts:-

London Times, 24th October

'It is now quite manifest that Mr. Larkin's action in outraging the feelings of the Roman Catholic Church was very bad tactics. *The priests have reasserted their authority over the women of the working classes* and it is no longer certain that Mr. Larkin enjoys the unquestioning obedience of the men of the Transport Workers' Union. The call of religion still retains its ancient efficacy in Dublin, and if Mr. Larkin wants to recover lost ground he will drop the deportation policy without delay. For the moment, however, it seems that he will persist in it.'

London Times, 25th October

'Mr. Larkin's influence is thought to be less powerful both in Great Britain and in Dublin than it was a fortnight ago. He has been badly beaten over the question of the deportation of the workers' children. As *Irish Times* says today, he has exasperated public opinion and shaken the allegiance of his own followers.

His prestige is hurt, and for a democratic leader prestige is everything.

Not content with 'reasserting their authority over the women of the working classes,' in other words, appealing to the ignorant bigotry of mothers to help in the starvation of their own husbands and children, the priests secured the arrest of the two ladies in charge of the deportation scheme.

Accusations that the children were being taken to England to be proselytised and weaned away from the true faith were spread and commonly believed. But the dirty reptile latent in priest craft could not rest content with that. The children were being deported for the white slave traffic!

How much truth there was in these reports and fomented rumours will be seen from the following taken from The *Times of* 24th October: -'Tonight Mrs.Montefiore was arrested as a result of her participation in the deportation scheme. The charge against her is practically the same as that preferred against Mrs. Rand.

A news agency states that Mrs. Rand is a Roman Catholic. She is a daughter of Senator Gage, ex-Governor of California and United States Minister of Lisbon at the time of the Revolution.Mrs. Pethick Lawrence writes that Miss Mary Neale, who recently conveyed some Irish strikers' children to Mrs. Lawrence's cottage, had before starting an introduction from a Roman Catholic priest to the Vicar-General guaranteeing that there would be no attempt to proselytise and that arrangements had been made for the children to hear Mass at a neighbouring private Roman Catholic chapel.'

With regard to the arrest of the ladies, I believe they did take charge of one boy with a view to his going to England who was farmed out between the neighbours, as children of incorrigibly drunken and negligent parents often are.

The drunken father was hunted up, made to state that he had given no consent to his son's removal, and this was made the basis of the charge.

I saw red; and when I see red I have got to get into the fight.

I offered myself to speak for the strikers in Beresford Place, the open space outside the Transport Union Headquarters, Liberty Hall, and my offer was welcomed. The sands of my gentility had run out.

CHAPTER 21.
THE GREAT STRIKE

The great strike of the Dublin Transport Union began about 20th August 1913, in Horse Show week. It began as a Tramway Strike in pursuance of a fierce struggle for mastery between James Larkin and James Martin Murphy, Director of the Dublin Tramway Company.

A day or two later the names of the General Staff of the Ulster Volunteer Force were published from Belfast.

I mention this synchronization because it is symbolic of a deep connection which is not visible on the surface. Time, the invisible dimension, brought out the hidden link between the ultimate forces warring respectively to sever and maintain Ireland's connection with the British Empire.

From the first the strike had a revolutionary character. The charge against Larkin, who was arrested within a few days of its commencement, was one of conspiring with others for the criminal purpose of disturbing the public peace and raising discontent and hatred between the working classes of Dublin and the police and soldiers of the Crown, and for the purpose of exciting hatred and contempt of the Government and of inciting to murder.

Larkin was released on bail. A meeting which he had vowed to address in O'Connell Street on Sunday 31st August 1913, was proclaimed. In the interval Larkin went into hiding, 1 think at the house of Countess Markievitch- Madam, as she became known to all Dublin. Anyhow, he was fitted out with a frock-coat and top hat belonging to Cassy Markievitch, Madam's Polish husband - a prince of playboys.

Thus disguised, Larkin, who I will allude to henceforward as Jim, appeared on the balcony of the Imperial Hotel overlooking O'Connell Street.

His appearance was the signal for an amazing outburst of police savagery. A huge force of police hurled itself from a number of side streets on the citizens of Dublin. No less than 479 people were injured; 57 police were injured also in the disturbances that Sunday and the following day, according to official reports but few, if any, police could have been injured in that particular charge connected with the meeting.

A photograph of this appeared in the illustrated English paper the *Sphere*. It was immediately withdrawn from circulation, but I have seen a copy. It shows about three policemen to every civilian and several of the policemen are engaged in having a second whack at a fallen foe, not always of the male sex.

Under such auspices began the Great Dublin Strike.

Say *The Times* of 2nd September: -

'Larkin's movement is not an ordinary trade union agitation. It is one of those challenges to society which must be put down with a strong hand, if anything like ordered society is to exist. In a speech last Friday Larkin told his followers that the head of a man, who had written a certain newspaper article, ought to be broken, and that any man who starved while there was food and clothing in the shops was a "damned idiot." Larkin's movement is a real and immediate danger to the public peace. It has also been suggested that his arrest was a mistake. The fact is that if, after his first arrest last Thursday, he had not been released on bail, the rioting on Saturday and yesterday might never have taken place.

Employment is found by Messrs. Jacobs (biscuit manufacturer) for three thousand men, women, and girls. Some of the employees - men and women - have become members of Larkin's union and latterly the relations of the company and some of their staff have not been so harmonious as hitherto. On Saturday the firm, owing to the friction in the factory, issued a notice prohibiting the wearing of Larkin's "Red Hand" badge during working hours. Later in the day three of the men, who refused to handle a load of flour sent in by Messrs. Shackleton, who have locked out their Transport Union employees, were dismissed on the spot.

This morning a number of Messrs. Jacobs' men and boys who are members of the Union refused to resume work. Their absence caused so much disorganization that the firm at once closed down the manufacturing part of the factory. In a notice which they issued today they announced that they will not reopen until they have received sufficient applications from men and women who are pledged not to belong to the Transport Workers' Union. They have no objection to their workers joining any trade union conducted on ordinary lines, but they will in future refuse to employ any member of the Transport Workers' Union, an organization which they say has been conducted with so much intolerable tyranny and injustice.

The closing down of so large a portion of the big factory has resulted in rendering idle many hundreds of workers, most of whom can ill afford one week's idleness. Later in the day another large firm of employers, Messrs. Tedcastle & Compan coal merchants, paid off one hundred men who were members of the Union.

Last week some of the carters who refused to deliver coal at a farm, where there is a strike of farm labourers, were dismissed. This morning one hundred of the carters refused to resume work unless the others were reinstated and the firm replied by paying off all the men. At the depot of the Tramway Company in Inchicore, where a fierce attack was made on a number of tramcars last evening, two men in the repair shop this morning refused to work on the damaged cars. They were immediately dismissed, whereupon all the other men in that department struck work.'

The above makes it perfectly obvious that there was concerted attempt on the part of the employers to crush Jim and his union.

In fact, the Times of 5th September says so specifically, and gives its blessing to the work: 'Things have come to such a pass that the employers must either kill Mr. Larkin's influence in the city or shut down their business altogether. At this moment the works of Messrs. Jacobs & Co., who export nearly half a million's worth of biscuits from Dublin every year, are closed owing to the activities of the Transport Union. It is stated on good authority that unless the employers win in their present struggle Messrs. Jacobs will move their whole business out of Dublin. The only hope of relief from an exceedingly grave situation is that the delegates from the Trade Union Congress will face the facts honestly and will report accordingly.'

A month later, the Times changes its tune. Jim and the Transport Union and were too difficult nuts to crack. What before had been 'one of those challenges to society which must be put down with a strong hand, if anything like ordered society is to exist' is now recognized as indestructible. Further, the naughty, cruel employers are lectured for having evoked any unpleasant idiosyncracies which Jim may have displayed.

Says *The Times* of 8th October: -

'Our Dublin correspondent says that the employers would accept a pecuniary guarantee from the English Transport Union, but the latter, who know that Mr. Larkin would pay no more attention to them than to anyone else, are very unlikely to give it. Perhaps the prospect of securing better wages and other conditions under the scheme suggested by the Court, coupled with removal of embargo placed on his union by the employers, would make him more amenable. In our opinion the employers can very well consent to both these steps without prejudice. Conciliation boards will eventually be formed in any case; they are inevitable, and it is impossible to destroy the Transport Workers' Union. It would only form again under another name if the attempt apparently succeeded. The day for suppression has gone by. All experience proves that it defeats its own object; if the Dublin employers do not know that, then it is time they learnt the lesson, and there is another. Mr. Larkin is their own creation. It is true that no evidence was offered of the sweating of which they are accused and the Court of Inquiry only speaks of low wages and unsatisfactory conditions of employment as alleged. But it regards the events that have occurred as indicating that grievances of considerable importance have existed. We agree with that view. It is not denied that wages have been extensively and substantially raised in consequence of Mr. Larkin's agitations, which means that employers have refused to have terms they could well afford until they were compelled. This conduct is playing into the hands of the agitator, as we have often pointed out. It gives substance to the charge that employers care for nothing but money, and justifies at once the agitator's denunciations and his promises.

This is the chief secret of Mr. Larkin's extraordinary influence, and the Dublin employers have themselves to thank for it.'

Of what I said to the strikers at our first contact I have neither record nor memory. Very likely I corrected their theology; anyhow, from my very first entrance I became part of the strike. Very early in the day I remember speaking on a platform with Connolly and big Bill Heywood, the American I.W.W. agitator. Heywood called for boos for the police, which were heartily given. This jarred my 'gentlemanly' feelings somewhat, and when it came to my turn to speak I expressed my disapproval. 'The police were only doing what they were paid to do,' said I. I did not know at the time of the amount of extraneous brutality they were guilty of. 'Anyway, booing them was only waste of energy against the day when we would have to fight them.'

Connolly took me to task for introducing this remonstrant note at the meeting.

The intellectuals of Dublin were in sympathy with the strike. There was the most astonishing body known as the Peace Committee, which consisted principally of poets and professors. The great George Russell (AE) was a member of it, so was Padraic Colum the poet, Robin Gwynn of Trinity College, and Houston of the College of Science. Sheehy Skeffington was on it, of course.

Soon after I came to Dublin this Peace Committee had a meeting intending to terminate its function, as peace was the last thing either of the contending parties wanted.

I was invited, to attend.

Tom Kettle was by way of being chairman and, as there was no sign of his appearance, we waited patiently for half an hour.

Then E. A. Aston, the man now connected with Greater Dublin building schemes, was voted in as Deputy Chairman.

He had hardly taken his seat when Tom Kettle arrived.

His arrival was spectacular. He carried in one hand a bunch of carnations, in the other a bag of oysters, and blood streamed from an open cut on his cheek. He was gloriously drunk, and he was witty enough even sober.

He took the chair, but the proceedings were riotously irrelevant.

Then I took a step, which had big consequences. I proposed that Kettle be asked to vacate the chair as unfit to conduct the proceedings. My lead was followed. Kettle left the chair and the meeting, and I was elected chairman in his place. We wound up the old Peace Committee and reconstructed ourselves as the Civic League. For what reason we chose this title I cannot say. It sounds like Aston preparing for his Greater Dublin. As a fact, we were indirectly responsible for demolition on a grand scale; for it was that innocent Civic League which actually passed at my instance the first resolution to drill the Dublin strikers and its treasurer, Professor Houston of the Dublin College of Science, received the first cheque to supply with boots and drill staves the Irish Citizen Army. I sometimes wonder how you sleep o' nights, Robin Gwynn, Padraic Colum and Co., knowing the subversive activities to which you lent your august names. Yes! And you thoroughly enjoyed it. We were all mad then but oh! How much pleasanter it was.

I find in my records an open letter to me addressed through the columns of the Irish Independent, which evidently belongs to this period. I give it in full. It seems more concerned with AE than it is with me, but that is just as well.

AE's adherence to the cause of the strikers is typical of the remarkable feature of this period in Dublin. The intelligenzia had ceased to be either prostitute or passive.

They were actively and wholeheartedly with the strike, denouncing the employers, in AE's case in a letter which deserves to rank as a classic of revolutionary literature, working in soup kitchens, entertaining Larkin and Connolly as honoured guests at their gatherings. The very students of Trinity College, the Protestant Unionist stronghold, broke out of college and marched to one of my meetings singing 'Oh! Oh! Antonio' in defiance of the prohibition of their Provost, the late Anthony Trail. The millennium had obviously arrived. Brain and muscle were united against mere Philistine greed. It was delightful while it lasted, but it was too good to be true.

Here is the open letter to me: -

To CAPTAIN WHITE, D.S.O.

'Sir,

It is stated in the public Press that you spoke from the platform of "Liberty Hall" last Friday. In your speech, as reported, you gave a certain amount of qualified approval to Mr.Larkin's party. You stated that you had not studied the question at first hand, but that you appeared on that platform as a result of having read a speech by, and enjoyed a conversation with Mr George Russell.

Now, is Mr. Russell a safe guide to follow in the exceedingly vital and practical matter of deciding on the merits of a labour dispute? I suggest that he is not, for the following reasons:

In the first place, Mr. Russell is somewhat of a mystic and a visionary. If we are to believe Mr. George Moore, Mr. Russell was capable of the rather unpractical act of going down into a subterranean chamber somewhere near Newgrange, and there endeavouring to invoke a visitation of the ancient pagan gods of Ireland, not desisting from his efforts until he was disturbed in his invocation by the arrival of two Presbyterian clergymen.

This incident may be entirely a creation of Mr. George Moore's lively imagination; but we have better and nearer evidence of Mr. Russell's incapacity for forming a clear and rational judgment in a case where his emotions are aroused. Looking at the present slums, and labour situation in Dublin, Mr. Russell saw slums and he saw employers. He immediately jumped to the conclusion that the employers are responsible for the slums, when a little calm thought should have shown him that the responsibility for the housing of the working classes in a town rests on the municipal authorities.

The municipal authority in Dublin is the Corporation, and the Corporation does not represent the employers. The franchise being what is called a low franchise, the great majority of the members of the Corporation are elected by and represent the working classes.

In the second place, I submit that Mr. Russell is in this matter actuated by personal spite. We had recently in Dublin a controversy concerning the erection of an Art Gallery across the River Liffey. Several citizens, including Mr. Russell, wished to have this gallery built. A good many others opposed the scheme, and a certain employer wrote many letters to the Press expressing his disapproval of the project. When the scheme for a trans-Liffey Art Gallery was defeated Mr. Russell appears to have said to himself, like a pettish child,

"You won't give me the Art Gallery I want, then I will do you some damage when I can."

The opportunity for attempting to do damage was not long delayed. The labour disputes broke out in Dublin, and the above-mentioned opposer of the Art Gallery was, rightly or wrongly, generally looked on as the leader of the employers. Mr. Russell was soon delivered of a violent diatribe, which purported to be directed against Dublin employers in general, but which was really a bitter and venomous personal attack on the employer who had dared to take a prominent part in opposing the suggested Art Gallery. Mr. Russell could not refrain from dragging the defunct gallery into his letter by way of showing that those who oppose his ideas are not possessed of souls.

If you think I am wrong in imputing venom and personal spite to the poet and idealist, Mr. George Russell, I would ask you to read the back numbers of Mr. Russell's paper, the Irish Homestead. In the files of that journal you will find bitter attacks on every one who does not happen to agree with the editor on the question of co-operative trading.

So much for Mr. Russell. Permit me now to turn to another point. As an officer of His Majesty's forces, and as a man who did his duty in fighting against the of enemies of his country in South Africa you are, of course, a man of honour and a gentleman. You believe that when a man makes a promise or enters into an undertaking he should keep his word. But what view is held on this subject at "Liberty Hall," from which you spoke on Friday? Mr. Larkin and his lieutenants have repeatedly declared that they will make agreements and break them as soon as opportunity offers. This Policy was summarized by Mr. Larkin in his now famous phrase, 'To hell with all contracts'; it has been restated by his viceroy, Mr. Connolly, within the last few days. And these statements are not merely examples of frothy platform rhetoric; it was proved by evidence at Sir George Asquith's enquiry that breach of agreements and breaking of the pledged word are part of the settled so-called 'Liberty' policy of the so-called leaders at the so-called 'Liberty' Hall.

Can you, as a man of honour, support these people?
IGNOTUS.'
And my reply:

OPEN LETTER TO 'IGNOTUS
FROM CAPTAIN J. R. WHITE
'Dear Ignotus,

I have to thank you for an open letter addressed to me in the columns of the Irish Independent of 10th of November. My attention was not called to it till the evening of that day, which is the cause of any delay in my reply.

I am glad you commence your letter to me with the words: ';It is stated in the public Press," for between what is stated in the public Press and the actual facts, there is, in Ireland, a deep gulf fixed, across which, sir, your winged words and mine can with difficulty pass.

For my part, I believe the filling of this gulf with the dead reputations of newspaper proprietors is the first duty of Irish patriots.

In my speech at Liberty Hall, I gave neither qualified nor unqualified support to Mr. Larkin's party, for the name of Mr. Larkin did not pass my lips, nor was his personality, since I have never met him, present in my mind.

Further, I would be unable, in any case, to regard a crowd of some two thousand or more men and women, eagerly seeking counsel in a great crisis in their lives, as the party of any less a Person than Almighty God.

Now, it may interest you to know what I did say. In my first sentence I disclaimed any partisanship on the ground of ignorance of the true facts, but I followed my disclaimer by a declaration, which I am prepared emphatically to repeat, that any man who wished to take a share in moulding the new Ireland 'was not much good' if he failed to inform himself, first hand and at the fountain head, of the causes which could bring such a crowd together as I then addressed.

You ask me is Mr. Russell a safe guide to follow in the exceedingly vital and practical matter of deciding on the merits of a labour dispute? I answer, 'Certainly not.' Neither Mr. Russell nor any other man is a safe guide for me to follow in any decision whatsoever on which my own future action is to be based; the only safe guide is my own conscience instructed by my own judgment after full personal investigation of the men and matters concerned.

I did mention Mr. Russell's attitude as a subsidiary reason for my presence. I wanted to pay a personal tribute to Mr. Russell, whom I have known fairly intimately for some time and remarked of him that what was good enough for his great mind and big heart to concern themselves with, was good enough for me to have a look at.

Now from you, sir, who know Mr Russell through the medium of George Moore's books, I learn that Mr. Russell is a great master of magic.

"I can call the spirits from the vasty deep,

Ay, so can I, but will they answer you?"

Evidently they will answer Mr. Russell, for a more direct reply to the invocation of the ancient pagan gods than the appearance of two Presbyterian clergymen could hardly be looked for if you have read some of their sermons on Ulster Day you will be obliged to admit this.

It is a little embarrassing to me that your open letter to myself is so largely occupied with a criticism of Mr. Russell, for whose character I am as little responsible as he is for my actions. But without consulting the back files of the Homestead, a task for which I have neither leisure nor inclination, I am in a position to speak as to whether Mr. Russell visits his "venom and personal spite on those who disagree with him. I have frequently disagreed with Mr. Russell, much more violently than I should venture to disagree with you, dear "Ignotus," if we should ever meet, and I have seen no signs whatever of Mr. Russell's venom and spite towards me in consequence. We must take people as we find them, "Ignotus," and even poets and idealists are apt to do so.

I come with some relief to the last paragraph of your letter, which concerns myself. You say Mr. Larkin and his lieutenants have repeatedly declared that they will make agreements and break them as soon as opportunity offers; that this policy was summarized by Mr. Larkin in his now famous phrase, "To hell with contracts," and that it has been restated by his viceroy, Mr.Connolly, within the last few days! If your version is correct I, as a man of honour, cannot support such sentiments nor the men who give voice to them. But, in the first place, that leaves my interest in the well-being of the workers and of the City of Dublin unaffected, and, in the second place, frankly, "Ignotus," both from your anonymity and your general temperament, as disclosed in your letter to me, you do not appear to me to rank as a final and infallible witness.

I have been told that Larkin's famous phrase, 'To hell with contracts,' has been deliberately divorced from its context; that he used the phrase in a quite different connection to that which you suggest, remarking, "To hell with their contracts" in answer to a plea of the employers that the strikers' action prevented the fulfilment of their (the employers) contracts with other firms. A man is bound to observe a contract entered into by himself, but C is in nowise bound by a contract entered into between A and B.

In conclusion, I will be most grateful if you will give, or refer me to, the evidence on which your statements are based, for, if true, it is the plain duty of every honourable man to dissociate himself from such a propaganda as you portray, and if false, it is as plainly he course of honour to assist in exposing the falsehood, and the falsifiers.

J.R. WHITE.

CHAPTER 22.
THE STRIKE ANALYSED

'The children of this world are wiser in their generation than the children of light.' Of course they are, for the children of this world have a closer concentration on a far narrower field. Whether in this world or another, concentration is the secret of success and the handmaid of wisdom, worldly or spiritual. The poor children of light do not know where to begin; they have no point of focus.

They get their values all mixed up among themselves, and hopelessly overlaid by worldly values with a spiritual veneer. To Irish eyes England is the great purveyor of this veneer; it is positively necessary to get outside the atmosphere of England and the British Empire to get any point of focus at all. Inside there is no touchstone for anything. God is British to the backbone, and the dangerous part of His naturalization is that nobody mentions it. It is taken for granted alike by Tory, Liberal, and Socialist, even by atheistic Communists, for the God they defy without escaping is the naturalized Britisher.

The attempt of a dyed-in-the-wood Briton to see the world as a moral unit is foredoomed to failure. To see the spiritual unity of things, moral purpose, or moral direction, it is necessary to have some point of focus either for the spread of the mustard seed of good, or, failing that, for the self-cancellation of evil.

Viewed from what I will call the inner Ireland, England and British Imperial values obscure the dividing line between good and evil. There is and can be no primary value in a community that increasingly every year puts first things last. England lives by industrial overshadowing and agricultural vampirization. She maintains her empire to perpetuate the perversion. All talk of moral aspiration on the part of this vampirizing octopus is to what I have called the inner Ireland a sort of bitter joke. For myself the English side of me recognizes that the English people are perhaps the noblest or at least the most benevolent and the fairest-minded in the world. But Ireland has taught me to recognize also that they have gained so much of the whole world that their own soul is irretrievably lost. Their very personal virtues blind them to the swelling collective damnation they sow and will inevitably reap. For this

Captain J.R. White

collective sin, which the Englishman's personal virtues are sucked in to nourish, Ireland is England's conscience. She is the only country near enough home to enable England to realize the effect of her own actions on others. She has not yet succeeded in doing so. The prickings of conscience can be suppressed, indeed in this case must be suppressed. There is no room for two diametrically opposed consciences in the 'British' Isles. A united and conscious Ireland would inevitably ask why, with ability to feed a population of eight millions, which she once possessed, she should be reduced below four millions to feed the neighbouring island, which maintains a population of forty millions on soil that could perhaps feed twenty.

This is the real angle from which to approach the Great Strike of 1913-14 in Dublin. It was the recoil of a people from an overstraining away from the balance of nature, which is also the balance of the human spirit. The land fight had been largely won under the leadership of the old Nationalist Party. But what did victory assuming it won, mean? It meant the freedom of the farmers to own their own farms But it meant equally the freedom of the farmers to export their produce to the best market, namely, England. Victory in the land fight did not touch the problem of the landless labourer in town or country. He continues before the Larkin strike to live on tea and bread, while his more prosperous English brothers ate meat, largely cut from Irish pigs or bullocks, twice or three times a day.

Did the Dublin labourer think about this? No, of course he did not. Things do not happen that way. In England where few are hungry or primitive enough to develop intuition, you have wait for the science of psychoanalysis to tell you that the unconscious is to the conscious in life, much as the submerged part of the iceberg is to the visible. But Ireland has suffered from a constant pressure on that very dynamic seat of the unconscious, the stomach.

So the Irish labourer heard Jim say that William Murder Murphy ought to have the tripes cut out Of him, or that some worthy in the next street to himself was a 'blasted yaller scab' with a vague but satisfying sense that righteousness was at last raising her diminished head. He did not ask to see the distant scene, one step enough for him. For myself, in contact with the strike I found a touchstone. I was too incurable, a

153

surveyor of the distant scene to give it up; but I begun to survey it from a new angle, which I felt, was the true one. Slowly but surely I became denaturalised as a Briton, supporting my religious temperament on the alternative God I had become acquainted with from Tolstoy and the Russians. I felt that hitherto my spiritual values had all run into one another for lack of an actual visible touchstone from which they could begin to deploy into action. Have you ever seen a company trying to extend, when the skipper has forgotten to mention the point of extension whether from the right left centre? It 'clubs.' That is if it moves at all. If it is wise it won't move, till the skipper has remedied his omission.

But we have all got a skipper inside us ordering us to move, and fearfully remiss about mentioning the point of extension. I found my point of extension in the Dublin Strike. Heretofore my values had been something like the Scriptural values in the story of the disgruntled American hobo. He complained to his pal that he was never able to get good hand-outs 'Why,' said his pal, you want to give them Bible stuff, and on the disgruntled one confessing complete Scriptural ignorance, coached him a bit in some out-standing incidents of Scripture history. On the next campaign, a dear old lady told him she hoped he read his Bible. 'Why, Marm,' said he, 'I just love to read about Joshua leading his army through the belly and that there strong man Simpson slaying thousands of them Philippine bastards with the arse bone of a cow.'

Whenever I meet an Englishman seeking outlet for the natural nobility of his sentiments in high social endeavour, he reminds me of the strong Simson, going forth against the Philippine bastard with the arse-bone of a cow. He has modernized himself so completely that he regards it as irrelevant if one mentions the age-old roots, planted by himself and still sprouting, of the evils he seeks to remedy. Samson has become Simpson. The good chap is not to be blamed for this. A moral historical sense is not given to many. Simpson has no incentive whatever to acquire it and much to lose by doing so. That is not the right line of approach. It is necessary for *the Irishman to modernize himself also;* shout at Simpson as he flourishes his arse-bone - that belonged to my cow, and you've eaten the rump steak.' In outraged disgust at the Irishman's descent to low personalities, Simpson may drop his weapon. Then, if the Irishman is quick, he may pick it up and biff the strong man over the head. But he's got to be P.D.Q.

This dainty parable puts the cause of the Larkin strike in a nutshell. What of the consequences? Remember we are approaching the Great War. England is about to make a very noble and sweeping gesture of world redemption. The Irish conscience also is about to prick, prick quite hard. I am about to provide it with a sharp instrument for the purpose.

My conduct was to all right-minded persons so deplorable that I may be pardoned for seeking to justify it both in advance and in retrospect.

It is now the fashion to emphasize the evil, even the futility, of war. No particular war is brewing for the moment, and mechanical murder on a big scale, if treated by a keen imagination, is nearly as good copy as individual murders for some motive of greed or passion. We can even afford to investigate possible motives of greed behind the big-scale murder. So the Su*nday Express* publishes serially Remarque's *All Quiet the Western Front*. Here is the 'spicy bit' in a square all by itself heading one Sunday's instalment (3rd November 1929):

THE DEGRADATION OF WAR

'I am young, I am twenty years old; yet I know nothing of life but despair, death, fear, and fatuous superficiality cast over an abyss of sorrow. I see how peoples are set against one another, and in silence, knowingly, foolishly, obediently, innocently slay one other. I see that the keenest brains of the world vent weapons and words to make it yet more refined enduring. And all men of my age, here and over there, throughout the whole world, see these things; my generation is experiencing these things with me. What would our fathers do if we suddenly stood up and came before them and proffered our account? What do they expect of us if a time ever comes when the war is over? Through the years our business has been killing, it was our first calling in life. Our knowledge of life is limited to death. What will happen afterwards? And what shall come out of us?'

'I see that the keenest brains in the world invent weapons and words to make it yet more refined and enduring.' I am writing of Ireland in November 1913. Another nine months and the keenest brains are going to get busy, with weapons and words; do not forget the combination.

It is difficult to meet weapons and words with words only. The whole of International Socialism discovered that. The threatened International resistance of the workers collapsed at the first sound of the trumpet and the empires drove their obedient sheep to the slaughter. Only in parts of Ireland was there a failure and a repudiation,' says Mr. Churchill in his '*Aftermath of the Great War*' 'and about that there is a lengthy tale to tell.'

Well, let's get on with the tale from a somewhat different angle to Mr. Churchill and a more intimate angle. I do not remember the exact date when I brought forward the proposal at a Civic League meeting to drill the strikers and form a Citizen Army. I do remember its enthusiastic acceptance.

Larkin and Connolly welcomed the proposal to drill the men. It was just the thing to put new heart into them. Larkin had bought for the Union an estate at Clontarf, a mile or so outside Dublin, called Croydon Park. Great meetings of the strikers took place there every Sunday. It was at one of these Sunday meetings I first propounded the proposal of the Citizen Army, to the huge enthusiasm and delight of the men themselves.

CHAPTER 23.
THE CITIZEN ARMY

The first appeal I made for an Irish Volunteer Movement which got Press publicity was at a meeting of the Trinity College Gaelic Society. A paper was read by a Mr. Joseph Bigger, one of the students, on 'Self-reliance, the Panacea for Irish Ills.' Then various 'distinguished strangers' invited for the evening addressed the house.

Arthur Griffiths was the principal speaker that night. At the time I had never met him and I never came to have more than a nodding acquaintance with him. Even so I did any nodding there was. I always thought him a very unpleasant little man. To me he seemed to emanate the suspicion of the professional Gael towards the foreign or Protestant interloper in the 'movement.' From his name I suppose he was of Welsh extraction, and I don't think he was a Catholic; but he personified to me the 'closeness' and suspicion of a persecuted race and a persecuted religion combined. Perhaps to do him justice that is why he had the intensity and concentration to build up a movement on a fixed idea for twenty-five years and carry it through to fulfilment. His idea and mine were poles apart. I can well believe that when Lloyd George presented the draft of the Irish Treaty to the Irish delegates in London, Griffiths, who read it first, declared immediately, 'I'll sign that, Mr. Prime Minister, whatever the others do.' I was told this on the best authority. In his speech that night, Griffiths said that if any degree of connection was to continue between the two islands it must be based on the Irish Constitution of 1782. John Dillon, as quoted farther back, had said of this Constitution it had one defect fatal to its existence, namely, that the executive Government was not subject to the Parliament, but was subject to the English Ministers across the channel and the revenue levied by the Irish Parliament was used by British Ministers to corrupt that Parliament and to sacrifice the liberties of the nation.

Griffiths concentrated on the attainment of fiscal independence, forgetting that while 'any degree of connection' existed between the two islands, it would be used by British Ministers secretly or openly, directly or indirectly, with the consequences alluded to by Dillon. Much proof could be given that the treaty, which was the crowning work of

Griffiths' life, has reproduced the defeat of the Constitution of 1782.
Following immediately after Griffiths, I struck deeper at the root.

I did not quote Wolfe Tone 'to break the connection with England,
the never-failing source of all our political evils.' I tried to incarnate the
spirit of Wolfe Tone in the treatment of existing problems.

I ignored the resolution I was supposed to speak to and concentrated
on the demand for an inquiry into the conduct of the police in the recent
'riots.' I asked the audience to press for an immediate inquiry into the
matter and to be insistent in their demand, even if they as students had to
tell their professors that they must close their college as they had more
important civil duties elsewhere to perform.' At this point a lady called
out, 'Speak to the resolution, and was seconded by some 'Hear, hears,
but I ignored the interruption and went on: 'If they wanted to be masters
in their own country, if they wanted to complain with irresistible force
against the ill-treatment of the citizens, they must prepare to control the
police force themselves; let them lay the foundation of a great National
Movement for the creation of that order and discipline they so sadly
lacked by raising again the standard of the Irish Volunteers.'

So I called for a Students' Strike and a Rebel Volunteer Movement in
Trinity College, the Alma Mater of the British Connection.

Under the circumstances it is not surprising that the old Provost, Dr.
Anthony Trail, kicked. Says the *Times* of the next day:

DR.TRAIL AND CAPTAIN WHITE

'The meeting of the Dublin Civic League this evening received a
valuable advertisement from the Provost of Trinity College. Dr. Trail was
so much annoyed by Captain White's political outburst at the College
Gaelic Society yesterday that he issued the following notice this morning:
- "Any resident student who attends Captain White's Home Rule meeting
this evening wilt be deprived of his rooms." This notice was founded
on a misconception of fact, and possibly on a further misconception by
the Provost of his powers. The Civic League meeting was not a Home
Rule meeting. The University Statute, now virtually obsolete, which
regulates the attendance of students at political meetings, ordains the
punishment of expulsion for a second offence only. The interest of the
position was increased by the fact that the Rev. R. M. Gwynn, a Fellow

of Trinity College, is one of the principal organizers of the Civic League. It is probable that for the Provost's threat not a single student of Trinity College would have been present at the meeting, but as a protest about eighty students marched to the hall in a body. They were received with cheers, and were accommodated on the platform behind the speaker. The meeting was quiet and unimportant. The O'Mahony presided, and the speakers included Captain White, and Mr. James Connolly, of the Irish Transport Workers. Captain White spoke rather vaguely about Mr. Larkin's volunteer movement, and Mr. Connolly described what the Transport Workers' Union had done for the conditions of the Dublin Working classes. The meeting passed resolutions of protest against the attitude of the employers and against the postponement of the enquiry into the conduct of the Dublin police.'

The same night as the Trinity College meeting Connolly gave it out publicly in Beresford Place that I had undertaken to organize a Citizen Army among the members of the Transport Workers' Union.

The limitation of membership of the Citizen Army to the Transport Union introduces the whole thorny subject of the relations between the Labour and National wings of the Volunteer Movement.

Without entering for the moment into the differences of idea and purpose in the National Movement itself, which developed in October 1914 into the great split between the Sinn Fein and Redmondite sections of the National Volunteers, I want to deal from the broadest angle with the governing principles of national and class revolt. I quote from a pamphlet of my own called *The Significance of Sinn Fein,* published in 1918.

'We see today two main kinds of collective revolt, that of subject races and subject classes. They may be (indeed, generally are) quite distinct. A class may revolt against the pressure of a social system, although the race of which it forms part has evolved that system as part of its character and culture. Or a race may revolt without formulating any distinct class protest. The race revolt corresponds to the sub-consciousness drawing its impetus from inborn racial instinct. The class revolt is an affair of the surface consciousness, concerned with the modification or reconstruction of external conditions. Where the two revolts unite in one the whole National Being is engaged.'

But what is the relation between the two aspects of revolt thus fused, differing as they do in their motive and inspiration. W. H. Myers has defined genius as subliminal uprush, that is to say, the emergence of elements which remain latent below the threshold of consciousness in less gifted men into harmonious fusion with the reasoning and expressive powers of the surface personality. Where such harmonious fusion is absent we have not genius, but madness or hysteria. It would seem, therefore, that the inborn race-inspiration of Ireland, which Sinn Fein represents, has got to be harmonized with the conclusion and demands of Irish Labour, drawn from and directed towards external environment. Failing that, Labour's efforts will lack the subliminal element of genius, and Sinn Fein be in danger of lapsing into hysteria.

The Irish race is pre-eminently intuitive, that is to say, it feels its conclusions rather than thinks them, and often proceeds direct from feeling to actions which subsequent events fully justify, though reasoned calculations would have condemned. Its genius in this respect rests on a radical difference in psychology, a scaled book to John Bull, and to all peoples devoid of the education of untamed suffering necessary to read it.

I cannot here write a history. I must assume it to be known that the Citizen Army under Jim Connolly made common cause with the Sinn Fein section of the volunteers, when the latter had definitely repudiated the control of Redmond and the Parliamentarian party.

Sean O' Casey in his little book, *The Story of the Citizen Army,* criticizes Connolly for the submergence of Labour in National ideals severely enough. Says 0 Casey, speaking of Connolly's assumption of command after Larkin's departure for America:

'Under Jim Connolly's leadership an appreciable change began to appear in the attitude of the Citizen Army Council towards the volunteers. The attitude of passive sympathy began to be gradually replaced by an attitude of active unity and cooperation. In their break-away from the control of the Parliamentarian party the volunteers had built a bridge over the stream of thought that separated the two forces from each other, and speculation became common as to whether the volunteers would absorb the Citizen Army or that body's influence would sway the councils of the volunteers. Jim Connolly had never associated himself with any of the attacks made upon the volunteers during their earlier history - indeed, whenever he had previously interested himself in the affairs of the Citizen Army, which was seldom, his influence had been invariably exerted to moderate the mutual hostility that smouldered, and occasionally flamed into passionate recriminations - and, consequently, the relations between him and the militant members of the Volunteer Council soon became cordial. It is difficult to understand the almost revolutionary change that was manifesting itself in Connolly's nature. The Labour Movement seemed to be regarded by him as a decrescent force, while the essence of Nationalism began to assume the finest elements of his nature. His articles that now appeared in the *Workers' Republic* with consistent regularity, the speeches that he delivered at various demonstrations and assemblies, all proclaimed that Jim Connolly had stepped from the narrow byway of Irish Socialism on to the broad and crowded highway of Irish Nationalism. The vision of the suffering world's humanity was shadowed by the nearer oppression of his own people, and in a few brief months pressed into a hidden corner of his soul the accumulated thoughts of a lifetime and opened his broad heart to ideas that altered the whole trend of his being. The high creed of Irish Nationalism became his daily rosary, while the higher creed of International humanity that had so long bubbled from his eloquent lips was silent forever and Irish Labour lost a leader.'

O' Casey is in a position to criticize Connolly, for he left all armies for the art of the dramatist. I am not; for I merged myself in the National Volunteer Movement, as I shall tell in its place, long before Connolly identified the Citizen Army with the National Cause. I am at liberty, however, to criticize myself; that, too, I shall do in its place. For the moment I want to advance what I believe to be Jim Connolly's strongest defence. He realized that the National Movement was the reservoir of the nation's subconscious power, that amalgamating with it he could tap mines of energy, which would ultimately produce the true revolutionary ore in Ireland, even if mixed with a mass of sentimental dross. He was a realist. He saw the British troops in Ireland. They are out of twenty-six counties now. That is Connolly's defence against O' Casey or even against me.

It is, I believe, a mistake to criticize or judge harshly any living soul on this reeling earth except oneself; and one ought not to be too hard even on oneself. Christ got there, as He always did, when He said, 'Judge not that ye be not judged,' and spoke of plucking the beam from one's own eye before the mote from other people's. I judged O' Casey once because he took a literary prize from the hands of Asquith, Prime Minister of the Government that shot Connolly, his old chief –for it may not be generally known that O' Casey was secretary of the Citizen Army Committee under Connolly and for a time under me; but men have their function at their time and place and according to their lights; O' Casey to write in ink, Connolly in blood. The nearest to Christ perhaps is the man who writes in his own blood to save the blood and the guilt of others. Such was Sheehy Skeffington, who, strange to say, was a member of the Civic League when it adopted my proposal to form and drill a Citizen Army. Stranger still, if I am to believe O' Casey's booklet, on a point of which I have no memory, he was a member of the first Citizen Army Council that was elected. If this is correct, it is proof of the pacifist purpose of the Citizen Army at the time, for Skeffington was a perfectly consistent pacifist, though, like all really sincere pacifists, the most Pugnacious of men. Someone wrote of him that there was no one in Dublin who had not at one time or another broken an umbrella over his head. It will be remembered he was shot at the whim of a British officer. He, Skeffington, was out in the middle of the 16 rising at the imminent risk of his life anyhow from stray bullets, trying to stop the people looting. The officer, who was proved in the subsequent, very subsequent, inquiry to have been stimulating his ferocity by Old Testament texts, had him arrested and shot against a guardroom wall with two other prisoners. I say 'very subsequent' inquiry, for the whole thing was hushed up till Sir Francis Vane heard of it and induced Kitcheners to take action.

To get the essence of O' Casey's criticism of Connolly, it is really necessary to read his appreciation of Sheehy Skeffington; it's worth quoting if only for the beauty of the language. Speaking of the ferment after the '16 rising, O' Casey writes in the same booklet from which I have already quoted: -

'In this new wine a lowly life like a pearl had been dissolved; a life untarnished by worldly ambition or selfish perception; a life of mourning struggle and valorous effort sacrificed humbly and fearlessly for the general good; sacrificed under circumstances that stripped the offering of all the draperies of martyrdom. Unwept, except by a few, unhonoured and unsung -for no national society of Sheehy Skeffington, like the tiny mustard seed today, will possibly grow into a tree that will afford shade and rest to many souls overheated with the stress and toil of barren politics. He was the living antithesis of the Easter insurrection: a spirit of peace enveloped in the flame and rage and hatred of the contending elements, absolutely free from all its terrifying madness; and yet he was the purified soul of revolt against not only one nation's injustice to another, but he was also the soul of revolt against man's inhumanity to man. And in this blazing pyre of national differences his beautiful nature, as far as this world is concerned, was consumed, leaving behind a hallowed and inspiring memory of the perfect love that casteth out fear, against which there can be no law.

In Sheehy Skeffington, and not in Connolly, fell the first martyr to Irish Socialism, for he linked Ireland not only with the little nations struggling for self-expression but with the world's humanity struggling for a higher life.

He indeed was the ripest ear of corn that fell in Easter week, and as it is true that when an ear of corn falls into the ground and dies it bringeth forth much fruit, so will the sown body of Sheehy-Skeffington bring forth, ultimately, in the hearts of his beloved people, the rich crop of goodly thoughts which shall strengthen us all in our onward march towards the fuller development of our national and social life.'

CHAPTER 24.
CASEMENT AGAIN

It is just like me to have jumped ahead from the first public appeal for a Volunteer Movement in Ireland to comment on an insurrection which took place more than two years later.

It may be a good plan, however. The events I have to describe are the seeds of greater events and have interest due to their culminating consequences. First the corn, then the ear. To the best of my knowledge, no one has ever yet succeeded in making Irish politics or its underlying motives intelligible to the English mind. If at this distance I can ignore the sequence of time and establish the sequence of cause and effect, I may succeed where others have failed, though I am not over sanguine.

The night following the Trinity College meeting, the Civic League held its first public meeting in the Antient Concert Rooms. Piers O'Mahony took the chair. Robin Gwynn, a Trinity professor, was on the platform. The poor old Provost, Anthony Trail, was honoured in the defiant breach of his authority by a band of some eighty students singing Oh! Oh! Antonio, as they marched into the meeting. I rubbed it in in my speech. What, I inquired, had led Dr. Trail so far from the right track as to attempt to debar his students from participation in this high social endeavour?

We were there to bring about healthy social and economic relations between all classes and interests in Dublin. I proposed that the League should prepare, with assistance from the right quarters, a list of firms which did or did not treat their workers fairly and that the public should be invited to patronize only those firms which gave fair treatment.

I then read the two following telegrams from Roger Casement. The first was, I think, addressed to myself. -

From Sir Roger Casement: 'Strongly approve proposed drill and discipline Dublin workers, and will aid that healthy national movement, as I am also prepared to aid wider national movement to drill and discipline Irish National Volunteers throughout Ireland. Please read this at today's meeting. - *Roger Casement.*'

To Professor Collingwood, Dublin 'Civic' League Meeting, Intient Concert Rooms, Dublin: 'I understand you begin movement drill and discipline Dublin workers. That is good and healthy movement. I wish to support, and I hope it may begin a wide spread national movement to organize drilled and disciplined Irish Volunteers to assert Irish manhood and uphold national cause in all that is right. It is time drilled and disciplined Irishmen stood up all over the land to give the lie to those who say we are a Quaker Oats sort of people, who take everything lying down.- *Roger Casement*.

We sent the following telegram to Jim Larkin, who was speaking in London at the Albert Hall the same night: 'Mass meeting of Dublin citizens records emphatic protest against employers' refusal to confer with Dublin workers against the pledge proffered to their employees, and against the postponement of the police enquiry.'

At the end of the meeting, a Trinity College student, whose name was given as Mr. Armstrong, explained that a large number of Trinity students who were at the meeting could not wait until that late hour, as they had to leave to attend roll-call at nine o'clock, but he assured us of their sympathy. He wished there were more students present to testify their sympathy.

At this point in my writing I go out to have my lunch.

At Bertorelli's, the only really satisfactory restaurant in London, I meet one F. R. Swan on the *Daily Herald.* He reminds me that he organized the Albert Hall meeting in London addressed by Larkin the same night as our meeting in the Antient Concert Rooms. The London students attacked the London meeting and were driven off by organized taxi-men with spanners. Once more the hidden dimension of time brings out essentials. In Ireland intelligence sways to the side of Labour the vehicle of progress; and it sways that way in direct connection with myself. Was this chance or had the slow and laborious transmutation of my own intelligence from its old environment acted as an occult magnet. In England on the same night unregenerate intelligence has to be reminded of its limitations with a spanner. Am I theorizing again? Admit, anyhow, my theories have a way of clothing themselves in very concrete symbols.

We see from Casement's telegram read at the meeting just reported that he was broadcasting his blessing to the Labour and National drilling alike, though the had not yet started. The greatest vagueness existed as to the aims of either or both. I find among my collection of cuttings the following undated, but evidently referring to this period. The 'Citizen force ready to uphold the authority of the Crown and Government in Ireland' is not bad. Of course the one thing the Labour and National wings had in common was the pious aspiration to overthrow the authority of the Crown and Government in Ireland. For this red and green ultimately combined. But how was a newspaper correspondent to see into the future? Casement wasn't likely to help him.

THE NEW PROTECTIVE FORCE

'Soon,' says the Dublin correspondent of the *Daily Chronicle, 'We* shall see the formation of an Irish National Volunteer Movement, which will have for its object the organization of a citizen force ready to uphold the authority of the Crown and Government in Ireland.

Like many other Irish movements of a national character, this one takes its origin amongst the Ulster Protestants. The rank and file of the Nationalists who have been watching the course of events in and around Belfast have not been prepared to sit down calmly and watch the parades and inspections of the Orangemen without raising a hand to defend themselves and their children from the attacks which have been so loudly threatened, and now two Ulster Protestants are about to place themselves at the head of the movement, and invite the Nationalists to come forward and do what is necessary.

These two leaders are Sir Roger Casement and Captain James Robert White. It is Captain White's intention to start with the men on strike in Dublin. They have leisure at the present moment, and will be quite ready to respond to his call. But these will only form a nucleus. There are thousands of men in all parts of Ireland who will be only too ready to come forward to enrol themselves in the ranks of the National Volunteers, not for any aggressive purpose, but merely as a protective measure.'

THE WIDER AIM

Interviewed on the subject by the *Daily Chronicle,* Sir Roger Casement, who is in London, said: 'I would like to see the movement that has been begun in Ulster in a spirit of sectional exclusion transformed by Irish national goodwill into an Irish Volunteer Movement, whose aim should be to inculcate patriotism and the duty and right of all citizens to defend their own country. My intention would be to say this: -

'You Ulstermen have set us a good example in the name of loyalty to Ulster. You say you are arming and drilling to suppress crime and disorder or an attack on your liberties. There we shall be with you. We believe it is our right equally with yours to arm and drill in the same good cause, and should any attack be made upon your liberties from any quarter, we shall be the first to come to your assistance and to stand beside you.'

I certainly had no clear goal of violent revolution, national or social. At first I just enjoyed the fun and excitement of the whole thing. There was so much enthusiasm about and such an apparent weight of intellectual sympathy that to my sanguine inexperience a bloodless revolution seemed well within the bounds of possibility. The Citizen Army, after teaching the police manners, could be the nucleus of industrial organization in the new era. But the following article written by me under a pseudonym proves that I had a fairly clear theory of social revolution. I wish now I had let that theory govern every step of my practice.

SOME THOUGHTS ON DISCIPLINE

'The ultimate goal of the workers is said to be to secure the whole produce of labour. If this is not their goal it ought to be, for only by securing the whole produce will they have enough to pay adequately people with brains like myself; and until they can do that the whole produce will not remain with them very long. In point of fact, the power of the workers to get the fruits of their labour and their power to keep them are inseparable.

The present capitalists get the fruits of their own and a good deal of the fruits of the workers' labour, because they know how to keep what they have got. Their machinery for doing so has gone through three stages - all three of which are still with us. First the soldiers to conquer the outside tribes and guard the spoil; then come the police to guard against acquisitive persons of the capitalists' own tribe; last, but incomparably most important, come the lawyers, who perpetuate on a sheet or two of foolscap paper what it has taken the capitalists by the aid of the soldiers and police centuries to accomplish; but once down on the lawyers' paper, the efforts of centuries, good and bad, humane or destructive of society, continue themselves automatically with the lady typist to circulate them, and the police and soldiers standing by for the rare occasions when someone is rude enough not to take the lady typist's word for it.

My brothers if you would only realize that society is now ruled through, and very largely by the lady typist, you would not talk in such a grandiose vein about social revolution. Certainly you must have a social revolution, but the heroic part of it won't come till it is over, and we settle down to live as, it is to be inferred from the New Testament, God meant us to.

The first step of the social revolution is to steel yourselves to an obstinate un-chivalrous refusal to take the lady typist's word for things. "But the police will insist on our attending to the lady," you say, "and after them the soldiers."

Oh no, they won't. All they will insist on will be to club you over the head, and put an odd ounce or two of lead into you, while you are really not sure enough of yourselves to contradict a lady at all. It is a delicate business anyway, but there is not a married man amongst you but knows it can be done - with the right combination of firmness and sweetness. Talking about this combination of qualities. Have you ever thought about drill? That requires a firm command from the leader and a firm walk and carriage from leader and men. But it makes for sweetness too.

It shows each man his place and enables him to work with other men with the least possible friction and delay. It has, if intelligently carried out, a considerable effect upon the character, and one most necessary for the workers' purpose. For supposing the whole produce of labour is at your disposal, its distribution among yourselves in proportion to the labour of each would be a mighty undertaking. You would have to have amongst you all, and more than all, the qualities now employed by masters and workers; you would have to do your work, but direct your own work, market your own produce and pay yourselves your own wages out of the proceeds. That will take discipline - discipline voluntarily undergone by yourselves to fit yourselves for the mighty task you have before you.

What about Carson and Murphy? Humble slaves of the lady typist both of them! But in case either or both of them intervene between you and that firm, courageous interview with "herself," which I desire you should have, a knowledge of some elementary military evolutions will not be amiss.

CHAPTER 25.
JIM LARKIN

The fact is, I was unconsciously sitting on the fence. In moments I saw the clear revolutionary principle; at others I was repelled by the bitterness of a philosophy fighting against the whole established order, imputing sinister motives to every 'bourgeois action, including my own. I clung to the comfortable suavities of my own class. I was not innocent of patronizing the cause I had adopted. I was definitely guilty of emphasizing this note of patronage in intercourse with my family and respectable friends. The following letter to my mother brings this out clearly: -

'Standard Hotel,'
Harcourt Street,
DUBLIN, *29th November.*
    My darling Mother,
    Thank you very much for your letter. I am sure you must be somewhat perturbed as to whether I am and will be rightly guided in what I am doing.
    I can only say that whatever I or anyone may think, it is fairly obvious that the working classes are bent on bettering their condition, and mean to change the old order of things at all costs. But there are few to tell them that the realization of a better state of society demands in the first instance a very high state of discipline among themselves. Without discipline their efforts will only destroy. With it I firmly believe they can make life a richer thing, not only for their class but for ours. Larkin and Connolly, for all the excrescences of their platform speeches, are men of ideals and ability. To earn their sympathy and trust now and to establish a bond between their class and the progressively minded people in ours will, I believe, bear golden fruit when the time comes to construct. I look forward to a conference when the strike is settled between the Labour leaders and such men as Sir Horace Plunkett and George Russell; the plans they devise will be very much easier to carry out with men who have been through a training which I am specially devising to bring out their intelligence and to discover in each small

group the men with most imagination and capacity for leadership.

I get weary of the whole thing sometimes, but I know at bottom I've got to go on with it, whether I like it or not, till I have accomplished something and can leave.

The Transport Union men are delightful to work with. I have what will probably be the biggest muster yet to-morrow at Croydon Park, quite a large mansion with large grounds, which Larkin bought for the Union. It is rather a colossal task to get three thousand men, as I shall very likely have to-morrow, into working order single-handed. To-morrow I am going to explain and illustrate to them my scheme of organization, which is based on a small working unit of eighteen - sixteen men and two N.C.O.'s, with a loose organization into companies and battalions when the sections of eighteen have to work together.

I met Ronald McNeill today in Grafton Street walking with Carson. He introduced me to Carson as 'the redoubtable Captain White.' Carson said, 'Oh! I know he's always abusing me,' to which I replied, I haven't abused you for two months.' Carson wasn't gushing, and I was not favourably impressed by him. Ronald, as usual, was delightful. I only walked a few steps with them.

I hope you will write often, and I will write as often as I can.

With love to the girls, -Believe me, ever your loving son,

Jack.

I speak in this letter of expecting a muster of three thousand men at Croydon Park. My expectations in the matter of numbers were subject to fantastic disappointment. The day the Citizen Army was actually inaugurated in Croydon Park by Jim Larkin and myself there were, I suppose, between five thousand and ten thousand men present, whom I fell in somehow and marched back to Dublin in military order.

The regular enrolling of recruits and the commencement of drill was announced for the next day. I expected anything from five hundred to one thousand men. Incredible as it may sound to anyone who does not know Ireland, when I arrived on the ground at the time appointed, I was literally alone. After waiting about an hour some fifteen men had dribbled in in ones and twos, several of them not members of the Transport Union to which the Citizen Army was confined, but ardent

Nationalists of the middle class anxious to instruct me how to organize-the- nation.

I made a start, however, the first day with a squad. Then at some drill, perhaps after a big meeting at Croydon Park, I would have four hundred or five hundred enrolments, 95% of whom would evaporate within a few days. I stuck at it and gradually got together a solid and reliable nucleus. Often when I had ordered a parade for them, after getting Larkin or Connolly's sanction for the time as not clashing with any of the political arrangements of the strike, my faithful commando would be taken off to appear at some speech-making or other without my being notified.

I don't think any man ever worked against greater odds. The men, when I had sifted them down to the ones that meant business, were all right. The leaders used me as a useful side-line to keep the men busy when they weren't doing anything else, and as a good publicity stunt. Moreover, I began to feel psychically the collective hostility of the upper and middle classes. I did not get enough psychic support from my adopted crowd to counteract it. I began to know the terrible strain of being in the middle of opposing mass-currents without belonging psychically to either. To keep going I had to depend on what I regard as the spirit, as distinct from the psyche, the mind reaching out to the unborn future founding itself on tendencies, directions of progress rather than any existing actualities. Ahead of me in the future lay a conflagration of 'existing actualities' and the birth of a new state from their ashes. The very men I was drilling were to apply the torch. My mind could not see so far. My psyche, the product of class training and tradition, and Imperialist class training and tradition at that, had no vital impulse in itself towards the changes, which my mind was galvanizing my often exhausted body to prepare. Small wonder that I sought bridges across to the unknown future by milder methods than destiny had in store. My reference to Sir Horace Plunkett and George Russell in my letter to my mother is very instructive. It illustrates so well the irreconcilables I was trying to combine. For Sir Horace Plunkett, the founder of the Irish Agricultural Organization Society was the supreme example not only of the mentality but the economic mechanism, which Connolly and the Citizen Army were out to destroy and supersede. In the main Sir Horace organized the farmers of Ireland to do with more ease and profit the very thing Connolly, and after him Republican Ireland, wished to prevent, namely, send their produce out of Ireland to the English market. If I remember right, part of the time I was drilling the Citizen Army, I was actually living in Plunkett House being 'vetted' as a possible Plunkettian young man.

George Russell (AE), the pen and the imagination of the I.A.O.S., editor of its organ, the *Irish Homestead*, came out nobly on the side of the strikers at first. His enthusiasm was regarded with extreme disfavour by Plunkett House. Eventually the indignation of the I.A.O.S. constituents at AE's revolutionary pronouncements became so great, that a kind of court martial was held upon him at Plunkett House. He bowed to discipline, partly because he is first and foremost man of letters rather than of action, partly out of personal loyalty to Sir Horace. The incident and AE's real spiritual leadership of the Irish Renaissance were closed.

AE informs me that no censure was personally conveyed to him.

I know I was ultimately rejected by Plunkett House as eminently unsuitable for one of their young men, because I kept reminding the public of AE's passionate utterances before policy quenched passion. So my pose to myself and my mother of self-appointed link between minds so different as Jim Larkin and Horace Plunkett, representing such divergent mass-interests was pretty thin. It was quite a natural line of least resistance to adopt none the less. It takes time to learn that the line of most resistance is almost always the line of fate.

The drilling of the Citizen Army went on varied by a good deal of speech making. I was a free lance politically, and could take part in any efforts at combination I chose. Madam (Countess Markievitch) was in the same boat. Her main allegiance was to the strike and Liberty Hall. She ran a soup kitchen there with indefatigable energy and good humour; but she took an active part in what may be called the Republican left wing separatist movement that was steadily gaining ground.

My first friction with Jim Larkin took place on an occasion when these divergent political activities converged. I have as yet given no sketch of Jim's character.

'Le etat c'est moi, said Louis Quatorze. So Larkin might have said of the great strike, of the whole beginning of the insurgency of Southern Labour, 'C'est moi.' 'Might have said' do I say! He did say it, tacitly all the time, often overtly; and he said it while Connolly was conducting a steady philosophic propaganda in speech and writing and I was drilling the Citizen Army to put some spirit in them, when all but in spirit they were beat.

The little clash between Jim and myself about to be narrated sheds the most vivid light possible upon his character. It is Jim at his worst, which perpetually dogs the heels of his best. In those days, at the height of his influence he was, what God meant him to be, great. He is so intrinsically great, that a great opportunity on the direct line of his genius, which is to be the mouthpiece and interpreter of mass-emotion, might even make him great again.

Let the incident referred to come in its place in the middle of the report of two great converging meetings as it appeared in the Irish Times of the following day. I give the report, for nothing could serve better to show the state of popular feeling, the particular points on which it was focused, and the interplay of movements and personalities. The first line of defence between a Government and revolution is the police. The use of the police had overstepped the mark in an attempt to cow the people. Popular feeling was concentrated on the effort to expose the excesses of the police and their instigators. The effort of the Government was to shield and whitewash their servants. The struggle against the police I am shortly to symbolize in personal physical combat. Out of that struggle with the police arose in due course the second stage, the challenge to the second line of defence, the military forces. The meeting now reported shows the first stage drawing to its climax.

RIOTS COMMISSION
PROTEST MEETING IN DUBLIN
MR. LARKIN AND THE BRITISH FLAG
A REMARKABLE INCIDENT
CAPTAIN WHITE AND THE POLICE

'Yesterday afternoon a meeting of a miscellaneous character was held in Sackville Street. It was called by a poster on the walls, for which no person seemed to be responsible, and it was stated that the object of the meeting was to protest against the constitution of the Viceregal Commission which is now engaged in inquiring into the allegations of the use of excessive force on the part of the police in dealing with disturbances in the city which arose out of the strike. Mr. Hobson, who was supposed to be the leader, or chairman, rose to speak, and at that moment Superintendent Quinn and Inspector Campbell, who were in charge of the police, approached the vehicle with some difficulty owing to the crowding, and, speaking to Captain White, said the wagonette and the people were causing an obstruction to the thoroughfare.

Captain White asked - What do you propose?

Superintendent Quinn - I request you to go away.

Captain White -Then I refuse. You have had plenty of opportunity of saying what you have to say before this. Go on, Mr. Hobson.

Mr. Hobson proposed the following resolution: Since, in response to a public demand for an inquiry into the conduct of the police, including the Police Magistracy, in connection with the Labour disturbances in Dublin, the Commission instituted by the Government does not fulfil the conditions publicly agreed to by the Chief Secretary, and is not recognized by the public as properly constituted, in view of the questions of official misconduct that are involved, and since on these grounds those capable of giving disinterested evidence do not wish to go before the Commission, this public meeting of the citizens of Dublin requests the Lord Mayor of Dublin to hold an independent inquiry at the earliest possible date, before which the evidence of the citizens can be brought. Should the Lord Mayor, for any cause, feel unable to-accede to the request of the citizens, this meeting calls upon the Corporation to undertake the inquiry.

The reference to the Lord Mayor in the resolution was greeted with groaning and booing.

CAPTAIN WHITE'S ADVICE

Captain White, who next spoke, said: The Lord Mayor was to be asked to hold an independent inquiry into the police outrages, which were reported on only too good, and undeniable grounds. He had written twice to the Lord Mayor asking him to give a definite statement of his views on this matter, and he had not received a reply to either of his letters. (Boos.) If their leaders didn't lead the people of Dublin, and if the people didn't want to be trodden down and treated like slaves, it was time that they should push the leaders aside, and relegate them to obscurity, from which they never should have emerged. This was a case in which any action could not be too strong. In spite of the denials of legal liars the photograph stood as proof that two or three policemen battened each individual that Sunday in the street when the people were trying to escape. (Hear, Hear!) The solicitors to the Civic League had in their possession over seventy signed statements showing that the people were hemmed in and battened in a way, as one man said, that you could hear the batons rattling on the heads of the people. The police broke into the Corporation Buildings, and they batoned women, and women with child in these buildings. He did not say that all the police were tarred with that shameless brutality which had been brought home to individuals of them. That was the result of the abominable system, for which the people themselves were to blame. Two Members of Parliament - one a Liberal, the other a Unionist - had given him an account of what they had seen. The Liberal said that he had seen four policemen arresting one man, and that he followed them to the station. He saw another policeman come behind and strike the prisoner on a delicate part of the body, and that prisoner was stunned. Next day, in the Police Court, a charge was made that there had been an attempt at rescue of the prisoner. There was no such attempt whatever. The other Member of Parliament to whom he referred was Mr. Ronald M' Neill, who had written to him a letter in reference to the charge made against Mrs. Sheehy Skeffington of having attempted to hand some suffragist literature to Mr. Bonar Law at the door of Lord Iveagh's residence. Mr. M' Neill said that the lady had done nothing to warrant her arrest and prosecution that he saw. Yet, said the speaker, the lady had to go to prison. That was Castle government in Ireland and it would go on, said Captain White, until you are ready rather to die than to bear it any longer." (Cheers.) "Now, " asked the speaker, "is that incitement to violence? (Laughter.) I have already broken the law once, by refusing the police to leave this place. (Boos.) No boos, you are not a lot of geese or sheep."

The Countess Markievitch then spoke.

While Countess Markievitch was speaking, there were loud cheers in the distance, followed by a movement on the outer fringe of the audience. Another brake was seen rapidly approaching, followed by a large concourse of people. The cry went up, 'Jim Larkin,' and there was loud cheering.

The second conveyance, which included Mr. Larkin among the occupants, drew up about three hundred yards away, near Nelson s Pillar, so that the respective audiences became merged in each other, and together they must have numbered over ten thousand.

At this point Madam and I, having done our talking, left our own lorry and walked through the huge crowd to join the party on Jim's lorry. The crowd made a lane for us and cheered us loudly - in the middle of Jim's speech, too - as we approached the other lorry. This was too much for Jim, as the following cutting will show.

MR. LARKIN'S REFERENCE TO CAPTAIN WHITE.

'Mr. James Larkin was received with enthusiasm on rising to address the meeting. He referred at the outset to the presence of Captain White (who had just reached the wagonette). Captain White, he said, was the son of Sir George White, who defended the British flag at Ladysmith, the flag under which more disease and degradation had been experienced than anything else that he (Mr. Larkin) knew of.

At the close of this sentence Captain White rose and hurriedly left the wagonette.

Mr. Larkin, continuing, said that if a man did not agree with him, he had a right to act as he thought right. As for himself, he was responsible for what he said, and Captain White, who held commissions in the service, was a man whose views as regards certain things were not in consonance with his (Mr. Larkin's), while as regards certain other questions they were agreed. They had a resolution calling on the Lord Mayor to hold an inquiry. With that resolution he had no sympathy. He would not call on the present Lord Mayor to polish his boots. (Cheers.) The Lord Mayor was not worthy of it. He was a tricky little wirepuller. If the Lord Mayor had done his duty when the crisis opened twenty weeks ago there would have been no need for an inquiry now. (Cheers.) Instead of asserting his right to control the streets of Dublin, he acted the part of a poltroon. The Corporation, of which he was the present head, had proved that they were only self-seekers and job-seekers, who masqueraded as men holding Nationalist opinions.'

My own attitude to the incident appears in the following account of an interview with me on the subject. I should like to emphasize that what I resented was the attack on the flag in connection with my father, who had died not a year ago.

CAPTAIN WHITE AND LARKIN
UNION JACK INCIDENT
From Our Own Correspondent
DUBLIN, Monday Night.

'Captain White, D.S.O., was interviewed this evening as to the incident at Larkin's meeting in Sackville Street on Sunday, when that officer left the platform during Larkin's references to the Union Jack as that "dirty flag."

Captain White said: "I considered that I had no choice but to do so. When my arrival was made the signal for an attack on the flag under which my father had fought I left as a personal protest, as I thought my personal feelings had been unceremoniously disregarded. You ask me will the incident affect my future connection with the Labour Movement? I cannot see why it should. I have certainly been to some extent indebted to facilities which Mr. Larkin has courteously given me for getting into touch with the men of his union. These facilities he is not likely to withdraw, from what I know of him, because I resent a portion of one of his speeches.

"If anyone were foolish enough to suppose that I would abandon my deep interest in the Labour Movement as a whole because of a personal disagreement with Mr. Larkin, the fact that I spoke last night in support of Mr. Carpenter, one of the Labour candidates for the municipal elections, is sufficient answer to them.'

I wrote to Jim telling him straight what I thought of his conduct, adding, I believe in my superior way, that it was the sort of thing that spoilt his influence and gave the ungodly occasion to blaspheme.

He gave me no apology whatever till about ten years later, when he suddenly took it into his head to make an impassioned defence of me from a bad heckling I as getting from Communists in Battersea Town Hall, because I had expressed belief in an intelligent Supreme Being.

The occasion was a meeting under the auspices the Irish Workers' League in London, of which I was then Chairman.

Jim was magnificent. He lacerated 'that woman here and that other woman (in trousers) over there' ho had dared to heckle 'his friend White, who like Saul of Tarsus saw a great light'; he told the most heartrending story, entirely fictitious, about accompanying me into some military club and all the other members getting up and turning their backs on my rival.

Finally he apologized for the Union Jack incident of ten years before, not to me, but the audience. That is Jim.

CHAPTER 26.
INTERVIEW WITH BIRRELL

The strike was dying as a strike and being reborn as a National Revolution, destined to fuse for the moment the Labour and extreme Nationalist elements.

Had I known then what I know now, had I been less sensitive to a certain natural suspicion of me on the part of the Labour leaders, and more alive to the power of popularity which an event to be recorded in the next chapter was to give me, I believe I could have brought off a revolution on the Russian model almost on my own.

It could not have lasted, for the North would have been hostile and the South was not ripe.

The parson could have played on political superstition in the North and the priest on religious superstition in the South, as he did in the matter of the deportation of the children. But if I had been at that time an active Labour Revolutionary of the temper of Connolly, he and I together could have made a purely Labour Revolution in Dublin before the Great War. In that case, a clearer precedent might have been established, with less blood.

If I had stayed with the Citizen Army instead of going off in a huff to the National Volunteers when the Transport Union appointed a committee to clip my wings and control me, I believe I could have merged National in Labour ideals instead of leaving the merger to come the other way round.

I cannot blame myself, of course. What Connolly said to me one day, when I remonstrated about my army being taken off to a political meeting without my being notified, was true enough, You're nothing but a great boy,' said he. 'Go to hell,' I replied. The incident was the first beginning of the dissipation of class-suspicion and the establishment of warmer relations between us.

Yet my ideas were revolutionary enough as the following the *London Daily Herald* of 5th," February will prove: -

'Captain White's address to the Independent Labour Party of Ireland, of which a brief mention was made in a previous message, was a wonderfully stimulating, confession of faith in the Labour and Socialist

Movement. Captain White went to fundamentals in few Socialist speakers have time to do, and showed the need for basing our economic and political systems on spiritual and metaphysical ideas.

The first necessity was a complete revolution in religious conceptions - an abandonment of the root principle of Western theology, that human nature was intrinsically bad. This theory was the basis of ecclesiastical authority, and of half the evils of the education and economic system. Secular life had broken away from religion in consequence, and both had suffered.

The class-war was a reality; Liberals and Tories were united, and, therefore, there must be no breach ranks of Labour.

His constructive plans for the regeneration of Ireland included co-operation, which he announced he was going to set on foot in Dublin immediately; and the Citizen Army as the reserve, in case the conquest of capitalism could not be achieved by peaceful means. He wanted no sporadic violence, but the gentleness that could only come from a consciousness of disciplined strength. The revolution of thought had come; force would be needed to compel legislation.

The ideas and enthusiasm of Socialism and Syndicalism -which were two aspects of the same thing were dying out because there was no one to translate them into action. "Give me twenty thousand men and I will remodel Ireland."

Connolly was, of course, more definitely revolutionary than I, and more prepared for violent methods. Here is a speech of his taken from the Christian Science Monitor sometime in December 1913: -

'The *Monitor's* Dublin correspondent telegraphs that at a meeting held at Beresford Place James Connolly announced that Captain White was prepared to drill men for a corps to be formed by the Irish Transport and General Workers' Union. This work, he declared, was not going to be left only to the Ancient Order of Hibernians and the Orangemen.

His idea of a self-governing Ireland was a republic among the nations. It was work such as they were engaged in which would make that great ideal possible. Continuing, he stated that workers all over Great Britain were prepared to co-operate with them. It will come, he said, with the same dramatic suddenness as the closing of Dublin Port a few days ago.

In concluding his speech, which was composed mainly of ultra-socialistic exhortations, Mr. Connolly declared they were engaged in a rebellion, and that the men would carry it to a successful issue. The rebellion was against the employing classes in order that the workers should have their rights, and to that end they meant to fight until victory was achieved. Before being beaten they meant to put up a bigger fight than has yet been attempted, for before they surrendered or were beaten they would pull down civilization and go down with it themselves.'

Jim Larkin, the big noise, had been to England 'to raise the fiery cross' as he put it. Failing to raise a crusade up to his hopes, he rounded with his verbally terrific but morally weak vituperation on the English Labour leaders. There is in pure-souled revolutionary theory a certain blinding influence akin to that of sexual love. Larkin and Connolly were in love with an idea. They represented two different types of lover. Larkin was the troubadour serenading with love-inspiring poems. If the lady proved difficult they turned to vicious lampoons. Connolly could sing a little, very little, rather raucously, like a crow in the mating season. But he held the cave man in reserve and relied on the cave man, not the troubadour.

I was seeking but had not yet found the happy and effective blend of troubadour and cave man. Even then, however, my tendency to transcendentalism gave me a natural insight into human psychology.

I had met some English Labour leaders. I had met Arthur Henderson, their great pattern and type. I did not expect them to be revolutionary. I did not expect them to admire or ultimately to support other people in being revolutionary. Instinctively in dealing with them I would have sung my sweetest and passed ammunition like hell to the cave man, I would have kept on singing till the cave man could stand a siege. I would have saved myself the trouble of composing lampoons because Arthur Henderson did not kiss the fiery cross. Not so Jim Larkin. His emotions of love or hate were too sacred and spontaneous to be repressed. The world must worship or vilify with him.

Here from some English paper is comment on the failure of Larkin's fiery cross campaign in England, with some instructive details about the gradual collapse of the strike. Connolly as cave man appears in reserve.

'Mr. James Larkin's latest manifesto has given rise to considerable discussion across the water, and it is regarded in Dublin as evidence that the strike leader believes that his mission to England has failed of the object he had in view. Those who think this say that the English people have given full justice to the good work Larkin has done in raising the standard of living amongst the quay labourers and unskilled workers in Dublin, but that they have begun to realize that he is a revolutionary and that his aim is to overthrow society. A leading employer in the city said yesterday that the man who can leave prison when he likes may easily delude himself as to the extent of his power, but now that he has found that he is not accepted in England as a great leader he turns upon those whose sympathy he hoped to enlist. On the other hand there are those who regard with satisfaction all that Larkin has done and see in him one who will bring their fight in Dublin to a successful issue.

No arguments, however, are put forward to prove to the man in the street how the present deadlock is to be ended by a quarrel between Larkin and the British Labour leaders, and that, after all, is the dominant question in Dublin.

In spite of all the discussions going on a new phase is being entered upon, from which it would appear that commerce will right itself in due course to a very large extent, whether the Transport Union men return to work or not. As is well known, the shipping trade has been diverted to other Irish ports, causing activity to be transferred to the railways, and all the lines running into Dublin are very busy. Indeed, the traffic is almost remarkable, and the congestion of goods has been shifted from the quays to the railway depots, where a large number of extra hands have been engaged. The result is that the railways have plenty to do. Traders are carting away their stuff freely, and it is noteworthy that only a small proportion of the vehicles have police protection. The quays themselves are quite deserted, but during the week a great clearance has been made.

There seems to be a general movement towards the formation of volunteers in Dublin, and apparently the strikers are going to take their part. Two weeks ago Mr. James Connolly announced that the members of the Transport Union would in future be drilled "for the purpose of defence." The following order has been issued by the Government of Liberty Hall:

"Transport Union Citizen Army. - All men wishing to join for the purpose of training must attend at Croydon Park at 6 p.m. on Sunday. Captain White will take charge. By order."

It will be remembered that Mr. Connolly said the union must be drilled first, and when arms were wanted they knew where to get them.'

Meanwhile the condition of the people in Dublin was desperate; they had neither food nor clothing. I expended a pretty big sum out of my own pocket for boots for the Citizen Army, a good many of which found their way to the pawnshop. The longer the strike drew on the more desperate the people's condition became.

It came to my knowledge early in I 914 that there was a sum of £2,000 from the British Treasury allocated to the Dublin Local Government Board for the relief of distress. This sum was to revert automatically to the Treasury if not expended in relief by a certain date. I did all I could to get the Dublin L.G.B. to spend it on some relief scheme, and suggested various schemes to them. Failing to get any move made, I crossed to England and paid a call on Mr. Birrell, the Chief Secretary for Ireland, in his room at the House of Commons.

Now there was a most admirable lady in Dublin called Miss Harrison, a member of the Corporation, with a heart as tender as her conscience and a great persistence in the cause of their joint dictates. The innumerable and glaring evils which cried to Miss Harrison and Heaven for remedy, led in the first place to the door of Mr. Augustine Birrell, the Chief Secretary. I believe Miss Harrison had chased Mr. Birrell away from his post, and he was skulking in the House of Commons to be safe in the body, but not the spirit, from her splendid importunity. Certain it is, that no sooner had I been bidden to enter in response to a knock on the door and stated that I came from Dublin, than the Chief Secretary shrank back in a very comfortable armchair with a look of genuine alarm on his face.

His greeting had been geniality itself.

'Well, my boy, where do you come from?'

The fatal word Dublin worked the change.

'Good God, I hope you're not a friend of Miss Harrison?'

'Well, sir, said I, I have the honour of the lady's acquaintance. In a certain sense we may be said to be comrades in the field. But I make bold to hope that I possess a power denied to her of crystallizing my business for presentation to the official mind.'

The dear old gentleman looked a little happier. He scanned me quizzically as much as to say:

'Although on business you are bent,
You have a kindly mind.'

Then catching the sympathetic twinkle in my eye, he decided to relax altogether; in fact, he decided to unburden himself of what was evidently the dominant phobia of his life.

'I call her the nine of clubs, the curse of Ireland, said he. 'That, sir,' said I, chidingly but still sympathetic, 'is because your unfortunate official position removes you from the sphere of the lady's excellent personal qualities.'

'Good God; my boy,' said he, 'you are the first to show me the least advantage in being Chief Secretary of Ireland.'

After that we were friends. I had gone to the heart of the Chief Secretary's complex. If Ireland was oppressed or ignored it was from no ill-will or indifference on the part of this kindly old man. It was because he regarded Ireland as an extended projection of Miss Harrison, and she had got him down, 'all-of a dither.' She had inhibited Ireland, produced complete paralysis of function; but let some other substitutional channel present itself for the old gentleman's natural kindliness, and all would be well.

I stated my desires as briefly as possible. I wanted the Chief Secretary's authority to get Henry Robinson, not yet, I think, Sir Henry, head of the Irish Local Government Board, to release the earmarked £2000 for any reasonable relief scheme I could put up to him. I would find the scheme and the men. Let Birrell and Robinson do the rest; but let Birrell make it quite clear that I had the support and goodwill of the supreme authority.

'Certainly, my boy, I'll do anything I can for you; I like you much better than Miss Harrison.'

I left Mr. Birrell with a letter for Robinson, instructing him to give me all the help in his power.

So far so good, but I had yet to learn the limitations Of supreme authority, the nest of squirming red-tape worms in Ireland herself battening on her carcase, while they deflected attention to the English connection as the root of all evil. So in a way it was; for before its removal no abuse could be tracked home, let alone remedied.

Returning to Dublin, I got busy at once. The following letter of mine to the Irish Independent dated 14th March 1914 will give an idea of the difficulties with which I was faced:

'Sir;

It is right the public should know that there are thousands of people in Dublin starving as a result of the dual causes of (1) the savage victimization by many of the masters of the Transport Union Workers, and (2) the apathy and red tape of the public bodies responsible for the inauguration of relief works.

I was invited by a high official to prepare a scheme whereby the grant supplied by the Treasury could be disbursed in relief work. If it is asked why such an invitation should be sought by and gladly extended to a free lance like myself, the reply is that the unwieldiness and inefficiency of Dublin municipal bodies is so notorious that no project dependent on them is expected to reach fruition unless some unshackled person can be found to galvanize individual members into action. The first scheme submitted, accompanied by detailed plans as to its execution, concerned Government property, and had been reported on by a Royal Commission as likely to be profitable. After some days of reconnaissance I discovered the official most directly responsible for its adoption, and was informed by him that some months at least must elapse before, following the prescribed official procedure, the scheme could be finally sanctioned.

Owing to this verdict, and the fact that this scheme from its magnitude involved the grant of money additional to the Treasury relief grant, I abandoned it- and turned my attention to seeing what could be done with the grant already lying with the Local Government Board. The body responsible for the disbursement of this relief grant is the Dublin Distress Committee, a large proportion of members of which are also members of the Dublin Corporation. Some co-ordination between the Distress Committee and the Corporation would seem to be demanded; as the innumerable sites where clearing and demolition is waiting to be carried out are under control of the Corporation. Anyone who has seen the photographs of the Dublin slum areas attached to that remarkable document, the Dublin Housing Report, will know there is no dearth of these sites.

The Distress Committee sat last Tuesday and settled nothing. The Corporation does not sit again till the first Monday in April. On inquiry from the City Engineer I was told that the allotment of sites for employment of men under the Distress Committee presented difficulties, as, for example, the serious problem as to who should indemnify the Corporation were a brick to fall from a roof on a Distress Committee workman's head. The City Engineer was unable to say who would indemnify the relatives of those persons who starved to death while this matter was being settled.

Another visit this morning to the City Engineer, accompanied by a lady, herself a member of the Dublin Corporation and the Distress Committee, resulted in a negative, or, at best, most discouraging reply to our question as to whether any sites were available for immediate clearance. That there are numerous sites over which arbitration has taken place and compensation been awarded is not denied, but some months' delay is deemed probable to enable the Corporation law agent to investigate the title of those who are to receive compensation.

The sites are in any case acquired and the investigation of title can take place with equal case after work has been commenced on them, but such fatuous reasons are gravely advanced, regardless of the fact that money is lying waiting to be spent on relief works - money, too, which has to be automatically returned to the Treasury if it is not allotted by the 31st of this month, while the utter destitution of the people grows daily more widespread and appalling.

I heard today of a man who had just died, according to his wife, of a broken heart" from the attempt to feed himself and his family on a loaf of bread per day. The people prefer death to going into the workhouse. Would to God they would seek their death in violent protest against the devilish apathy of those responsible for their relief. Every avenue is blocked to them.

Fifty locked-out tramway men applied a day or two back through the Labour Exchange for the same number of posts on a new line opened at

Torquay. They were led to expect they would be engaged, but later were told there were no places for Dublin men.

The attitude of the Dublin public is little short of devilish. The Lord Mayor of Dublin told a friend of mine today that he thought feeling was too bitter to make an appeal by him for funds from the public likely to be successful. I have had evidence myself of the attitude of a large section of the comfortable classes. It can be summarized at "Let them starve; it will teach them a lesson."

The present state of the workless poor in Dublin, and the callous apathy with which it is being met, is a blot on civilization and an outrage on the name of Christ.

J.R. WHITE (Captain).

The remarkable part about this letter is that it is dated a day after I got my head battered to pulp by the Dublin police in an effort to call attention to the evils of which it speaks.

I cannot explain this. Probably I had reached the point when I knew that words were futile and had decided to act first and talk afterwards on my favourite maxim, Action must always precede knowledge.' If I wrote the letter after the battering I got from the batons of twenty of the Dublin Metropolitan Police, whose average height at the time was about 6 feet 3 inches, I must have been a better man then than I am now. I may have written the letter before and arranged for it to be published afterwards in preparation for all eventualities. Anyhow, the letter sets forth the sort of thing that made me see red and decide to stand no more nonsense.

CHAPTER 27.
NEARLY SCALPED

Called or got called a meeting in Beresford Place outside Liberty Hall on the afternoon of I3th March. By that time the strike had so far collapsed that most of the Citizen Army men, who were nearly all fine hefty chaps, were back in work. At the meeting, at which Connolly also spoke, I stated our intention of marching on the Mansion House at the end of the meeting to demand work. My speech was pretty violent. I did not incite to any initiative in violence, but I remember saying that if our march was interfered with, I for one would fight while I had breath in my body.

To be prepared for eventualities I had bought a blackthorn, not a walking-stick, but a shillelagh with a loop for the wrist. I made the mistake of getting it too thick, and when the fight came I was afraid to hit out for fear of committing murder. I had given the Citizen Army staves to an odd lot of unemployed, who had neither the Citizen Army's discipline nor physique. Numerically they made a pretty good show, probably two or three hundred men.

As soon as the meeting was over our march to the Mansion House began, the unemployed substitutes for the Citizen Army in the van; there were, I think, four real Citizen Army men in the front rank.

We had not gone a hundred yards when a big horsedray attempted to drive right through the ranks; the horses were halfway through the sections of fours, when the men seized their bridles and forced them back.

Whether the occurrence was arranged by the police or not I cannot say. It had the appearance of an act of deliberate contempt. I ran across to the driver and struck the footboard at his feet with my shillelagh as a forcible hint to pull back out of the ranks, which he did. Then I ran back to my place in the column. A moment later, a police inspector laid his hand on my shoulder as though to arrest me. I wheeled sharply and struck at him. He let go quick enough for my shillelagh was a desperate weapon.

Then the band played. The police charged at once, and to my sorrow be it said the substitute army melted away like smoke before the batons of some twenty, at most twenty-five, policemen. My sorrow but not my shame-, for the four genuine Citizen Army men held their ground, but their heads were too thin and they went down at the first blow. That left me to face the twenty police. Though I say it, I think I put up a good fight. I kept them at bay for a minute or two, but when some of them got round and began clubbing me from behind the odds were too heavy. They managed to seize my shillelagh on a back swing and disarmed me. Then they pinioned my arms and began to lead me away to Store Street Police Station, a couple of hundred yards away, I was so fighting mad by this time that I got an arm free no less than three times on the way to the station, and punched one of my escort on the jaw each time. The police were a queer mixture of kindliness and brutality. I distinctly remember one chap saying as I struggled with them, 'Arrah., now, captain dear, come quietly; sure they're cowardly devils, they're not worth fighting for.' The next moment I got an arm free and a punch in, and received a baton blow from behind, though one man amongst twenty, unarmed, bleeding like a pig, and almost finished.

The last whack I got, just before we got to the station, was from Sergeant M. W., the biggest man in the biggest force in the world. I thought it had done for me. The noble blow was observed by a British civil servant out of the window of the Local Government Board Offices. To his credit, be it said, he was so horrified by the savage brutality of it that he reported the donor to Sir John Ross of Bladensburg, who was then in command of the D.M.P. Sergeant W. was transferred out of Dublin.

It came to my ears that the civil servant, O'Connor, had reported Wolfe's blow, and I made great use of it at the trial.

My head was a bloody pulp, but my spirit remained exalted from the joy of battle. Madam Markievitch had hung on the flanks of the enemy throughout, darted in and tried to trip up a policeman when possible. Now she was magnificent at the station. She forced her way in and demanded that a private doctor should be sent for at once. The first time they flung her out, but she ducked between policemen's legs and got back again somehow. The police were trying to reserve my battered pericranium for inspection by their own police surgeon. Madam insisted on getting a solution of Jeyes fluid and bathing at once for fear of its getting septic, and got her way in having a private doctor summoned at once. I give the report on my scalp furnished by the said doctor for my solicitors later.

'Dear Sirs,

In reply to your request for a report on the injuries I found Captain White suffering from, in consequence of his trouble with the police, I beg to say that he had two scalp wounds: one on the interior and right aspect of his scalp which was about two inches long, and presented the appearance of a wound such as a baton would produce. The other lesion was situated nearer the middle longitudinal diameter of the skull at its posterior and right region. This wound was what would be honestly implied by the expression "horrible." It consisted of a linear split of about two or two and a half inches long, with two smaller splits extending outwards from its right border. The most probable explanation of the appearance of this wound is, to the best of my knowledge, that Captain White was struck at least three times over the same area of skull, one blow being from behind and the remaining two being from the side. Nothing else but an imaginary miniature weapon representing a rake could with one blow produce three distinct lesions resulting in a break of the continuity of the scalp.

Both wounds extended down to the membrane immediately covering the bones (periosteum) and on this account had an added danger to that of any ordinary wound. If they become septic, the matter could freely move like a fluid support all over the skull and raise the scalp. The periosteum becoming inflamed would from its direct connection with the bones and more indirectly with the meninges of the brain lead to most critical complications. Apparently these complications did not occur. I disinfected, sutured, and dressed the wounds, after which I understand Captain White came under the care of Dr. Joynt. Sepsis having been avoided, I do not consider the wounds injurious to health.

I am, Yours truly,
Seymour Stritch.'

Meanwhile in the Police Station there was a lively time. Besides Madam, a Mr. Verschoyle had gained admission. He was a magistrate and a landowner, but none the less a gallant soul for that.

He had seen the fight when I was alone at bay against the police, and observing one stalwart policeman raising his baton to club me from behind, had rushed in at the imminent risk of being batoned himself. He stood by me manfully, not only at the police station but the subsequent trials.

I asked for Sir Horace Plunkett to be rung up to see if bail could be arranged for me. He and Professor Houston stood sureties, and I was released with my head swathed in bandages, about nine o'clock that night. Marvellous to relate, I never had so much as a headache. I must have a phenomenal skull.

Here is a letter to my wife dated 14th March, the day after the fight.

'Standard Hotel,
Harcourt Street,
DUBLIN, 14th March.
My Dear Dollie,

I have been hoping to hear definite news of your arrival, and you will, I am sure, be anxious for news of me. I told Madam Markievitch to wire you before I was bailed out yesterday and she says she did.

I'll send you some papers with accounts of yesterday's most inspiriting row, but all the paper accounts are false or garbled, so I may as well tell you the correct story.

Well first, as I think I wrote you, I have been busy since I came back here trying to get some scheme of work adopted to set all the victimized strikers to work, and have found myself blocked everywhere by the apathy and red tape of the Dublin public bodies. Meanwhile the plight of the people was becoming more desperate, and I was beginning to lose patience. Also over the National Question, by this absurd Lawyer's Home Rule Settlement, to which the wretched Nationalist Party has agreed, the last sparks of Irish manhood and nationality are likely to be killed. I felt that firstly national freedom can only keep pace with the freedom of the most subject class in the community, and that to stir the national spirit one must first stir the spirit of this daily growing more dejected class, and also that I must come into prominence to pull all the most virile elements on the national side together, and to heal the breach which has so far existed between official Nationalism and Labour. Therefore though I by no means went out yesterday meaning to provoke a row, I went out determined not to go an inch out of my way to avoid one.

As though by fate, immediately we marched off from the meeting in Beresford Place, a big mail-van drove right into the ranks of what the papers call the Citizen Army, but were in reality a scratch lot of weedy-looking individuals I had mustered with not more than two or three Citizen Army men among them, as most of the Citizen Army are back at work, and this meeting was for the out-of-works in the afternoon. I rushed straight at the driver and made as though to strike him with a big shillelagh I was carrying in readiness for emergencies' I do not think I actually struck him. I am not charged with doing so, anyway, in the police charge, only "attempting to strike." The driver then pulled the van back and I ran back to my former position at the head of the men. Before or just as I got there a police inspector came and caught hold of me, apparently to arrest me. I struck at him and he let go, and then I stood at bay swinging my shillelagh. None of them would face me in front, but they clubbed me repeatedly from behind and finally disarmed me, striking me again over my hands which I had placed above my head to protect it. If I'd had my back against a wall, I believe I might be there yet. They knocked out the three or four men who alone out of the crowd of about one thousand five hundred put up any kind of a fight, and having battered me till the inspector told them to put up their batons, they pinioned my arms and led me off to the police station. On the way I broke loose two or three times, and got them some grand punches in the jaw. I was calling on the crowd to rescue me all the time, but the poor half-starved creatures hadn't the guts.

Each time, or certainly one time, I broke loose the rear files of my escort clubbed me over the head with their batons. The last blow nearly finished me, and as we were close to the police station and the crowd were making no attempt at a rescue, I thought honour was satisfied and made no more resistance.

I am charged with assaulting the van driver, a police inspector, a police sergeant, and two constables, so that's not so bad. My friends all assure me that I put up a very good fight, and from the feel of my head I think I must have.

They kept me in the police station three or four hours, during which Madam Markievitch and others bathed my cuts with disinfectants, though at first they refused to let her in to do so, and pushed her out of the station when she refused to go.

A doctor I had sent for arrived before the police doctor, and he was not let bandage my head for some time, waiting for the police doctor to arrive. You see my head was no longer a part of a human body, but a piece of evidence.

However, finally they let my doctor go ahead and he stitched up two cuts and bandaged me. About nine o'clock they let me out on bail. Meanwhile all my friends had been to the police station to see me, till I got heartily sick of them.

This morning I appeared to answer my bail in the police court, and the case was adjourned till next Thursday for both sides to get ready, and also as I had a medical certificate that it would be inexpedient for me to be subjected to the strain of police court proceedings. We will make a huge case of it, and I have no doubt that, in conjunction with a letter I sent off yesterday to all the leading papers in the British Isles setting forth the devilish apathy of the public and public bodies about the starving people, something will now be done.

I doubt if they dare to put me in prison. I shall certainly refuse to pay any fine, and I suggest that you come over and stay with Madam Markievitch, Surrey House, Leinster Road, Rathmines, Dublin, who will be delighted to have you, and see me before I have to go to jail, if I do. I shall not be happy if I don't see you, and I am certain you must want to see me.

Will you show this letter to mother?

Your loving

Jack.

At the police court proceedings which followed I engaged James O'Connor, who afterwards became Master of the Rolls, to defend me. He adopted an apologetic tone on the first three days of the case so I dispensed with his services. Some delighted Junior came up to congratulate me. 'I am telling them all, Captain White,' said he, 'you're the first man to teach the Irish Bar manners.'

I must admit I enjoyed the police court proceedings.

I brought cross-summonses against the inspector (Purcell) and one of the constables for assault, and against the van driver for having driven a van to the danger of the public. I'm afraid I played to the gallery pretty shamelessly. I refused to take an oath on the testament proffered me. The grounds I gave for refusal were, that on the first day of the case, when the police, had given evidence, I had heard so much barefaced perjury committed over this testament that I preferred being sworn in some other manner. I was sworn by the raising of my right hand.

I seem to have been fair to the police, especially to Inspector Purcell, to whom for some reason or other had taken a liking. In the newspaper reports I have before me as I write, I see that I charge Purcell with laying a hand 'firmly but without undue violence' on my shoulder. I express regret for having struck him as he was weaponless. But I claim he assaulted me non the less by laying a hand on my shoulder, 'I not having committed any illegal action.' I denied the legality of my arrest. I complained that after I was disarmed put my hands over my head to protect it, but the police continued to strike at and threaten me with their baton till a voice, believed to be Inspector Purcell's, said in tone of remonstrance, Put up your batons.' The reason for my liking for him, no doubt.

Accused of calling a certain Superintendent Quinn a bloody hound,' I decline to deny that on oath, but honestly believe it to be false. I admit calling him an ill-conditioned hound, when I saw him pushing Countess Markievitch out of the police station. I state my belief that the police acted from bias against me, but make a exception of Inspector Purcell, who I 'believe to be a honest man.'

There seems to have been some argument as whether a certain Constable Butler was on point duty at the scene of the fight. I am very positive he was not. The question arose over what my action would have been if I had seen a policeman signal the offending van to go on. I reply I would have stopped the procession. Asked by prosecuting counsel what would I say if Constable Butler's presence on point duty was sworn to, I reply, 'If all the police in Dublin swore that Constable

Butler was on traffic duty on the occasion I would not believe them if they had an object in perjuring themselves.'

'That is very candid,' said the magistrate.

'It is candid, but not conciliatory, said prosecuting counsel. (Laughter.)

I make a concession. 'Of course there are one or two exceptions. I would not like to tar all the police with that brush.'

'I see you looking at Inspector Purcell, Captain White,' says the magistrate.

'Yes, I have a kind of sneaking kindness for Inspector Purcell,' says I. (Loud laughter.)

After this sort of good-natured banter, dear old Verschoyle's introduction of a harsher note was naturally resented. He deposed that in the police station I had been treated with the grossest insults.

Prosecuting counsel was up in arms in a moment.

'I will not extend the latitude to Mr. Verschoyle that I extended to Captain White, and I will ask him to conduct himself like an ordinary witness in this Court.'

Of course! Verschoyle was only a magistrate in the execution of his duty. I was up for damaging an inspector and four policemen. Why wouldn't I have some latitude? I'd take it, anyway, so it was more gracious to give it.

My newspaper report ends with Verschoyle's protest.

'I am quite sure your worship wants a true story.'

The probability is his worship wanted to be amused like every one else.

The episode of the Battle of Butt's Bridge may close fittingly with the note from the doctor who sewed up my head thanking me for the cheque I sent him.

'Dear Captain White,

Many thanks for your cheque (£1,10s, 6d.) for fees due me. I regret the necessity that compels me to accept it; as I realize you are in a very gratuitous if not a thankless position on behalf of men kept in a condition of depravity.

Yours truly,
Seymour Stritch.

And I regret the necessity that compels me to this day to get into 'very gratuitous if not thankless positions.

CHAPTER 28.
AN EASTER BENEDICTION

The case was put back for trial at the Assizes.

The preparation for it was wearisome and costly, and I was bored with the whole thing before the case came on.

This time I engaged a Unionist to be my counsel, feeling rightly, as the event proved, that a Unionist would put up a better fight than a 'Cawstle Cawtholic' lawyer. The latter were all too afraid of the suspicion of pronounced national views interfering with their prospects.

Cecil Fforde, my counsel, put up a magnificent fight and got the sympathy of the jury from the first. The civil servant, O'Connor, who had seen Michael Wolfe club me over the head as I was being dragged into the station, proved invaluable. He gave his evidence reluctantly, but his very reluctance made it the more telling. I began to feel sorry for the police; they were shown up as such inhuman brutes; for there was some-thing in what O'Connor said to me:

'After all; White, you were fighting like a bull.'

Lord Justice Molony, who tried the case, was suave and courteous throughout. After two or three days of it a proposal took shape, whether originating with Molony or the opposing counsels I forget, that the charges against me and my counter-charges against the police should both be dropped with expression of mutual apology and regret. The case had already run me into about £70. There was no more fun in the thing. I am not a vindictive nature, and something in me disliked all this fuss about a good fight, in which I had not been exactly a sacrificial lamb.

I agreed to the compromise. Molony made a speech which was a sort of Easter benediction. It was Easter, of course; everything in Ireland culminates at Easter; which fits in with my vision of Ireland's destiny. You know my views about time, the hidden dimension, showing the inner connection of things outwardly distinct. Anyhow, both from natural kindliness and boredom with this legal aftermath of a good fight, I was disposed to show a Christian spirit. Inspector Purcell and I had been good friends all through, though he was the only one of the policemen I had damaged badly enough for a bandage. When the compromise was agreed to, Purcell came up to me in court and said I'd have to give him the shillelagh. Some wag had tied a green bow on it where it lay on the judge's table, the sole 'exhibit.' 'All right,' said I, 'there it is.' 'Oh, that won't do at all, captain,' said he, you'll have to present it to me with proper ceremony.' So I picked up the shillelagh and handed it to Purcell with a little bow. God Save Ireland.

I was blamed by my own side for weak good nature and waste of the opportunity to score a decisive victory over the police. But then my own side were not shelling out some £10 a day for the case

Jim Larkin comments on the situation with his usual trenchancy in the following article. I think there is no mistaking his style. His attitude to me is psychologically continuous with the Union Jack incident. He does not like anyone to steal his thunder.

'If ever a case proved the foulness attached to the administration of the law in this country, Captain White's case surely proved it up to the hilt. We can quote thirty cases of alleged assault against the police by men locked out during the last-dispute. Alleged assaults, we repeat, when the men charged - common workmen -got two and three months as an average sentence, no option. One case we know of - the man charged got seven months; witnesses swore this man was working nearly half a mile from the scene of the alleged assault! It mattered not! The law, moryah! must take its course. We say because Captain White is Captain White he is allowed to go free. It was proved he struck an officer of the law. He actually presented Purcell with the stick he struck Purcell with. We have counsel repeating and admitting Captain White maybe was justified in calling Superintendent Quinn a b - y hound. That is a libel on the hound; Quinn is a sanguinary cur. And the puny place-hunter and carpetbagger, Molony, talks of an Easter benediction. What hypocrisy! When this Christian gentleman, disappointed at not being able to assume the black cap in Daly's case, bided his time, allowed Captain White and his counsel to turn the court into a theatre and enact a farce. But what a change when a poor, hard-working man who honestly admitted he had committed a common assault on a scab who was taking the bread and butter from the children of Daly's comrades! This Daniel! Yea, a wise young judge; a judge who knows on which side his bread is buttered; a judge who would be in the obscurity of a

briefless barrister - an obscurity he would well adorn but for the foulness of political life in this unfortunate country; this Daniel drops the mask. No benediction, but takes away from two long Daly's children and wife their breadwinner for years. This Catholic Christian gentleman!'
And so on. . . .
My own attitude is expressed in the following letter to my mother: -

'Standard Hotel,
Harcourt Street,
DUBLIN, 16th *April.*
My darling Mother,
Thank you for your letter the other day. I don't quite take your view of the settlement of the case. I think I had the police beat and no jury would have convicted me, but on the other hand they might have disagreed, and in any case each day the case dragged on was costing me heavily.
The general opinion seems to be that I scored a moral triumph. I don't believe any honest man can keep clear of prison at least once, but when I do go in I want to be sure of its having the maximum of moral effect. It is only a matter of time till I rally all the progressive and honest forces in Ireland, a long time maybe, but it will come.
Dollie and I and Larkin motored to Bray in the car last night and held an open-air meeting there to extend the Citizen Army. Larkin spoke like a man inspired, and Dollie was very much impressed with him, but says she is not going to be carried away till she has seen more of him, in which I commend her prudence. We have been having the most gorgeous weather, each day finer than the last. Dollie is very fit. We went one night to the Abbey Theatre with the Misses Yeats, the sisters of the poet, and met Yeats himself, who had just returned from America. The principal activity I am now engaged in is a campaign to spread the Citizen Army. I think it will result in compelling the National Volunteers to cease from their suspicious aloofness from anyone connected with Labour and draw together the Middle Class and Labour National Movements, if it cannot succeed as a Labour National Movement alone.
Your loving son,
Jack. '

To draw together the Labour and National elements in Ireland was not and is not possible.

A common emotion of patriotism cannot reconcile a concrete and fundamental antagonism of interest and objective.

The most pure-souled Nationalists in Ireland, who do not belong to the ranks of Labour, are not freed by their purity of soul from the necessities of their body.

If they live by hiring the labour of others instead of selling their own, they will tend inevitably to hire it as cheap as they can; and the worker who has his labour to sell will tend to do so as dear as he can. The two opposing interests cannot blend. They may combine to kick out foreign interference preparatory to having a straight fight between themselves. This as much as they can do and, what in point of fact, they did.

CHAPTER 29.
DERRY AND DONEGAL

I have already forecasted my resignation from command of the Citizen Army. When the strike was over, the Transport Union had leisure to realize that an uncontrolled military dictator in its midst needed a check. A committee was appointed to assist, advise, and shepherd me. I am not easy to shepherd yet; then I was impossible. After a few meetings of the committee the storm broke. I don't remember even what the particular point of rupture was, very likely something affecting my personal vanity. If it had been an important point of principle, I would have remembered.

I turned to Connolly saying: 'All you'll do will be to destroy my work,' and to Sean O'Casey, who was secretary of the committee, saying: 'And it's all your fault'; what I alleged to be his fault I forget. Then I marched out of the room, a free man, to spread myself with the rapidly spreading Irish National Volunteers; say rather a swollen-headed young ass looking for limelight in a movement with which spiritually I had little or nothing in common. Perhaps I am too hard - on myself. I was looking for scope for my abounding energy as much as limelight. That is no excuse, though; the hardest thing in life and the most valuable is to control congested energy till one gets exactly the right line. The Irish National Volunteer Movement had no definite ideals and no definite objective. I was a blind leader of the blind. I won't go as far as a remark once made to me by Bishop, later Cardinal O'Donnell, that the whole movement was 'a vulgar and too late imitation of Carsonism, but the movement as a whole proved its lack of solidity of purpose by the evaporation of 95 per cent of it. The remaining 5 per cent made the 16 rising and beat the Black and Tans. I got plenty of scope and limelight. I had big commands. In Derry I organized and commanded a brigade of men, mostly old soldiers, which I brought to a parade efficiency almost equal to the Brigade of Guards.

Derry was a powder mine at the time. Once a week at least I would be called out of bed by an orderly with some report that 'the other sort' (the Orangemen) were mobilizing for a secret attack on the Catholic

Quarter. By sifting and dissipating these false rumours, I preserved the peace, but I did not make myself popular.

There was one incident where I almost incurred an open mutiny by resisting this atmosphere of neurotic mutual suspicion that might easily have led to open conflict.

A battalion of ours was out for the day at a place called Molennan some miles out of the city. Separated from them by a few fields was a battalion of Unionist Volunteers. I was reviewing another of our battalions across the river on what is called the Waterside, when a police inspector came up to me during the review and said he wanted to speak to me urgently. He told me that a third battalion of ours was marching out to the support of the one encamped at Molennan; it was almost certain the Unionist battalion, seeing our people reinforced, would assume the object of the reinforcement was to attack them. Needless to say, our battalion had marched out on some rumour that attack was contemplated by the Unionists.

The inspector begged me to come at once and turn back our battalion marching out.

I thanked him for his information and told him I would certainly do as he suggested. I was furious at the breach of discipline involved in the marching out of the extra battalion without orders from me.

I told the inspector to get into my car with me and we started in pursuit. Probably I committed an error of tact in taking the inspector with me. For the moment he was my ally in motive in wishing to prevent a conflict, which would have had most disastrous consequences to the whole cause of Irish unity and might have set Protestant and Catholic at each other's throats all over Ireland. I did not stop to think of the unfortunate symbolism of having a policeman in the car with me. It is hard for an honest boy to remember that he will never be given credit for honest motives either by friend or foe, though honest men have sooner or later to learn the terrible lesson.

We caught up with the main body of the battalion half a mile out of the city. Commandant McGlinchy, an old regular sergeant major, was in command of it. He was a fine type, but as obstinate as a mule, as indeed most Derry men are.

Knowing the advance guard was in front of him, I got out of the car and, marching beside him for a few yards, told him my opinion of his conduct. I said I was going forward to catch up and turn the advance guard, and ordered him to turn about and march back, as soon as he saw the advance guard coming back.

He was more than half inclined to be mutinous, but his sense of discipline just held. I motored on and turned the advance guard. McGlinchy turned the battalion, though I did not feel sure he would do so till it was done.

I think it was over this incident that I sent for publication in the *Derry Journal,* which published my brigade orders twice or thrice weekly, an order dismissing M'Glinchy from his command. My order did not appear. On inquiry from the paper, I found that such strong influence had been brought to bear to prevent publication that they had not dared to publish. Obviously my authority was being undermined. There were influences in Derry, as there are to this day all over Ireland, that wanted a sectarian victory, not national unity.

At last a deputation waited on me and asked me straight if it came to a fight would I fight against my own co-religionists.

I answered as straight that I would not; that I was there to keep the peace between Irishmen and combine them if I could against the English connection.

After that my command plotted against me and eventually ousted me.

Dollie was with me for a month in Derry. She worked splendidly to help me, filing my voluminous correspondence, an efficient but not a wholehearted secretary. She did not like my connection with latent rebellion, which she was psychic enough to sense.

Casement was backwards and forwards to our headquarters in Derry, and Dollie has told me since she had a waking vision of him one day as he sat in the sitting-room at McMahon's Hotel with a hangman's noose round his neck.

At the end of a month's dutiful co-operation, Dollie told me I was behaving exactly as if I was God, and soon after took herself off. I did not think of replying at the time that one had to arrogate to oneself divine powers to handle such a job.

I was brigadier, colonel, and sergeant major, and orderly room staff of four regiments, and storm centre of a delicate and dangerous political situation all at once. I even organized field days of which the *Derry*

Journal, the local Catholic paper, printed the scheme of operations and the umpire's reports in full. I was scheme-deviser and umpire. So I take it is God, though He prints nothing about His schemes or their consummation.

Years later, during the petering-out stage of the Republican Free State civil war in 1923, there was an interesting sequel to the Derry incident, which I have described.

A paragraph suddenly appeared in the *Independent* saying that I had been invited to stand as a Workers' Republican candidate for Donegal at the election then in progress.

On investigation I found that the moving spirit behind the issue of the invitation was one Boyle, stationmaster at Raphoe, who had been a member of the deputation of Derry Volunteers, to which I had given such an uncompromising reply.

Boyle had respected me for my straightness, and in the interval had come to realize the truer patriotism of my motives. Hence his fathering of the invitation to stand.

Alas! I had to disappoint him again. In the interval I myself had come to realize that the only way to over come the deep-seated damage done to the national life by the sectarian issue in Ireland was to strike at the theological root. Common labour ideals and common economic interests represented in the slogan 'Workers' Republic' were not enough in themselves alone strong enough to bridge the religious division. That division could only be healed by the healing influence of the reconciling and incarnating spirit of Christ, superseding the destructive dichotomy of the warring creeds. So I made a speech at the Mansion House in Dublin the night before going up to Donegal to accept the invitation to stand. In this speech I condemned the whole Republican physical force movement as morally and politically unsound. I said that the Free State was so morally unsound that it would have perished of its own moral rottenness, had it not been strengthened and given a false sanction as the Government of Law and Order in the panic induced by the civil war.

I spoke of my invitation to Donegal and my intention to accept it, *if* I were permitted to stand, not as a Workers' Republican, but openly as a Christian Communist, thus tending to unite the workers north and south not only in a common economic interest, but in a common and individual Christianity.

The papers containing my Mansion House speech reached Donegal before I did.

Boyle met me at his own station. He was not enthusiastic. Knowing the Catholic mind and its terror of words, I didn't expect him to be.

With a little coaxing out came his trouble: 'He'd look well gandhering about hell, because I had corrupted his soul.'

I did not stand either as a Workers' Republican or a Christian Communist. My backing melted away as I knew it would. A man who ploughs down to fundamentals sows for the future not the present. But I got in one speech in Letterkenny in which I predicted another great World War, more widespread and destructive than the last, as the inevitable consequence of the rejection of Christian principles by the whole world as the organizing principles of life.

One man at least understood me, a working farmer who came up and wrung my hand, as I refreshed myself after my oratorical effort in my friend Conal Carberry's pub.

'You told them the truth, captain, but it was too much for them; they're not fit to bear it.'

Yet they bore the last war, various civil wars, and they'll bear the next.

Men can bear anything on earth or out of hell but the effort of thinking for themselves and living out their thoughts.

CHAPTER 30.
WAR IN TYRONE

When I was ousted from Derry, I was invited immediately to take command in Tyrone. There on paper I had a force of something like ten thousand men under me. I was there with my headquarters at Omagh when the Great War broke out.

It is my reaction to the Great War I want to come to. By the time of its outbreak I was absorbed in the efficiency of the Irish Volunteers, or rather in their obvious inefficiency. My one object was to take the necessary steps to overcome it. Characteristically enough, I decided to use the Great War, if possible, for the benefit of Ireland the Irish Volunteers, and my own main objective to get them efficient.

While in Derry I had been on the point of starting a, training camp for officers as outlined in the following project published in the *Derry Journal.*

McMahon's Hotel,
East Wall, Derry.
Sir,
I understand the Irish Volunteers to aim at being a military force with a national purpose, and that their power to achieve this purpose depends on their military efficiency.

Every day's experience of the movement convinces me that the sole hope of making them a force whose efficiency and discipline will be a strength and a credit to Ireland, lies in the taking of immediate steps to overcome the natural ignorance of all matters and methods military, which almost universally obtains. No National Army worthy of the name can be formed by the reiteration of fine sentiments or the elementary training of any number of individual companies, with the supply of competent instructors and the growth of military cohesion throughout the whole force treated as negligible details.

With regard to the present dispute as to 'control' of the Irish Volunteers, I am surprised that the patriotism of Irishmen permits them to wrangle about the plans of the superstructure, while the earth is in danger of falling in on the nobly-laid foundations. Of all the paltry factions that have stood between Ireland and the fulfilment of her hopes, surely this, if permitted to continue, would be the most foolish and the most ignoble. Like most factions, too, it is utterly beside the point, for the Irish Volunteers are not yet ripe for a central control, and the men who are arguing about its constitution would be better occupied in encouraging the growth of effective military organization locally, so that the central control can be built up eventually on a sure basis representative of the volunteers themselves. If the nominal headship of a civilian secretary for war of the British Army is sometimes made matter for ridicule, surely the entrusting of the formation of an Irish army to a committee of fifty civilians, looking askance at each other's claims and motives, would be the broadest farce, if it were not certain to be of such tragic consequences to the country and the movement.

What we need now most urgently, and what we must have if the splendid outburst of a people's patriotic enthusiasm is not to be wasted and betrayed, are a score or two of organizers and instructors combined, men of energy, capacity, and initiative with the qualifications of good regimental adjutants. These men we must first create, as we do not possess them. I propose a means of doing so.

I have arranged an excellent site for a camp of instruction in Eastern Donegal, and all arrangements for the camp can be completed by the 3rd of July next. I hereby invite those willing and able to pay £2 a week for a fortnight or three weeks' course (the sum named to cover messing tent or house accommodation, and instruction) to send their names to me with the least possible delay. I will be guided chiefly by the order of receipt of applications in selecting fifty of the applicants. The site for the proposed camp contains a fine flat park for "barrack square" drill, and wood, mountain and meadowland suitable for every variety of tactical exercise. Applicants are requested to state in their replies whether they can come for three weeks or only a fortnight. I will communicate later with each of the fifty applicants selected as to the kit and equipment they should bring with them to the camp.

After a start has been made it may be found possible and advisable to extend the camp to deal with a much larger number. For the present it seems to me essential to make a start with the least possible complication or delay.

I am, yours, etc.,

J.R. White. (Captain).

I abandoned the whole scheme of the training camp after I had received enough applications to promise success. De Valera was among the first to apply. I did so because in the fight between the constitutional and revolutionary elements struggling for control of the Irish Volunteers, the constitutionalists, that is John Redmond, scored a sudden success. Up till then the volunteers had been controlled by a provisional committee of twenty-five, mostly young rebellious spirits. Redmond forced the acceptance of an equal number of his own nominees to serve with the original committee. I saw this must lead to an eventual split throughout the whole force, and called off my training camp till the split should take place. It came in October 1914, the volunteers dividing into two sections, the Irish National Volunteers (Redmondites) and the Irish Volunteers (Separatist).

When world-war broke out I was not long trying to turn it to the advantage of volunteer efficiency. The following circular letter issued by me from Omagh, County Tyrone, to various leading personalities is dated 17th August 1914, not a fortnight after the outbreak of war:

Omagh,

17th August 1914.

Dear Sir,

The one and only guarantee we can have that the Irish Volunteers become efficient and remain distinctly Irish and a genuine national force, is that they should be trained and officered by Irishmen. It is a task beyond our resources, I fear, to run and equip camps for the training of these officers ourselves. Therefore, I think we should invite Government help in a manner which I will define more specifically in a moment. Firstly, I want to make the point that we can truthfully represent to the Government that they will have an incomparably finer force for Home Defence if they help us to train the officers and send them back to us to train the men, thus preserving the magnificent spirit of the movement, which would evaporate immediately a large number of volunteers passed under purely Imperial military control. From our own point of view the advantage of getting trained officers of our own would be simply immeasurable. The old soldiers and militiamen who have now, I am glad to say, been for the most part recalled to the colours, were 95 % of them quite unfit for the task of training a Volunteer Force. Our men respond in a way that is little short of miraculous to an appeal to their collective intelligence in real military work. These old soldiers were, most of them, far from perfect in the "barrack square" drill, the petty points of which, or their confused memory of them, they were inclined to grossly over-emphasize, thus acting as stoppages to the force becoming permeated with an intelligent grasp of the essentials they must learn. There is quite a large enough percentage of smart, intelligent young fellows of some education to fill with far more ability the places vacated by the Reservists. It is of the first importance to seize the opportunity of having two thousand of them trained for a three weeks' or month's course - say a camp of five hundred in each of the provinces of Ireland. Care must be taken to select the right men. They should be paid and fed when in camp, and given travelling expenses to and fro. With encouragement through the Press and from leading men, a very large number of applicants would be obtained. These should be subjected to some preliminary test of general intelligence before acceptance as cadets, similar to the Admiralty Examination of candidates for Osborne, namely: a test of general "horse sense" and having their wits about them.

I suggest that the expense of the camps should be borne jointly by the Imperial authorities and the representatives of the Irish people, the latter paying what they can to safeguard national self-respect. The camps should be under the charge of Irish Volunteer officers, but the military authorities to have a representative present with control, if they wish, of the instructing staff, and a large say as to the hours of work, nature of course, etc. But disciplinary matters touching the cadets should be in the hands of the Irish Volunteer officers.

Of course, the normal military man will say that a course of three weeks or a month for the training of officers is no use. I deny this objection, and would beg you not to be overborne by it. Quite enough of the essentials of squad and company drill, skirmishing, musketry, and outpost duties, can be learnt in three weeks by men of intelligence eager to learn to enable them to go back to the units from which they have been drawn and leaven the whole lump.

Two thousand cadets should be able to supply an officer and someone answering to a colour-sergeant to every fifty men of a force of fifty thousand, and that is I all that is really necessary. I have found the greatest obstacle to efficient work the number of would-be instructors anxious to hear their own voices. As soon as you shut them up, the men prove that they are natural soldiers.

Six weeks, or at most two months, would, therefore, by my plan turn out enough leaders for a force of one hundred thousand men, and I suggest that the Government be asked to provide one hundred thousand stand of arms and ammunition and equipment for one hundred thousand men, arms and equipment to be issued to units as they reach a state of efficiency to satisfy a joint Irish Volunteer and Imperial Inspection Staff.

No notice should be taken of unreasonable clamour for arms to insufficiently drilled or leaderless men. On the other hand, the Irish Volunteers should know without possibility of doubt that the reward for the attainment of a certain degree of efficiency will be the issue of arms. That is my plan in outline. The Military Authorities will not, I expect, jump at it; but I believe they will take it if they are given clearly to understand they won't get anything else.

I was profoundly misunderstood. I was taken to be recruiting for Britain, whereas I was trying to use Britain to put Ireland into a position to enforce her own claims.

Some of the Sinn Fein leaders saw the sense of what I was after, and promised me support if I would do the underground work and bring the scheme to the point of materialization with British and Irish support.

Here is a letter from a priest, the finest priest and one of the finest men I ever knew, which has some bearing on the subject, though exactly what bearing I can't remember. The Moore referred to is Colonel

Maurice Moore, brother of George Moore the author. Colonel Moore was nominally in command of the whole movement.

6th September 1914.

Dear Captain White,

I was very sorry to hear in Omagh yesterday that you had been unwell. I hope you are feeling better today, and that you will soon be quite well again.

I would have replied to your letter sooner but I did not know where you were. I had left Dundalk before your letter reached me, and as I was moving about from place to place I did not get it till I returned here last Thursday. I wired you then that in my opinion your proposal to Moore was essential for the movement, but how that proposal can be carried out is not easy to see. If all the fools at headquarters could be put aside, and you and Moore act together, good work would be done in a short time, but I cannot see how this can be done at present. If a convention of one representative from each County Board in Ireland were called in Dublin, I fear it would break up in hopeless confusion. How the present deadlock is to be got over is hard to know. Were you to go on the staff as at present constituted you would be obstructed and tormented, and I fear it would not be possible for a practical man to remain long with such men. For my part, I think it would be better to try to organize a few counties, or even one county well, and thereby prove to the rest of Ireland what can be done, and then you would be in a position to dictate your own terms to the rest of Ireland. Of course there is a serious drawback to this, which you foresaw when you made your proposal to Moore, namely, that by the time one county was well organized, the movement would have died out in the rest of Ireland. From what I can see it is fast falling to pieces. It is impossible to take a bright view of it at present. !ts present state proves your statement: (a) the utter incompetency of the so-called leaders of the movement, *(b)* the incapacity of National Ireland to organize. That two or three thousand pounds should be spent on the purchase of useless and obsolete rifles while not a penny would be given for the training of officers, shows the incapacity of these men to lead such a movement, and makes Ireland a laughing-stock amongst the peoples where such arms were purchased.

The Italians are not supposed to be very up-to-date, but they must have a fine laugh at the Irish fools that bought rifles dated 1874.

By all means let us do all we can to get up the camp of instruction as soon as possible. If you can see your way through, we will do all we can to help you. The men you train in it will be loyal to you, they will recognize your ability and practicability to lead such a movement. It will be a small beginning, but out of such beginnings great things will come.

Yours very faithfully,

This priest[1], an ardent Sinn Féiner at that time and an influential man in the movement, was one of those who promised me open support, if I could bring my scheme to the point of fruition.

But no one would openly face the music. Men with a Sinn Féin outlook were not ready to court suspicion of being pro-war and pro-British, by a scheme which involved the co-operation of the British authorities. I can see now they were probably right.

It was left to me to get hooted at a Sinn Féin meeting in Dublin where I brought forward the scheme openly. I turned the hoots into a laugh by remarking that I did not believe in righteous wars (someone had sneered at England's righteous war); the last righteous war I had heard of was when I fought the Dublin police. That vindicated my rebel spirit a bit but not enough. ' For influence With Sinn Féin I was damned, and, I was elbowed out of command in Tyrone.

Before closing the Tyrone chapter, let me touch on the nature of the efforts I made to get my command efficient. I find among my records a newspaper, the *Ulster Herald* of 12th August 1914, with a great headline, 'England declares War on Germany,' in the centre of the page and my orders for a mobilization of all the volunteers of a district of Co. Tyrone in the adjoining column. With the publishers' consent I will put the latter in the appendix as illustrative of the difficulties of volunteer organization and the ambitious scale on which I was trying to achieve it. On that particular occasion I had some fifteen hundred 'mountainy' men out on a mountainside on a wet night. To get them on to the mountain I had to clear one pub myself by brute force.

[1] The writer of this letter asks me to omit his name. He says he will be a marked man in N. Ireland, where he still resides, if his name appears.

What a night it was. Contingents kept marching in long after the time appointed for the general rally. Luckily there was a farm, which did a big milk trade, just below our camping-ground. We cooked tea in huge milk cans set on turf fires till the small hours of the morning.

We enlivened the 'troops' by a singsong at which, strange mixture of those strange days, Darrell Figgis, hero of the recent Howth gunrunning, and Mrs. Noel Guinness and her daughter Margaret were present by my invitation.

Towards dawn, utterly exhausted, I tried to lie down on the mountainside and snatch a little sleep. I had given instructions for silence in camp, but there was a constant buzz of conversation round the damp-fires. The men, unused to sleeping in the open, seemed to discard all notion of sleep.

I shouted out several orders for silence. The conversation always broke out again. At last, irritated and overtaxed beyond endurance, I gave vent to a passionate tirade of abuse, so unbridled in its fury that for a while it achieved silence and permitted me a short spell of sleep.

Poor Figgis said to me next morning about this outburst of mine:

'No man ever yet spoke to Irishmen as you spoke last night, White, and lived to tell the tale. Only three things saved you - your absolute spontaneity, your unparalleled violence, and your complete and staggering unreason.' I'm afraid he was about right.

Next morning Figgis rescued me out of a very unpleasant situation. I record it gratefully. Figgis was an egotist, but so am I. On this occasion he got a friend out of a nasty fix, when he might easily have got kudos by his downfall.

I had given orders for the whole force to parade early in the morning to march to early Mass. One old dugout N.C.O. in charge of a company, with whom I had had words the previous night on account of his having 'drink taken,' came to me and objected to falling in his company. According to him it was against Catholic doctrine to do any work before going to Mass. The objection was, of course, frivolous, and meant to be obstructive. When he persisted in it, I ordered his arrest. His own company refused to act as guard on him. When I called on another company to supply a guard, his own company prepared to defend him forcibly. At this juncture Figgis interposed. He proposed that I should retire from the field for an interval and leave him to settle the matter. I did so, and on returning found that Figgis had induced the old N.C.O. to retire and pacified everybody.

We then marched to Mass. Figgis and I sat together in the gallery, of the chapel. Then we returned to our mountain and carried out manoeuvres at which I was astounded, as always, by the natural military aptitude of the men, not for barrack or camp discipline, of course, but for fieldwork. In the evening, for my part exhausted as I never remember to have been in my life before or since, we sent our volunteers packing homewards and struck a local hotel for a meal.

Figgis pinched the only sofa, so I collapsed on the floor.

CHAPTER 31.
THE WINNOWING OF WAR

The War then forced on me the necessity to choose between my two selves, or find a compromise between them -, my old self of ex-British officer and son of a British field-marshal, and my new self of rebel Irishman. The compromise I attempted was dictated by the fact that I was keen as mustard on the efficiency of the Irish Volunteers, and far from indifferent to the maintenance of my own position as the livest wire in the movement.

It is remarkable how thoroughly the great winnowing fan of the War sifted the chaff from the wheat among human souls. I write, of course from the standpoint that only those who held aloof from the War entirely can be reckoned as wheat. The Socialist or Trade Union leader who 'went wrong on the War' has never regained and never can regain his position in the trust of the revolutionary workers. So with the Irishman who succumbed to emotional influences, obscuring Ireland's rights under those of Belgium, his name is blotted henceforth off the scroll of clear-headed national thinkers. If, from the point of view of his national reputation, he was lucky enough to be killed, he is spoken of as 'poor So-and-So.' I have never heard Irishmen speak of poor Erskine Childers or poor Cathal Brugha or even poor Roger Casement. They live on in the trail they blazed with their lives.

Committed to a volunteer movement which was rapidly evaporating into the British recruiting offices, it may be asked how did I, as an ex-British officer, escape going with the tide and succumbing to influences all the stronger in my case that they were allied to the influences of my training and heredity?

The answer is that however mistaken I may have been in throwing myself into the National Volunteer Movement at all, I was faithful to the preservation of its separate Irish individuality.

I used the treatment of the Volunteer movement in England as the touchstone of England's *bona fides* in the whole question of Irish self-government.

Weighing England's action in this balance, I found it fundamentally wanting. I should have stuck to the Citizen Army, where I had the clear guidance of international revolutionary principle, undercutting and outlasting the conflict of national interests that caused the Great War. On leaving the Citizen Army I should have stood back and waited as I was ultimately compelled to do. I have confessed that I joined the National Volunteer Movement for 'scope and limelight, but as in the subalterns' court martial upon me in Edinburgh, 'on account of the youth and general imbecility of the prisoner' the sentence was remitted, and I was not condemned by taking part either in the Great War or a primarily National Rising to go back on and belie the deeper and wider motives of my life. I said a while ago that I could only permit myself to criticize Connolly by criticizing myself. I have done so in the foregoing words.

I claim no credit for my salvation. It was forced upon me bit by bit in applying the touchstone I have described. A kind though temporarily highly unpleasant fate saved me from becoming one of those strange hybrids, the imperially minded Nationalist or the nationally-minded Imperialist.

Having become badly jammed between two stools in Ireland, I crossed to England. I sent memoranda to Lord Kitchener and to Sir Ian Hamilton, and later, in default of any satisfaction from the two first, to Lord Roberts.

I give my letter to Sir Ian Hamilton as indicative of the whole burden of my song.

'The Wilderness House,
Hampton Court,
19th September 1914.
    Dear Sir Ian,
    Mother showed me your letter today, returning the cuttings which she had forwarded to you.
    If I write to you now at some length it is because I feel I have intimate first-hand knowledge of the situation in Ireland, possibly a more exact knowledge than the Irish party, who can never bring themselves to believe that any appreciable feeling exists in Ireland except that which they wish to create.
    Having written to you now I will be in a better position to appeal for your assistance if things get as critical in Ireland as I think it extremely

likely they will. Looking at things from the purely Irish stand-point, I realize that England's extremity is Ireland's opportunity in exactly the reverse sense to that in which the phrase is generally used.

It is Ireland's opportunity to train and discipline her own manhood with England's help. It is practically impossible for her to do so unaided, but till she has done so she has no instrument through which she can worthily express her own national ideal. Owing to the whole energies of the people having been absorbed for so long in a political struggle outside their direct ken, the idea of Irish Nationality is at present little but a source of profitless bickering among Irishmen as to the right means of its realization. Ireland must clearly evolve her spiritual ideal before it can be realized, and I am convinced she can only do so by such a mobilizing of her material forces as military organization would effect. But England's aid in the process must be conditioned throughout by willingness to help Ireland for Ireland's permanent, as well as England's temporary, benefit, and must therefore endeavour from the outset to evolve in Irishmen the quality of leadership. An opportunity for the concrete application of this principle is offered by the present situation, and the object of this letter is to emphasize the importance of its being recognized and acted upon.

The immediate issue between Ireland and the Empire is now the treatment of the Irish Volunteers; both stand to gain greatly by the settlement of the question in a manner satisfactory to both. The Irish political party have voluntarily come forward to impress on the Irish people their duty to co-operate with the Empire; but, and here lies the great danger, the Irish party come forward under this handicap, *that they have done nothing to promote the efficiency of the Volunteers as a self-contained organization and are suspect in the minds of many of the most virile Irishmen of having desired and still desiring the destruction of an organization which might predominate over their own.* It is surely natural and deserving of every sympathy that such a spontaneous national movement as the Irish Volunteers should be very jealous of its individuality. Had the Irish party done anything to promote the healthy growth of this individuality, so that in forming part of a vastly larger organization it might still be preserved, they could appeal now on behalf of the Empire to the Irish fighting spirit, with the certainty of commanding sympathy and success. But, as it is, it is to be expected that every hare-brained parochially-minded crank in Ireland will accuse them of dealing the death-blow to a movement which, had they been able, they would have strangled at birth. There will be enough truth in this to make the danger of the Irish fighting spirit devoting itself to self-preservation instead of expansion a very real one. It is because I believe this course of supposed self-preservation can only end in self-destruction that I hope you will do all in your power to make the measures of the military authorities compensate for the omissions of the Irish party. The crucial point is really the officering of the new Irish Force. To be in keeping with Irish aspirations the new force must be officered by Irishmen. The great disadvantage under which National Ireland labours is that only a very small minority of the Irish gentry identify themselves with her; there will therefore be few men of the class to which it is usual to look for officers available for the new force.

This leaves the authorities confronted with two alternatives: the drafting in of young Englishmen of good social position, or the concentration of effort on the creation of officers from the ranks of the new force. I venture to prophesy that this will be the point on which the success or failure of recruiting for the new force will be found to hang.

I enclose a letter I have just received from the best man I know in Ireland, a priest called Father -, who has worked with me untiringly for the efficiency of the Irish Volunteers in his district. The "camp" he refers to is a camp of instruction for officers which I have been unceasingly advocating should be started by ourselves in the interval of waiting for the Government's action. But it was hopeless to get anything done under the existing control of the Irish Volunteers. The Provisional Committee supposed to be responsible is universally discredited, and all its own members worth anything advocate its destruction. At the last meeting the members actually drew revolvers at one another. But it is capable of a tremendous lot of mischief, and may infect the whole country with its personal factions.

But to return, a guarantee on the part of the Government that officers from its own ranks would be trained simultaneously with the new force would, I believe, relieve the situation of its greatest element of danger. In Tyrone, where I have been in command, I could put forward twenty or thirty young fellows whom I have myself selected, and to whom I have given some instruction.

In that county I have had mobilization, field days, and classes of instruction. I don't think any serious attempt towards efficiency has been made anywhere else except Cork, Limerick, and Dublin, and to some extent Derry. I suggest that the officers might be selected partly by observation in the first drills, partly by an examination in general intelligence such as I understand the candidates for the Navy undergo. I can answer for it there are plenty of men of the right stamp, quick intelligence and imagination and much military aptitude. All they want is confidence in themselves to make them better officers than the kind of callow youths we'd be likely to get from outside.

I think it is my duty to impress on you, asking you to make only such guarded use of it as you think fit, my conviction that it is not a question of merely the failure or success of a recruiting campaign. It is a question of Ireland actively loyal or actively disloyal. There was a tremendous amount of enthusiasm and potential energy generated by the Irish Volunteers. This will not simply evaporate in the event of the failure of Redmond's campaign. It will turn into a more violently bitter anti-English feeling than ever before. The Irish Volunteers came into being to exert a force in support of Home Rule equal to or greater than Carson's force exerted against it. I think Redmond will find it hard to satisfy them with the Home Rule settlement as they realize that Carson will be in a far stronger position than ever to nullify it at the end of the war. They may not exactly realize what Home Rule is going to do for them but the desire for it is a consuming passion. Unless by wise and generous handling they can be induced to advance towards the real attainment of Home Rule by service to the Empire, no consideration of its impossibility will, I believe, prevent them from trying to get by the wildest means what they think they have been cheated of in the constitutional struggle. There are not wanting men who preach the most thorough-going treason, and there is practically no limit to the fantastic conceits which an Irish crowd can be got to pin its faith to, when its national pride and bitterness is played on. The men who trade in the bitterness of the past for the gratification of their own vanity can be silenced once and for all now by care and judgment. Once allow them to get a seeming modern instance of England's treachery, and repression of their propaganda or themselves would only fan the flame of suspicion and discontent.

I may exaggerate the tendencies I have observed in Ireland in the interval between Redmond's speech in the House offering Irish Volunteers and the present. They have taken no shape, but they might. The reception of Redmond's manifesto will show how things are going, but if there is a hitch, I hope you will take steps to make the views expressed in this letter known in the right quarters, as I know that by wise action the difficulties can be removed.

Yours sincerely,

J. R. White.

I sent a shorter memorandum to the same effect to Kitchener. The memoranda to Kitchener and Ian Hamilton bear the same date.

This document is not entirely sincere. It was no good telling a British general who ultimately put my views before Asquith, the British Prime Minister, that I was seeking a practical guarantee against England defrauding Ireland of all she had promised her. I was trying to be diplomatic. Admitted it doesn't suit me. I was doing my best.

Sincere or not, the document is unquestionably prophetic.

From September I 9 I 4 to Easter 1916 is some twenty months. That period before the Dublin Easter Rising I could write to Ian Hamilton, 'It is not a question of merely the failure or success of a recruiting campaign. It is a question of Ireland actively loyal or actively disloyal. There was a tremendous amount of enthusiasm and potential energy generated by the Irish Volunteers. This will not simply evaporate in the event of the failure of Redmond's campaign. It will turn into a more violently bitter anti-English feeling than ever before.

How did I know this? I sensed it with my cursed sixth sense. And I tried to wangle a compromise out of Destiny, which, as I said in reference to Casement further back in this book, can never be done. Destiny mangles the would-be wangler and wrings him clean.

Kitchener answered me briefly: 'It is impossible to give official sanction to what you suggest.' Ian Hamilton was very helpful and sympathetic. On receipt of my letter he asked me to come and see him.

He was then Commander-in-Chief of the three armies of Territorials called the Central Striking Force, and he seemed enthusiastic about the idea of a big fresh contingent being created. He weighed what from his point of view was the risk that when created they might turn against the British, but said that war was always a matter of taking risks and this was a good risk. Here I could sincerely agree. with him. I had as little desire for the Irish contingent to turn against the British as he had. I wanted an Irish Army officered by *Irish Irelanders* to defend Irish rights. Let the British train it for us and get their quid pro quo in what voluntary service units the natural fighting spirit of Irishmen would provide. Better for us, I thought, and better for them than what I sensed was bound to happen otherwise.

I knew Ian Hamilton had imagination. I had hung his coat up once when he came to lunch with my mother, and feeling a book in the pocket had pulled it out to see his taste in literature. It was *The Pilrim's Progress* - Bunyan I had thought at the time was incompatible with the more callous bunions of the military mind.

By good luck Sir Ian had a chance of speaking to Mr. Asquith after dinner within a few nights of our interview.

He wrote me: 'I met Mr. Asquith at dinner and told him of your keenness to raise a big force of Irish Volunteers exactly on the lines of our own Territorial force, i.e. without any obligation to go abroad or do military work beyond the defence of Ireland. I told him you were confident that if we did so, we could raise a considerable army and I added from myself that I was sure once that Irish Army was in being, we would be able to get them, first, to come over and complete their training with my central striking force; secondly, to volunteer for service abroad. Asquith, though he took up his favourite *non-possumus* attitude, shook his head somewhat sadly, I thought, as he replied, "Hors la loi," as if that ended it all. I suppose it does for a lawyer.'

Put brutally, my reaction to this letter of Sir Ian's now is that if Asquith had had as much imagination as Hamilton they could easily have fooled me and fooled Ireland. I would have had little cause of complaint, for I suppose at bottom I was trying to fool them. The relations between England and Ireland could not then and cannot yet be those of mutual trust. Hamilton wanted his central striking force to be increased, and was ready to take a chance in deflecting the patriotism of Irishmen to his purpose. I wanted my central defending force to be increased, and to be made capable of striking if England tried to double-cross us. It is as natural for men to draw other men into their own purpose as for a magnet to draw iron filings.

I see now that the risks and results of the '16 rising were preferable to this British trained force. Ian Hamilton was right. Trained and equipped with British help they would have 'come over to complete their training' and no doubt volunteered for service in the Antipodes. If not, means would have been found of despatching them there without consulting their volition.

The blunter intelligence of a great Figure saved me from prostituting mine. Sir Ian has told me since that when shortly after his interview with Asquith he saw Kitchener on the same subject, he encountered, not sad shakings of the head, but bedrock opposition. With startling energy Kitchener declared he would not trust one single Irishman with a rifle in his hand one single yard, and that he made no exception in the case of Redmond or anyone else. Kitchener is dead and so are Connolly, Pearse, and Casement. I am alive. I state the full facts to establish that the British at any rate had no right to shoot or hang me, though I don't imagine they would have hesitated had I happened to be in Dublin around Easter 1916. From Asquith's sadness and Kitchener's severity, Sir Ian passed to talk to Lord Roberts. Here it was a case of 'almost thou persuadest me.' I have it from Sir Ian that Bobs was certainly attracted by the idea, which is verified by facts I give elsewhere. It only carried him a step further in a project he had already envisaged of going over personally and carrying on a big recruiting campaign. Now he seemed almost prepared to consider whether he might not undertake the whole supervision of recruiting equipment and training of a great Irish Volunteer Army. But before deciding anything he said there were two men he must consult. From something he said Sir Ian was sure that one was Lord Milner. The other (according to Sir Ian's surmise) was probably either Sir Henry Wilson or Mr. Brodrick. Anyway, about a fortnight later Sir Ian met him again, and he (Bobs) had definitely made up his mind to turn down the whole project, lock, stock, and barrel. With no knowledge of Sir Ian's efforts at the time I myself turn to Lord Roberts.

I write to my mother from Hotel Metropole, Dublin, on 7th October.

Hotel Metropole,
Dublin, 7th October.

My Darling Mother,

I have written by same post as this a most important letter to Lord Roberts to Englemere. I told him of my previous intention to interview him, and my eventual decision not to do so.

Strictly private. Sir Horace showed me a letter from him (Bobs) today in which he proposes to come over to this country for a recruiting campaign. My letter to him is to dot the i's and cross the t's of Sir Horace's reply to him pointing out the dangers and difficulties of the situation here, yet emphasizing my belief that he is the one man who could save it under certain conditions. *I have not, of course, mentioned my knowledge of his correspondence with Sir Horace,* but harked back to my own previous intention. I mentioned being dissuaded by the emphasis laid by "my mother and others" on the improbability of his accepting Home Rule as a fait accompli and associating himself in the National Volunteers.

What I want you to do now, and what I hope you will not let anything prevent your doing, is to write him verifying my previous intention of seeing him, and dilating in your own manner on my intimate knowledge of the feeling in Ireland, and such inducements to him to throw himself into the subject with a reliance on my information as you can supply.

This is the last chance for the real welding of England and Ireland, and I believe I'm the only man who can understand how it is to be done and carry it into execution.

If this fails, things will go with a run the other way, and as I'm an Irishman first I shall probably go with them.

Your loving,
Jack.

On 31st October 1914 Bobs writes to my mother:

'Englemere,
Ascot, Berks,
31st October 1914.

My Dear Lady White,

Yes, your son did write to me, on a subject upon which he and I had some correspondence a short time ago, and I quite understood how impossible it was for him to remain on in Ireland under the present atmosphere of politics. I would have responded to his call to go to Ireland had I felt there was the slightest chance of his being able to do any good, but from what I heard from every one in Ireland of whom I knew enough to write to, I was satisfied that it was a hopeless task to undertake, and I most reluctantly gave it up.

I trust Jack will get on well now in the work which I understand he has undertaken on the Continent.

Please forgive a typewritten letter.

From yours very sincerely, Roberts.

CHAPTER 32.
PARIS AND PRISON

I write to my mother: 'If this fails, things will go with a run the other way, and as I'm an Irishman first I shall probably go with them.'

I wish to qualify this statement. I am not an Irishman first. I am a human being first, a very violent, affectionate, God-fearing, law-abhorring human being. I am more an Irishman than an Englishman, because I believe in the function of the Irish race to resist being mechanized.

I knew in my bones before it spread to my mind the truth of Freud's words written during the Great War.

'The individual in any given nation has in this War a terrible opportunity to convince himself of what would occasionally strike him in peace time, that the state has forbidden to the individual the practice of wrong-doing, not because it desired to abolish it, but because it desires to monopolize it, like salt and tobacco. The warring state permits itself every such misdeed, every such act of violence as would disgrace the individual man. (' Freud, 'Thoughts on War and Death.'- Collected Papers.)

My real vision of the future Ireland was - dare I say is? - a state that shall rise above the monopoly of wrongdoing to become the organic collective expression of free individuals. I have tried to hint at that ideal from time to time throughout this book. That is why I quoted O'Casey about Sheehy Skeffington's death and prolonged the story of my Derry Volunteer command to include my offer to stand for Donegal as a Christian Communist.

When I saw the British military and political powers were incapable of conceiving the idea of Irish independence, let alone of giving it practical recognition in their treatment of the Volunteers, I got an ambulance body on my Ford two-seater, at my own expense, and went out to France with an Australian Ambulance Unit.

As said unit seemed destined to stick about Boulogne, I quietly deserted it one night and drove to Dunkirk. I never needed much training in resistance to being mechanized. At Dunkirk I got an introduction to some Belgian general and authorization from him to join the Belgian forces right at the front. My passes were a bit shaky. I thought it advisable to proceed to take up my new duties under cover of dark.

The road from Dunkirk to Furnes had a number of sod-barriers built across it blocking direct passage. In front of me was a car driven by two French officers going at a great pace. It struck one of the sod-barriers at about forty miles per hour, and I cannoned into the back of the Frenchman's car. I smashed my radiator to scrap. My poor Ford was towed home by an artillery lorry. and I was left kicking my heels at Dunkirk, while a new radiator came out from home.

It was during this interval I noticed that I was being cold-shouldered. It became so marked that I inquired from Holland, who was, I think ' representing the British Red Cross Society, if he could give any explanation of it. He told me straight my position was causing comment and mixed up with the comment were remarks about my connection with Irish rebel or potentially rebel armies and Sir Roger Casement. Casement was by then (1915) in Germany on the mission that ended so fatally for himself. In short; if I wasn't suspected of being a spy, I soon might be.

I waited for my radiator. I believe Dollie accompanied it across from England and nursed for a while with her usual splendid efficiency at the Duchess of Sutherland's hospital in Dunkirk.

For a time I fetched carloads of blasted humanity off the 'wounded' trains and distributed them round the Dunkirk hospitals. I saw enough to intensify my instinctive loathing of the whole filthy mechanical slaughter - yes, and my contempt for the mentality that could accept it as all in the day's work. I wanted to get outside, above it all, get behind the roots of the filthy thing in the human mind and soul.

With the complete freedom of movement I seem always to have assumed to myself, I got Dollie's agreement to the plan, and we drove in the now restored Ford ambulance to Paris.

Dollie was dressed as a nurse, I in some kind of a uniform that suggested a British officer. We saw the 'sights of Paris' for a few days, taking up our quarters in a little hotel off the Rue Bonaparte on the left bank. Then Dollie remarked: 'The fact is, Jack, we're a couple of frauds.' We were. Conscious of our fraudulence, she went back to her mother at Gibraltar. I divested myself of the hybrid uniform, and began to build a philosophy of life on a foundation of the reckoning saucers at the Dome and the Rotonde. This means that they bring you a saucer with each drink, and then count the saucers to reckon the score. Here I was, then; in the Paris Latin Quarter within occasional sound of the guns. But the War was over for me, or at least outside me. Its disturbance of my consciousness was finished so far as any question of my participation was concerned.

Arthur Lynch, the man who was tried for treason for commanding the Irish Brigade with the Boers, met me in Paris about this time in the circle of Maud Gonne. whose 'apartment' in Passy was my chief resort. He reminded me recently of some verses of mine, written during the Paris interlude, which had tickled his fancy:

Now goodness only knows
Why it snows
In the latter end of March
When the larch
Greener grows.

I am very glad I'm drunk
And have sunk
An infinity of drink
And of ink
For a monk.

In a word, I was leading the contemplative life, trying to get behind the roots of the war in my own personality as a preliminary to discovering its root-cause in humanity. The drink was only an aid to quiet my surface-mind and open my sub-conscious. I have never drunk to get drunk, always to get sober. In some trepidation I give the key I found to the root-cause of war.

It came to me through a little love affair, slight in itself; but having tremendous consequences in my subsequent mental life.

I met a young American artist and his wife, Harriet Bruce we will call her. The husband was an excellent chap, a passionate idealist in his own line. He had thrown up a position in the States as an architect of rising fame to come to Paris and study the Gauguin, Van Gogh school of painting. He painted all day and all night, and his wife sat as his

228

model. Neither of them spoke a word of French. They had not a single friend till they met me. The husband felt no need of any. The wife did. The affair was perfectly open. Its results were so obviously beneficial that within a fortnight of its commencement the husband thanked me for saving him from unconscious murder. For Harriet, utterly absorbed in the husband's life, with none of her own, had been on the verge of nervous collapse. She gained over a stone in weight and became a natural sociable woman. Then all three of us went off together for a walking tour in Cantal. Later Harriet left the husband painting in Paris, and went back to some American university to study for a career of her own.

There can be no doubt that marriage is a very frequent field for the surrender or suffocation of the soul, a kind of psychic cannibalism, in which one of the parties devours the other, or the cannibalism may be mutual. Many women enter it either for subsistence or to escape from the restricted scope of the family. Many men stay in it from weakness or fear of public opinion, suffocated, deviated, in all but name murdered, by a wife who takes them right out of their natural bent and renders impossible the expression of their natural personality. Families founded on such marriages perpetuate and intensify the destructive in-growing energy. As I thought and reflected and observed, I became convinced that in-growing love, or so-called love, and outgoing exploding hate were in direct ratio the one to the other. The ultimate root of war was not hate, for what hate was there in these cattle driven to mechanical slaughter of each other? Greed there might be in the drovers, but that greed again was at bottom greed for life, greed for love. Behind all, there was love, life-energy simply unable to express itself in the present state of organized society. The economic causes of war were potent and glaring, but behind them lay a moral competition and a moral possession. Men competed for women mentally unready to be the arbiters of their own fate, and possessed women unable and unwilling to possess themselves. I saw humanity as a bird with one wing, attacking itself as a crippled bird is attacked by the flock. Women were not yet functioning as free individuals. The War would ultimately cure the root evil which had caused it by completing the freeing of women, which it had begun; but that completion would pass far beyond the political and economic emancipation.

I saw the free woman remodelling and expanding the narrow isolated family which embodied her possessed status.

God ordained the family! Of course He did, since it exists. But why limit the divine inventiveness to this very faulty institution? This was the kind of platitude by which high dignitaries of Church and State disguised their bankruptcy of any vision or creative imagination. The family is the source of life! Certainly, and a stream cannot rise above its source. Therefore if the stream runs turgid; if there isn't fall enough to generate power, have a look at the source.

We will now jump forward to 1916. Things have 'gone with a run the other way,' and I 'as an Irishman first' have definitely gone with them. In short, I am arrested in the South Wales coalfield for trying to get the Welsh miners out on strike. Why? To save Jim Connolly being shot for his share in the Easter Rising in command of the Citizen Army. Had I succeeded I would have crippled the coal supply for the British Fleet.

I failed. The very day, I believe, of my arrest, Connolly was strapped in a chair wounded, and shot by a firing squad. He prayed with his last words for all brave men who do their duty. I got three months in Swansea jail. A week before conclusion of my sentence I was transferred to Pentonville the night before Roger Casement was hanged. To point the moral, I was placed in the prison hospital which was fifty yards from the hanging shed. The hospital authorities were very kind. They allowed me to exercise at will in the hospital compound. Ten yards the other side of a low chain rail was Roger Casement's grave. It was not the Government's intention, but Casement and I were reconciled, even united, at last.

I have said a lot about myself, little of other people's opinion of me. How can I close better than by a sympathetic and disinterested opinion from an outsider of eminent respectability.

Sir Horace Plunkett writes to my mother, dated 22nd May 1916, on hearing of my arrest in Wales.

Plunkett House,
Dublin, 22nd May 1916.
Dear Lady White,
I have heard with much sorrow that your son has been arrested for some conduct which I take to be regarded as, technically, treasonable. I think it ought to be known that, at the beginning of the War, he did his utmost to get the Irish Volunteers, with whom he was personally connected. to regularize their position and to come under Government discipline and control. In other public matters I have always found him to be absolutely disinterested and zealous for public service; but, unfortunately, he is so impulsive that when anything excites him, he is hardly responsible for his actions.
You are at liberty to make any use you like of this letter.
Believe me,
Yours sincerely,
Horace Plunkett.'

A bad trait that, to lose responsibility for one's actions when excited. There's only one thing worse, to lose the power of getting excited. Thank God, I haven't lost that.

I find life increasingly -painful, but increasingly exciting. It begins to be shot with streaks of a strange joy that might even become peace.

I would like to tell you more about that. Now I must take hounds home for the day. I am only nominally master of this hunt.

Warrior, Rover, and Rebel have given tongue, but we have done little more than whip on to the line. It's a job getting on to the right line in life. It takes a good few casts. There are the scurrying rabbits and the timid hares. There are illusory beauty, false romance, partial deceptive ideals. I am reminded of the words of the old huntsman in Punch - "Ow can 'ounds 'unt with all them stinkin' flowers?'

Some day I want to follow up the line we have found clear of cover.

Captain Jack White 1879-1946

White Hall, The Family Home

MISFIT 2.
BY PHIL MEYLER

"I have the strongest and deepest objection to the all too common Irish habit of breaking a man's heart by misunderstanding him while he is alive and canonising him as soon as he is dead. I might almost say, because he is dead."

(Where Casement Would Have Stood Today, 1936. Jack White)

Misfit traces Jack White's life up to 1916. His life after that is somewhat sketchy. He went off to France as part of an ambulance crew in late 1915 for The First World War. It was here that he heard of the ill-fated 1916 Easter Rising and returned to Ireland immediately and was active in the campaign to oppose the execution of the 1916 leaders. In April 1916 he was arrested in south Wales for attempting to organise a miners' strike in support of his erstwhile friend, James Connolly. He was charged under the Defence of the Realm and jailed for sedition, being transferred to Pentoville prison in London on the eve of Casement's execution.

White wrote *"The Significance of Sinn Féin"* in 1918, a short pamphlet that attempted to explain the political and parliamentary success of Sinn Féin in the aftermath of the execution of the Rising leaders. However, increasingly influenced (like many of his contemporaries) by the news of the successful Russian Revolution, his politics moved sharply leftward.

After a series of arrests and prison terms for agitating (Dublin 1920, Edinburgh 1921) he was proposed as a candidate 'in the interests of the Workers' Republic' for Donegal in the 1922 Free State elections. At this time Donegal was a hotbed of worker militancy and political struggle and possibly could have won a seat but White soon withdrew his candidature, declaring he was a 'Christian Communist'. He declared that 'he was not prepared to go forward as the representative of any class or party, but only on the principle of voluntary change to communal ownership of the land and the gradual withering of the poisoned branches of standing armies, prisons and the workhouse system.' It was not quite what the Donegal electorate wanted to hear.

Jack White, throughout the 1920s, was active in a host of organisations including *The Irish Workers League* and *The Workers Party of Ireland*, moving between Dublin, London and Belfast and now clearly identified himself with left republican politics. A regular public speaker, he also wrote for many publications including *An Phoblacht*. In 1930, his autobiography, *Misfit* was published in London by Jonathan Cape and is an invaluable insight, from the point of view of one active participant, into the history of this period.

Jack White was active in the *Revolutionary Workers Party* in Belfast in the early 30s. In 1931, he was involved in a bitter street battle between unemployed workers and the RUC on the Newtownards Road in Belfast where he was arrested and his Crown Court appearance was widely covered in the media. After being found guilty and imprisoned, he was served with an exclusion order under the 1922 Special Powers Act (Northern Ireland) prohibiting him from residing in any part of Northern Ireland other than in the district of Limavady. The exclusion order caused him considerable distress not least because his daughter Avé, from his first marriage, was then at school in Belfast. This Order remained in force until 1935.

In the mid-30s White gravitated to the *Republican Congress* and was associated with the ex-Serviceman's section in Dublin. Here he was a familiar figure to many contemporary activists including Peadar O'Donnell and Frank Ryan. In 1934, he took part in the now famous march to the Wolfe Tone monument in Bodenstown as a part of a contingent from the Protestant Shankill Road in Belfast, carrying a banner that proclaimed *'Break The Connection with Capitalism.'* The IRA prevented the contingent from attending the commemoration.

At the age of 57, in 1936, White travelled to Spain (as part of a Red Cross ambulance crew) to help fight Fascism. Here he made contact with the members of the Anarchist CNT-FAI and POUM, just as Orwell had done, as described in *Homage To Cataluna*. White was forceful and always pushed himself up to the front line and insisted on meeting everyone of any interest to him. Impressed by the social revolution that was unfolding in Spain, he was further attracted to the Anarchist cause and especially the CNT-FAI, though criticised their decision to enter the Popular Front Government in 1936. He wrote the short pamphlets *"The Meaning of Anarchy"* (1937) and *"Anarchism –A Philosophy of Action"* (1937) in order to explain the background to the May '37 street battles and the struggles between the workers, the POUM-CNT and the

Communist Party members in Barcelona, a struggle which has been depicted quite well in the Ken Loach film *"Land and Freedom."*

In December 1936, the Socialist Party of Cataluna (PSUC) (Communist) which had shared power with the anarchist CNT-FAI in the Popular Front Valencia Government had declared their intention to do away with the duality of power which existed in Cataluna where armed militias had taken control of the streets and certain strategic public buildings and wanted to return control to the National Republican Guard (police) and the Assault Guards. Armed militias erected barricades and a General Strike was called which spread all over Barcelona. The anarchist Minister in the Popular Front Central Government, Garcia Oliver, called for an end to the barricades and the CNT and UGT as well as the Trotskyst POUM (which did not want to alienate the CNT, their conduit to the Valencia Government) called on the workers to return to work.

Only some small organisations, like The Friends of Durutti, named after Buenaventura Durruti, the skillful militant anarcho-syndicalist and military tactician who had been killed in the attempt to save Madrid from the assault of Franco's army, (Anarchist) and some elements of the IV International (Trotskyst) acting alone, joined the barricades, against the orders of these organisations. They were nicknamed 'The Uncontrollables'. For almost a week Barcelona was in the hands of its inhabitants when the Stalinists sent in 5,000 Assault Guard troops resulting in 15,000 deaths, thousands of wounded, the banning of POUM and the CNT and the end of the revolution.

White was radical in his Anarchism, as he had been radical in all else. He wrote in *The Meaning of Anarchism*, republished below; "So I must perforce be an uncontrollable...An uncontrollable is an anarchist who has stuck to Anarchy and who is not, therefore, primarily, concerned with the shades or strata of Capitalism but with revolution by direct action; who believes with Marx that the emancipation of the workers must be the work of the workers themselves and with Bakunin and Kropotkin and Maletesta that free humanity must be substituted for the State and that when Anarchists take part in a Government, they allow themselves to be deflected from their proper task and become corrupted by association with the instrument of tyranny. The first false step in Spain was the association of Anarchist leaders with the Government and the State. Had they given all their energies to co-ordination and unified command of CNT Collectives and Anarchist military units, instead of sacrificing Anarchist principles and control to compromises with a Government, the uncontrollables would have remained in control of themselves and ready for co-ordinated action with other sections instead of being sacrificed to a State dictatorship through a political party." It was about this period that he had written his second part of Misfit and it is a shame that no legacy of this is available today.

Jack White was unlucky in marriage; he was married twice, both to middle-class devote Catholic women. His arguments with his wives are infamous and renowned. It was an unfortunate and contradictory side to his troubled life that he never found a proper soul mate; a protestant looking for the nationalist Catholic wife who could temper his aristocratic background; he was a military captain to the end. These were his personal failures. The only thing is that he admitted them and criticised himself for them.

Returning to London from Spain in 1937, he worked with '*Spain and the World*', a libertarian propaganda group active in Britain in support of the Spanish anarchists. While in London, he met his second wife, Noreen Shanahan, the daughter of an Irish government official, while attending the same Spanish language school. Noreen Shanahan came from a well off south county Dublin family and was a practising Catholic. They had three children together, Anthony, Derrick and Alan.

However at the time of his death, White had completed a second part of his autobiography, a Misfit 2. Moreover, Albert Meltzer who knew White from his days with '*Spain and The World*', states that White, around 1937-8 worked with Matt Kavanagh, a Liverpudlian anarchist of Irish extraction, on a 'survey of Irish labour and Irish aspirations in relation to anarchism'. In the same article Meltzer also mentions 'White's study of the little known Cork "Soviet"', which was influenced by his exposure to the workers self-management movement in revolutionary Spain in 1936-37. Unfortunately these writings have been lost to history. The writings, which did survive, are now preserved in the Kate Sharpley Library in London (www.katesharpleylibrary.net).

Although it has not been conclusively established as to why these documents were destroyed, there is little doubt that White's second wife,

Noreen Shanahan, either alone or in conjunction with the White family, disposed of the bulk of her husband's papers in the aftermath of his death. It is possible that this may have occurred through neglect or simple expediency, but it is more likely that it was driven by White's conflict with his wife, an ardent Catholic, about his views on the evils of the Catholic Church and Catholicism itself; see his article *"The Catholic Church; Fascism's Ally"* which follows. It is quite probable that other articles in a similar vein existed in his notes. Whatever the exact circumstances, the destruction of these papers is a tragic loss for Irish history and especially for the history of Anarchism in the Spanish Civil War, as well as anarchism in relation to the revolutionary struggles in Ireland.

White inherited the family home and lands of White Hall by his father's will in 1912, but the inheritance was deferred as long as his mother lived; she died in 1935. In the interval, White had received a regular income from the rent and sale of the lands attached to the estate; this had been supplemented by occasional income from journalistic efforts. Although he had spent short periods at White Hall (and nearby Cushendun) in the intervening years, it wasn't until 1938 that he was able to live at the family home in Broughshane for any prolonged period. But despite the relative isolation of Broughshane, he appears to have remained in regular contact with his political associates, although the outbreak of World War 2 was to paralyse any real work.

White made a final and brief reappearance in public life during the 1945 General Election campaign. Proposing himself as a 'Republican Socialist' candidate for the Antrim constituency, he convened a meeting at the local Orange Hall in Broughshane to outline his view. But he never actually got his name on the ballot paper.

Six months later Jack White died from cancer in a Belfast nursing home. After a private ceremony, he was buried in the White family plot in the First Presbyterian Church in Broughshane.

In many ways White is an unsung hero of the Irish Revolution and sadly forgotten by all but a few on the international scene. He is barely cited in Irish academic history. *"The History of the Irish Working Class,"* (Berresford Ellis, 1972) fails to even refer to him and outside a certain few anarchists groups there has been no talk about him at all. The semi-official academic version of Irish history, *"The Making of the Modern*

Ireland, 1603-1923" (J.C. Beckett, 1966) mentions him only once in relation to the setting up of the Irish Citizen Army[1]. Beckett writes that "the strikers and their supporters, claiming that the police had acted in an aggressively brutal manner, organised a military force, the Irish Citizen Army, for their own defence. Its first leaders were J.R.White, an Ulster protestant nationalist who had served with distinction in the British army, and James Connelly, who had returned from America in 1910, and had been trying in vain to convert the Belfast workers to socialism until he was called to assist Larkin in Dublin."

Albert Meltzer, the London Anarchist who knew White well in the 30s wrote "He told me once he had originally accepted the principle of libertarian socialism in Bohemia, but had been 're-introduced' to socialism, as syndicalism and as Marxism, in Dublin. He was always more of a syndicalist than a Marxian Socialist and described himself at the time as a guild socialist"[2].

It is a shame that Jack White's later autobiography was lost, as it could have shed much light on both the Ireland of the 30s as well as his involvement in the Spanish Civil War.

The White Family Tombstone. The gravestone records Captain Jack White,, D.S.O. son of the above (Field Marshall Sir George Stuart White. Born May 22nd 1879. Died Febuary 2nd 1946.

[1] The Making of Modern Ireland, 1603-1923, J.C Beckett, Faber and Faber, 1966.
[2] Anarchy, JR White. With an introduction by Albert Meltzer. entitled "From Loyalism to Anarchism". (1981). Much of the information here is taken extensively from the excellent article by Kevin Doyle (2001) on the Workers Solidarity Movement website at http//flag.blackened.net/ revolt/anarchists/jackwhite/bio.htm. It is by far the most thoroughly researched article on Captain Jack White to date.

A REBEL IN BARCELONA:
JACK WHITE'S FIRST SPANISH IMPRESSIONS
(First published. November 11th 1936)

I came out to Barcelona as administrator of the second British Red Cross Unit. Two nurses and myself came on in advance to find a site for the hospital of the Unit somewhere on the Teruel front.

Unfortunately the Unit had been cancelled all except four ambulances which are now en route somewhere between Paris and Barcelona. Some of these ambulances are to go, I believe to the first Unit at Grañen. Till they arrive in any case, I am left with no one to administrate and nothing to do, so a friend in the CNT-FAI has asked me to write my impressions for broadcast or the press.

My first and deepest impression is that of the natural nobility of the Catalan people. I got that impression as early as Port Bou, where we had to spend six hours waiting for the Barcelona train. A bright sun was shining which tempted me to bathe in the bay. After undressing I left my coat, with some 80 English pounds in the pocket, on the rocks close to a frequented path with a sense of its perfect safety. Half an hour in Cataluña and a few conversations in my faulty Spanish had made me feel I was among friends, who appreciated the effort of the British workers and intelligentsia to help their cause. I would not have dared to risk such a large sum of money unguarded at any English watering place. Here I felt it was guarded by the revolutionary solidarity of Cataluña and even of the international solidarity of the working class of which Cataluña is now the bulwark.

This impression of revolutionary honour and revolutionary order has been maintained by all I have seen and experienced during the week I have been in Barcelona. On one occasion after a trying morning rushing round after the necessary passes to go on to Valencia – that was before the cancellation of the unit and I wanted to go on to the front to find a place for our hospital as soon as possible – I inadvertently paid my taxi driver four pesetas more than his fare. He brought it back to me remarking "eso sobra". This happened as I was entering the door of the Regional Committee of the CNT-FAI, the headquarters of those terrible

Anarchists of whose misdeeds we read so much in the Capitalist Press now. I am not going to enter into controversy, philosophic or political, I simply record my experiences, without fear or favour. It is a fact, that the Barcelona churches were burnt, and many of them, where roof and walls are still standing, are used to house medical or commissariat stores instead of, as previously, being used by the fascists as fortresses. I suspect their present function is nearer the purpose of a religion based by its founder on the love of God and the Neighbour. However that may be, the destruction of the churches has not destroyed love and honesty in Spain. If they are not based on the love of God, they are based on brotherliness, selflessness and self respect, which have to be experienced to be believed. Never, till I came to revolutionary Barcelona, had I seen waiters and even shoeblacks refuse a tip. Here the refusal of anything in excess of the exact bill or fee is as invariable as the courtesy with which it is done. This very courtesy makes one feel mean for having offered it, a benighted bourgeois, automatically continuing bourgeois habits and unable to grasp the self- respect of the workers now they are so largely in control. My first day taught me my lesson. I never offend now.

You will have heard no doubt about the Dublin Rising of 1916. That rising is now thought of as purely a national one, of which the aims went no further than the national independence of Ireland. It is conveniently forgotten that not only was the manifesto published by the "bourgeois" leaders conceived in a spirit of extreme liberal democracy, but, associated with the bourgeois leaders, was James Connolly, the international socialist, who some regarded as the greatest revolutionary fighter and organizer of his day. In command of the Irish Citizen Army, which I had drilled, he made common cause with the Republican separatists against the common Imperial enemy. It is said that he threatened to come out with the Citizen Army alone, if the bourgeois Republicans shirked the issue.

It was then the middle of the great war. The rising was ruthlessly suppressed by England and sixteen of the leaders were executed. Connolly himself, badly wounded in the Dublin Post Office, which was shelled to ruins by a British gunboat, was strapped in a chair and shot by a firing squad before he recovered.

Here in Cataluña, the union of the working class and nation starts off under better auspices than were possible in Ireland. In Cataluña the internal socialist reconstruction goes hand in hand with the armed fight against Spanish and international fascism. You are in advance of us in Syndico-Anarchist and Socialist construction. You are advance of us in dealing with the clerico-fascist menace. Again and again in Ireland the revolutionary Republican movement comes a bit of the way towards Socialism, and scurries back in terror when the Roman Catholic Church looses its artificial thunder of condemnation and excommunication.

I come of an Ulster Protestant family. There is a saying in Ulster "Rome is a lamb in adversity, a snake in equality and a lion in prosperity". I am glad that in Cataluña you have made Rome into a lamb. In Ireland Rome is still a lion, or rather a wolf in sheep's clothing. The priests inflame the mob and then pretend to deplore the mob-violence which they have instigated. Last Easter Sunday, I had myself to fight for three kilometres against the Catholic actionists, who attacked us on the streets as we were marching to honour the memory of the Republican dead who fell in Easter week 1916. The pious hooligans actually came inside the cemetery and tore up the grave rails to attack us.

In Ireland, as in Spain, it was the priests who started methods of fire and sword against the people. Yet they complain bitterly when their own weapons are turned against themselves.

Comrades of Cataluña! In your hour of trial when you hold the barricades not only for yourselves but for us all, I greet you with the voice of revolutionary Ireland, smothered awhile but destined to regain its strength. I hold myself honoured to be among you, to serve if I can in whatever capacity I can be most useful.

J. R. White
CNT-AIT Boletin de Informacion.
No. 15, November 11th 1936.
(donated to Kate Sharpley Library by Federico Arcos)

ANARCHISM - A PHILOSOPHY OF ACTION
[From *Spain And The World*, February 5th, 1937]

The following is the speech made by Jack White at a Meeting held at Conway Hall, January 18th under the auspices of the London Committee of the CNT-FAI.

Our comrade, Emma Goldman, is an anarchist and I should like to give a word of explanation why I stand beside her on this platform. I want to sketch in what, as I understand it - and my knowledge of theoretic anarchism is as yet very small - is a fundamental of anarchist philosophy. I believe, then, I am right in saying anarchism is a philosophy of action, because it is pre-eminently the philosophy of individual spontaneity. Every free and spontaneous individual knows that it would be highly desirable and convenient if knowledge could always precede action, and we could advance rationally step by step to a foreseen goal; life, and especially the deeper aspects of life, will not permit this; in the deepest crises and conflict of life, whether individual or social, action has to precede knowledge, and if we wait too long to calculate results and fail to obey our emotional impulses to stand for what is right, or resist intolerable wrong, regardless of consequences , we miss the psychological moment; somehow we are devitalised by our own prudence, and we are left to face wrong, morel deeply entrenched by our inaction, with less "elan vital" in our ourselves to give us assurance of future victory. Reason, or rather the passive attempt to calculate consequences without creatively contributing to them by the magic of the deed, has betrayed us. The highest reason is incarnate in action and often cannot explain itself till after the actions. Reason is latent in the pent-up emotion that drives to action. It is emotional reason, creative reason; the other kind of reason is dead.

At moments of revolution, the higher emotional reason is especially necessary, because it breaks through the old forms, which are the premises of the dead reason; it creates new forms, which have their seed primarily not in the mind but in the heart of man. He may not be able to foresee or define the new forms; but he knows the old forms are dead and will destroy his heart and spirit unless he bursts through them.

Non-Intervention A Verbal Screen

Nothing has been sadder to watch for the past five or six years than the way in which fascism has gained victory after victory by acting from its evil heart, while socialists and democrats reasoned and talked; in Germany and Austria. Fascism waited its moment and struck, quite regardless of the pathetic faith of its opponents in the compelling rightness of democratic theories. In the international parleys about Spain, talk of non-intervention has been noting but a verbal screen for armed fascist intervention on an even larger scale.

We have to look to the internal struggle in Spain for the first real meeting of fascist action by revolutionary action, first in the magnificent struggle of the Asturian miners, so ruthlessly suppressed, and later on the July 19th of last year in the historic defeat of the fascist coup by the workers of Barcelona. At last the philosophy of action of the fascists had met a revolutionary philosophy of action strong and direct enough to master it. In one day fascism was conquered in Barcelona. Machine guns and batteries of artillery were taken by the invincible rush of the people dependent for the most part on nothing but their bare hands with about one rifle per 40 men. The guns were turned against the barracks, their walls were breached and their stores of arms captured while the rank and file of the troops joined the people. In three days fascism was liquidated in Catalonia.

In addressing an audience like this to make known the work of the CNT-FAI, it is a little difficult to puts one's finger on points whether of theory or practice, which differentiate the Anarcho-Syndicalism or Libertarian Communism of Spain from, say, the more highly centralised system of Russian Communism. I have not the knowledge to descant on the points of theoretic difference, and, if I had it might be inadvisable to do so.

It might, however, be interesting to trace the historical foundations of anarchism in Spain and to indicate the roots of anarchist divergence from the brand of communism with which we are more familiar in this country. Mr John Stachey writing in the Left Book Club News of the working class movement of 1860 says, *"It is a pity that into the new born movement of that date had strayed the brilliant, erratic, disastrous Russian aristocrat, Michael Bakunin. He became far more influential in Spain than the Marxists. He split the International and set a great section of the Spanish working class movement in the rigid anarchist mound."* Whether Mr. Stachey is right in speaking of the anarchist movement as "Rigid," we will investigate later. I can only say that if I agreed with him I should not be on this platform now.

Out To Organise A New Spain

I want, if I can, to give you some notion of the respective characteristics of the authoritarian and libertarian groups in Spain, not in any spirit of invidious comparison, but to illustrate as far as possible the difference of outlook and temperament. Sir Peter Chalmers-Mitchell, writing in *The Times* of his experience in Malaga in the early days of Franco's rebellion, mentions two points in comparing the UGT and the CNT-FAI which are, I think, characteristic. Both, he says, organised Militias, but the former tried to attract recruits by promising them permanent service in the Standing Army afterwards, while the latter were bitterly opposed to all Standing Armies, and even their leaders refused to accept Commissions.

In their attitude to economics, he adds the former tended to concentrate on raising wages at the expense of capital, while the latter were out to organise a new Spain based on creative work.

Many impartial observers have spoken of the self-imposed discipline in the factories taken over and controlled by the workers, and realised that underlying this voluntarily discipline was great enthusiasm and revolutionary faith; hence the impression of dignity emanating from the workers.

While no doubt, the voluntary discipline and the enthusiasm that begets it, is not confined to the CNT-FAI, it is unquestionable that the policy of the Industrial Revolution simultaneous with the anti-fascist fight is the anarchist policy carried into practice in spite of the opposition of the P.S.U.C.

As to the dignity emanating from the workers, I saw enough with my own eyes while in Spain to verify the proof of the reports I have quoted.

I found Barcelona, a clean, well-run, orderly city, with trams and trains running to the minute, restaurants and cinemas open, and all run as collectivised institutions by their courteous and efficient staffs. Never before had I met waiters and even shoeblacks consistently refusing tips, so great is the self-respect engendered in the workers by their new status of the collectivised owners of the industries they control.

We are then bound in justice to give to Anarcho-Syndicalism and the CNT-FAI the credit which is their due for the magnificent creative work that results from their philosophy, individual and social.

Of all the Spanish workers, well may we say, with Langdon Davies, "We turn in humility to the humble fold of Spain, Republican, Socialists, Communists, Syndicalists, Anarchists, who are groping in horror with their bare hands to save the Light from flickering out. We turn in anger to those in England who want the Light to die and we cry in words to which Spain is giving a new meaning: 'No Pasaran.' "They Shall Not Pass."

J.R. White

THE MEANING OF ANARCHISM

---

*This article was originally published by Freedom Press, London 1937,
as a response to the May Day events in Barcelona in May 1937.*

THE MEANING OF ANARCHISM

PART I

There has been bloodshed between Anarchists and Stalinist Communists in Catalonia. Many are asking: (1) Is there so deep-rooted a difference of principle as to provide a philosophical basis for a physical clash? (2) What is the fundamental principle of Anarchism? (3) If the Anarchists have a definite and different philosophy, will it work in this wicked world? I propose to contrast Anarchism with Socialism and Communism, confining my use of the word Socialism to include points where Socialists and Communists agree. The Socialists say:

The State has been formed on a class basis to preserve the domination of one class by the domination of the others. To achieve liberation, therefore, we must get possession of the State. When we become masters by election or by insurrection we will abolish its *raison d'etre* which is the division of society into a possessing and an exploited class. Then the State will wither away and will give place to an economic administration of things, which will no longer have to safeguard the privileges of a minority but to minister to the needs of all. But to abolish the State one must first capture it and use it to destroy the cause which has given it birth - the inequality between the majority which produces everything and the minority which consumes a disproportionate amount of the product of the majority's labour. That is why it is all-important to secure the election of as many M.P.'s and Municipal Councillors as possible. Their installation will mean so much less to accomplish on the day of the revolution, when we shall have in the persons of our elected representatives guards within the citadel to throw open the gates to us.

To this the Anarchists reply:

The State contains a corrupting influence in itself. The people have

246

always been deceived (when they are not machine-gunned) by the revolutionaries who in their ignorance the people have hoisted to power. Consequently, to destroy the State, one must not begin by *becoming* the State; for in doing so one becomes automatically its preserver. One becomes so by force of circumstance, without conscious dishonesty, inevitably, because things appear under a different aspect and so many difficulties and duties crop up that no revolutionary turned politician can remain a single-minded revolutionary. The State corrupts the purest and the best. So to keep our revolutionary virtue, we must not expose ourselves to its pernicious infection. It is not from above with the machinery of the oppressive State, that one can abolish class-society. It is from below that we must wage the war against the privileged class and undermine the foundation of their privileges.

"We will expropriate them by law," say the Socialists.

"We can do it without you and your laws," reply the Anarchists. "We know how to strip the bourgeoisie by direct action. Our direct action is a series of attacks incessantly renewed, delivered at one point today and another tomorrow; an endless sequence of major and minor crises, schooling the exploited in practical war against the exploiter and preparing them for the final crisis of the general strike. We feel no need of voting to impose masters on ourselves. We are anti-parliamentarians, abstentionists. In one thing we are faithful Marxists: Did not Marx say 'The emancipation of the workers must be the work of the workers themselves'? Well, we are workers and we will emancipate ourselves. As for you, Socialists who offer to liberate us, if we listened to you we should only prepare one more disillusionment for the proletariat. For once you become a Government, you would do to us who are the people just what every Government has always done."

It would seem that the Anarchists have justification for their mistrust, not only in the lessons of history but also in the nature of things. Anarcho-syndicalism applies energy at the point of production; its human solidarity is cemented by the association of people in common production undiluted by mere groupings of opinion. Affinity of interests is more stable and more powerful than affinity of opinions. Disunity begins where differences of abstract opinion can no longer be harmonised and resolved in collective work. We cannot surrender the cause of human freedom to any combination of incongruities, to any 'Popular Front' whose incompatible elements can guarantee nothing but the obligation to compromise. In any Popular Front, groups and elements are accepted whose economic interests run counter to those of the proletariat.

In the people who compose it there are intellectual and moral affinities, which may disappear under pressure. It is dangerous to place people between the appeal of the conscience and reason and the appeal of these interests. These fragile affinities cannot exist in the groupings of anarcho-syndicalism; stronger than any bond of sentiment or of reason there is a bond of interest which unites them, the only stable and solid bond of unity.

The Socialists reply that Anarcho-Syndicalist propaganda, just because it makes flank attacks and raids on Capitalism, because its primary object is the defence of local and regional interests, is inadequate to make conscious revolutionaries. Anarcho-syndicalism is good for guerrilla but unsuited to serious organised warfare. Its efforts must automatically be lacking in concentration. Coordination and centralisation of effort can be the work only of a Party whose horizon is not limited to a town or an industry but embraces all the complex factors of a national or international situation. In our common interest of the revolution, Socialist and Anarcho-Syndicalist action must combine.

The Anarchists answer the Socialists: "Where is your logic? You assert that in the society which you intend to build, - economic groupings will be the only ones and public authority will be limited to the necessary administration to ensure the production and distribution of objects necessary to people's existence; why then wait for the revolution to give to economic groupings their vital creative function? Let them take the importance today they will have tomorrow. You admit the State is the effect of class exploitation and its function is to maintain it. We prefer to attack the cause. Leave the workers to fight their own battle on their own ground. Don't ask them to saddle themselves with political masters, who the day after they conquer state power will want, like all conquerors, to remain the masters.

Between employer and worker there is a brutal vis-à-vis.

Against the tremendous power of the State one must stoop to tactics;

sometimes one has to combine these tactics with those of other Parties. The proletariat finds it hard to follow these long-range operations, or it gets concerned with their detail, missing their whole scope; thus it risks contradicting a political habit of mind, which slowly atrophies the revolutionary spirit.

The working class, "economically organised, is sufficient unto itself, it needs only to be conscious of its power; electoral and parliamentary combinations can only delay the day of self-realisation."

Steklov, in his history of the First International, speaks of the split in it as caused by the past of the international proletariat rising in revolt against its future. He means by this that Bakunin and the Anarchists thought it was possible to jump straight from the decay of feudal aristocracy, which, from 1848, began definitely to collapse in favour of bourgeois industrialism, to the proletarian revolution.

"The broad masses of the workers," says Steklov, "for the time led astray by Bakunin, returned to the broad river of International Socialism." Dare we reply that the broad river of revolutionary destiny, for a time mapped correctly by Marx over a stage of its course, shows signs of reverting to a deeper bed charted by the genius of Bakunin.

Marx was, "par excellence", the prophet of the industrial proletariat; any developments depending solely on that proletariat had to await its growth and class-conscious solidarity; and that growth and solidarity had to await in turn the maturity, not to say the over-ripe bursting, of the bourgeois order. This patient dependence on ripening external conditions gives to Marxism an element of fatalism in sharp contrast with the unconditioned spontaneity of Anarchism.

"Anarchism does not wait. It acts in the individual and in small groups to build up social forms, which shall be, as near as possible, embryos of the fully-developed Anarchist society."

"Hope deferred maketh the heart sick," and any philosophy of action preaching present revolt as the best preparation for future revolution on a wide scale starts with an appeal to the fighter and people of action rather than the theoretician, which is psychologically sound. To the seer, the Kingdom of Heaven is always at hand, and its proximity calls for immediate preparation. And though the seers are generally wrong in their time forecast, they are often more right than the scientist about the fundamentals of cataclysmic change.

Bakunin was a seer, Marx was a Scientist. Bakunin was greatly influenced by the just and elemental protests of the peasants ruined by a dawning Capitalism, and he believed he could enlist the revolting bourgeois intellectuals in the service of complete social liquidation. He was wrong as to the time. But Marx was wrong in his scientific belief that revolution would spread automatically out of the most highly industrialised countries. The revolt, not of Germany or France, but of Ireland and Russia during the Great War is one up for Bakunin's *rapport* with the elemental human and one down for Marx's analysis of the scientifically conditioned masses.

"What!" I hear someone exclaim. "You place the Irish National Rebellion on a par with the Russian proletarian revolution and use both to discredit the accuracy of Marxian analysis! What heresy run to insanity is this?"

Just a minute, friend. I am pleading for two things: spontaneous voluntarism versus scientific social conditioning, and the elemental vitality retained by a peasantry, as indispensable features in revolution. I am suggesting that though the industrial proletariat has the strongest incentive to make the revolution, they are too mechanised and lack the vital force ever to do so unaided, and that therefore a social science based on industrial economics alone as the determining factor is inevitably misleading. Do the facts support me or do they not? Has successful revolution ever been achieved in a highly industrialised country? It has not. If we analyse the factors in the most recent revolutions we are familiar with, those of Ireland, Russia and Spain, in conjunction with the frustration of revolution in highly industrialised countries, we may have to conclude it is something deeper than bad tactics and treacherous leadership which has thrown out our calculations. Perhaps the Marxians and even Marx have omitted elemental and human factors, which can express and manifest themselves better through the vehicle of Anarchism. I am not saying Marx was wrong. Obviously he was very largely right. I am suggesting that he did not say the last word about the individual and collective "unconscious" when he interpreted so scientifically the consciousness of the industrial worker.

If we compare the Irish and Russian revolution, the former has two advantages over the more exclusively proletarian nature of the latter. It preceded it in time, the Dublin rising of 1916 antedating even the Kerensky Revolution by about a year, and it is surpassed in its voluntarism. It was essentially an insurrection of a conscious and voluntary minority forestalling and creating mass conditions rather than awaiting their ripening. If Nationalism has any function in paving the way for International Revolution, Ireland showed that function at its best. In Ireland, Republican Nationalism combined with Irish International Socialism (Connolly and the Citizen Army) against the common Imperial enemy, and in so doing made the only repudiation of the Great War in Western Europe long before the chaos and social military breakdown caused by the war compelled that repudiation, as in Russia, and later to some extent in Germany.

This voluntarism, scorning to calculate consequences and creative of new mass-conditions, is the essence of Anarchism with its distrust of majorities and "L'illusion majoritaire" and its respect of spiritual quality rather than numerical quantity. The Anarchist recognises, implicitly if not explicitly, that there are two reasons, one emotional and creative, arising from inner-spontaneity, the other "rational" and dead because its premises are in the past or present *status quo* and it is therefore reduced to calculate consequences in terms of the past or present *status quo* rather than create new forms.

The State-worship of Communist and Socialism has its source in the failure to lay enough stress on the inner spontaneity of people, and a consequent enslavement to outer externalised forms, such as the State as the source and key to power. The people's only road to real freedom lies in the voluntary coordination of their maximum individual spontaneity. All social panaceas that seek to supersede that coordinated spontaneity, even as a means to the alleged end of restoring it, must lead not to freedom but to the loss of such freedom as the people have achieved and to increasing depths of tyranny.

PART II

Having brought the Anarchism v. Socialism argument, with which this article opened, to its psychological and philosophical head, let us apply it to recent history in Spain, recent history still pregnant with problems of world-shaking importance.

If people's inner spontaneity is a factor of importance in revolution, increasing in direct ratio with the mechanical perfection and international consolidation of the forces of Fascist repression, are we not apt to overlook the surprises in the unknown destiny of people in our scientific forecasts of the mechanical destination of society? May not our oversight damage our insight into unexpected factors in revolutionary development? We must not divorce the spiritual qualities of a people from our scientific assessment of their place in economic evolution. Almost we might say that if human spontaneity has to become more dynamic and intense to triumph over intensified and universalised reaction, each succeeding revolution must be more Anarchist in its principle and practice than the last. Socialistic centralisation would thus become counter-revolutionary in effect and have latent affinity with counter-revolutionary forces, no matter how revolutionary its slogans or even its intentions.

Now Spain is deeply impregnated with the psychology, the principle and the practice of Anarchism. It would, I think, be false to insulate this principle and practice of Anarchism from the Spanish racial characteristic of human dignity. The sense of human dignity seems to be consubstantial with every Spaniard and undoubtedly it inspires the Anarchist goal of general freedom and solidarity and the educational voluntary associative methods leading towards it. The situation in Spain today compels us to ask the question: What is the surest guarantee against the triumph of Fascism? Is it the Anarchist psychology and tradition of the Spanish people expressing itself in its own Anarcho-Syndicalist forms or is it centralised State Socialism imposed, or alleged to be imposed, in the interests of maximum military efficiency and the maximum efficiency of production to feed the fighting fronts? May not this efficiency be too dearly bought, if it is bought at the price of damping the revolutionary enthusiasm of the Spanish people and splitting their revolutionary unity even in the interests of a unified command? One might even add with trepidation a further question: Whither is this

State centralisation in the interests of Spanish "democracy" leading? We are assured it is aimed at, and will lead to the speedy defeat of Franco. Have not the Second and Third Internationals agreed to meet to further that most desirable object? So, I note, have the Ambassadors of the capitalist Powers already met and conferred with the Valencia Government. Let us hope they have agreed to cooperate in the speedy defeat of Franco. That, however, is uncertain. One thing is certain. Anarchist leaders have been displaced, imprisoned, murdered, groups of Anarchists have been massacred by Socialist-Communists and the Anarchist idea of revolution, collectivisation of industry and as far as possible the agricultural village - communities, is being stopped and undone. The Anarchists had defeated not only Franco in Catalonia but had superseded the economic order, which Franco is fighting to save and restore. Now the Socialist-Communists are saving and restoring it instead, not for him, of course, but to speed up his defeat. Meanwhile large sections of the Spanish people have misunderstood; things were too puzzling.

When they saw their worker's military and economic committees dissolved, their worker's militia abolished, themselves disarmed, and finally the telephone building which they had won by repeated attack from the Fascists in July, forcibly seized from their syndicate by the Govt. Assault Guards they came out on the streets and erected barricades. They thought their revolution was being destroyed instead of saved. Their misunderstanding was increased by the arrival of French and British warships in Barcelona and the landing of French marines, while the open allies of Franco, the Germans and Italians, continued to blockade them outside the three-mile limit. The strange coincidence of the arrival of the French and British warships just at the moment when the workers came out on the streets to save a revolution they believed to be threatened, has been mixed up in their simple proletarian minds with the previous fact that the French and British had been blockading them all along under cover of a non-intervention pact and that the Valencia Government sent troops and threatened to send more to suppress what they thought was the defence of their revolution.

These simple people have been called "uncontrollables". In point of fact they were very easily controlled and went back to their work after six days of almost entirely defensive fighting. One can only hope they will not regret their docility.

I note that the epithet "uncontrollable" is reserved for my Anarchist comrades. Their fellow criminals in the joint misunderstanding are mostly "Trotskyites". A "Trotskyite", so far as I understand the term, is someone who thinks Marx meant what he said when he spoke of the necessity of the dictatorship of the proletariat in the transition period from Capitalism to Communism. Mr. Emile Burns, in his book Communism, Capitalism, and the Transition, has put the matter in a nutshell, not only as regards what should happen in theory but what did actually happen in the Russian Revolution. He might have been writing of the revolution that the simple Spanish "Trotskyites" thought they were defending. "All executive positions," writes Mr. Burns, which had formerly been filled by appointment from above had to be made elective and the elected persons had to be subject to recall at any moment by the bodies that elected them; therefore from the first day of the revolution the command of armed forces was taken over by elected deputies; the factory workers were armed and fought all the most vital battles; the officials in State Departments were replaced, by workers; the managers in the factories were replaced or controlled by councils of workers; the existing Law Courts were abolished and Worker's Courts with elected judges took their place; wherever Soviet order was established, elected worker's Committees took the place of appointed officials."

Now that is precisely the kind of order that the Spanish "Trotskyites", in common with other Spanish "uncontrollables", thought they were fighting to preserve and maintain from May 2nd to 7th in Barcelona.

But I would hate to be thought a "Trotskyite", for I remember it was Trotsky who helped to smash all that sort of thing at Kronstadt. So I must perforce be an uncontrollable.

What is the difference between a "Trotskyite" and an "uncontrollable"? I expect I am simple, too, but I will give the only definition my simplicity can rise to. A Trotskyite is a Marxist who has stuck to Marx, who believes for instance, that it is their converging or conflicting economic interests which will determine sooner or later perhaps sooner, alas! -Whether the Capitalist "democracies" will or will not help the Spanish people, led by the present Valencia Government, to defeat Franco and the relics of the clerical aristocratic order, which he seeks to preserve.

Not being a Marxist, I offer no opinion.

And an "uncontrollable" is an Anarchist who has stuck to Anarchy and who is not, therefore, primarily concerned with the shades or strata of Capitalism, but with revolution by direct action; who believes with Marx indeed that emancipation of the workers must be the work of the workers themselves, but with Bakunin, Kroptkin and Malatesta, that free humanity must be substituted for the State and that when Anarchists take part in a Government, they allow themselves to be deflected from their proper task and become corrupted by association with an instrument of tyranny. The first false step in Spain was the association of Anarchist leaders with the Government and the State. Had they given all their energies to co-ordination and unified command of CNT Collectives and Anarchist military units, instead of sacrificing Anarchist principles and control to compromises with a Government, the uncontrollables would have remained in control of themselves and ready for co-ordinated action with other sections instead of being sacrificed to a State dictatorship through a political party.

THE CHURCH: FASCISM'S ALLY
AN INTERPRETATION OF CHRISTIANITY
By J.R.White

(Published in 'Spain and the World', March 5ᵗʰ 1937. Courtesy of the Kate Sharply Library)

I should like to discuss this subject from the standpoint of a Christian Anarchist, which, if I am to have a label at all; and I hate all labels; is the nearest label to fit me. From that standpoint I define my conception of Christianity as Perfect Freedom, which coincides with my conception of Anarchy. In my opinion there are two conceptions of spirituality: the one that only in the fullest attainment and expression of his freedom can man attain to the spiritual life, individual and social. And the other that he must seek the high goal of his spirit not by self-expression and freedom, but by self-repression and obedience to external authority.

I believe the first conception to be that of Christ, and the Gospels read with any intelligence, and the second to be so foreign to the whole sprit of Christ that it is not only un-Christian, but positively anti-Christian. It follows that any Church which bases itself on the second, that of obedience to the external authority and denial of the individual's right to experiment and judge for himself, above all in those realms of faith and morals where his own soul must find its own unique path, is not, in my opinion, a Christian Church, even though it arrogantly claims the monopoly of Christian inspiration.

Subordinating Individual Freedom
From this standpoint I could have foretold the association of the Roman Catholic Church with Fascism, not only in Spain, but everywhere else, on philosophical grounds, because that Church and Fascism have the same fundamental philosophy of subordinating individual freedom to the totality of Church and State.

For the present, however, I must stick to the subject and cannot do better than by examining a controversy between a Cardinal Archbishop of the Spanish Church, Cardinal Goma, and Senor Aguirre, leader of the Basque Catholic Nationalists, who support the people's cause in Spain. This controversy brings out clearly the conflict between the Pope and almost the entire Hierarchy and controlled Press of the Catholic Church and the small but honourable number of Catholic priests and laymen, who have dared to follow their conscience against the overwhelming weight of their Church's authority. It is a conflict not only of ideas, but also of facts, and I hope to show that the Cardinal cannot defend his perversion of ideas without a direct and complete falsification of the facts.

Senor Aguirre writes to the Cardinal:

"The war has arisen between an egoistic Capitalism, which has abused its powers, and a deep feeling for social justice. It is not a war of religion."

Now you will see at once that in an argument whether, the Spanish struggle is or is not a war of religion, some definition of what is meant by religion is necessary, and my preamble about two different and irreconcilable conceptions of religion, namely, of freedom and authority, were not out of place.

"I do not believe that there are a dozen men who have taken up arms; to defend their property or to defend themselves from the persecution of those who hold or administer property. I admit social injustice is one of the remote causes of the struggle, but I categorically deny that this is a class war. A pretext is not a real cause, and the championship of the working classes has been only a pretext for this war."

The full insolence of the Cardinal's inversion of the facts lies in the last sentence, for it implies that on the sham pretext of labour demands for social justice, the Spanish people took up arms and started a war. Now let us have the truth, which the Cardinal inverts, in the words of Father Lopo, one of the few priests who have been faithful to their people.

"When the people were roused to demand their rights, when they asked for the universally claimed transformation of the land-owning System; when they asked for access to the great heartless machine of industry to humanise labour there - when we stopped our ears; we gave them a few crumbs in the name of charity and refused to envisage the solutions which reason and justice forced on every Christian conscience;

And there appeared immediately in the midst of the conflict a word lacking all meaning and reason for those who were to use it as a terrible weapon of attack. There appeared the word 'Order'; they talked of the established order and fortifying themselves against the workers, they called them with infinite scorn, 'enemies of order."

'Let everything go on as it was', was the supreme aspiration of those who were comfortably placed in life, who were little if at all perturbed by the Existence of the disinherited; yes, disinherited, a term and a conception which fill the mind with horror, so clearly do they speak of fratricidal and anti-Christian cruelty.'"

I am reminded of Francis Adam's lines:

Sometimes the heart and brain
Would be still and forget
Man, woman and children
Ragged down the pit
But when I hear them declaiming
Of Liberty, Order and Law,
The husk-hearted gentleman
And the mud-souled bourgeois
A sombre, hateful desire
Creeps up slow in the breasts
To wreck the great guilty temple
And give us rest.

"The great guilty temple," there is the position in a nutshell. Guilty priests of that guilty temple who refused to envisage, who from atrophy of soul and mind were, I believe, incapable of envisaging, the solution which reason and justice forced on every Christian conscience.

Wolves In Sheeps' Clothing
But when the disinherited, claimed their human inheritance, they were not allowed to claim it legally and peacefully, as they sought to do. They were attacked by their disinheritors.

They had to fight to defend more than their property they had not secured: they had to defend their liberty and their lives from the Fascist wolves, led on by the viler wolves in sheeps' clothing: the guilty priests.

Not a dozen men, says the Cardinal, took up arms to defend themselves from the persecution of those who hold and administer property. We answer him, "Foul bloated blasphemer! The whole Spanish people took up arms to defend themselves against the treacherous, rebellious attack of those who held and administered property and cared little, if at all, for those they had disinherited."

"They took up arms," do I say? They took up sticks, they took up stones, they fought with their bare hands for they had no arms to take. And in the sacred passion of the right for which they fought, and the burning determination not to be robbed once more by the treacherous violence of the inheritance, of which they had been robbed for centuries, now almost within their grasp, they wrested the arms from the hands of their persecutors and created a great people's army.

And then what?

The bullies and thieves could not depend on their own conscript army to shoot down their brothers. They imported more and more infidel Moors to massacre their own countrymen in the name of the highest God.

But the Moors were not enough. They had to pawn their country to foreign butchers, till whole army corps of Germans and Italians came to help the holy massacre.

I pray to the God of Justice, whom I believe can never be mocked in the end, that the peoples of the whole world will rise at last to take just vengeance on the spiritual criminals, who in frightful blasphemy pervert religion and encourage the slaughter of the poor and humble whom it is their duty to defend.

J.R. White